POP EDITION
THE BEST of the 90's ...So Far

Design: Odalis Soto
Editor: Carol Cuellar

ISBN 0-89724-463-X
9 780897 244633

CONTENTS

ALL 4 LOVE

Lyric and Music by
COLOR ME BADD and
HOWARD THOMPSON

Rock ♩ = 108
N.C.
mf
Verse:
D
G
1. I'm so glad you're my girl, I'll do
2. I will nev - er leave U, sug - ar,
an - y - thing 4_ U.
this I guar - an - tee. I
Call U ev - ery night and give U
look in - 2 the fu - ture and see
flow - ers 2.
U and me.
I
thank the Lord for U and think a -
Knight in shin - ing ar - mor, I will
bout U all the_ time, and
B your fai - ry_ tale. I

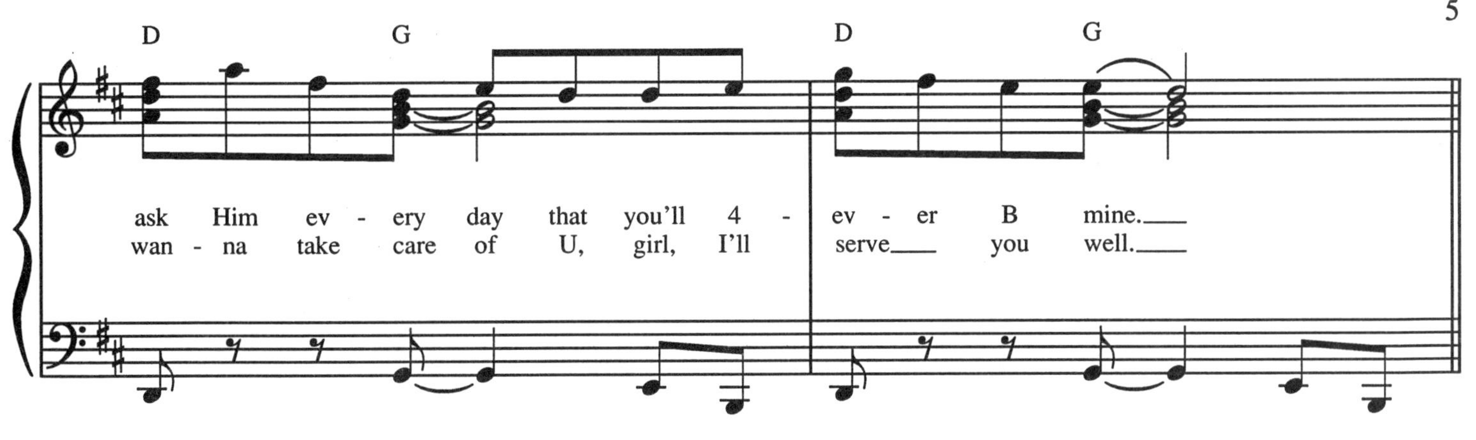
D G D G
ask Him ev - ery day that you'll 4 - ev - er B mine.
wan - na take care of U, girl, I'll serve you well.

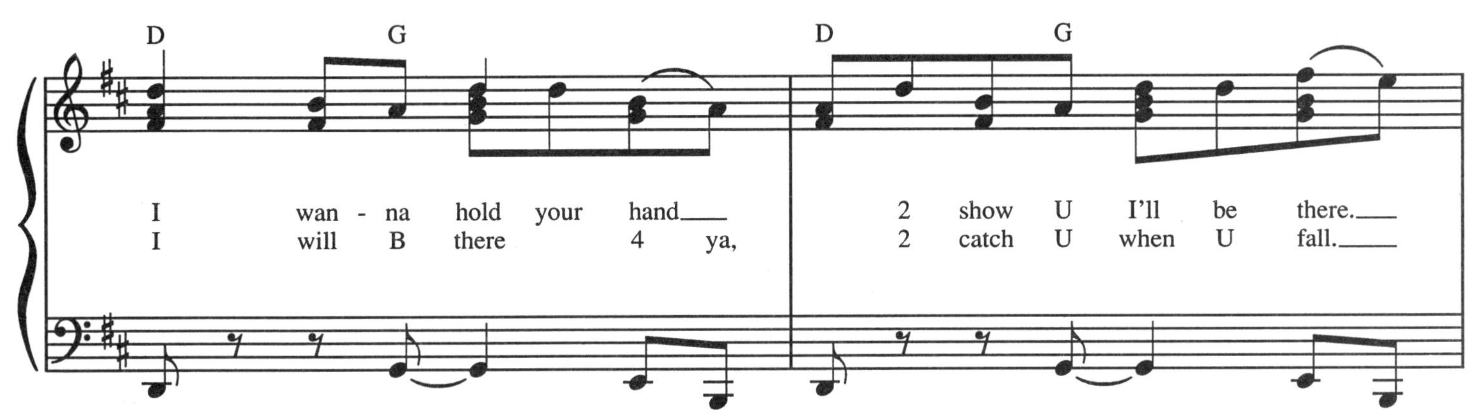
D G D G
I wan - na hold your hand 2 show U I'll be there.
I will B there 4 ya, 2 catch U when U fall.

D G D G
I like 2 do the things that let U know I care.
I'll hold U in my arms, that's where U be - long.

D G D G D G
I sing this lul - la - bye 'cause girl, U fill me full. I look in - to / in - 2 your eyes,

1.
To Next Strain
2.
N.C.
D
G
D
G
you're so beau - ti - ful.
you're so beau - ti - ful...
beau - ti - ful...
N.C.
Chorus:
D
G
D
G
yeah!
Oh, girl, I think I love ya.
I'm al - ways think - ing of ya.
D
G
D
G
I want ya to know I do it
all 4 love.
D
G
D
G
I love it when we're to - geth - er.
Girl, I need you 4 - ev - er,
1.
D.S.
2.
To Next Strain
D
G
N.C.
N.C.
and I want U 2 know I do it
all 4 love.
all 4 love.

3. 4. etc.
Repeat ad lib. and fade
N.C.
D
G
D
G
all 4 love.
all,
Spoken: Yo! Come here, sweetheart.
The distance B-tween us,
all,
I want U 2 know something, alright.
an ocean of tears.

1.
2.
D
G
all, all, all, all, all,
See, every day N my life without U would
See, all the things I do 4 U
all.
B like a hundred years.
all.
are 4 love.
Dig it.

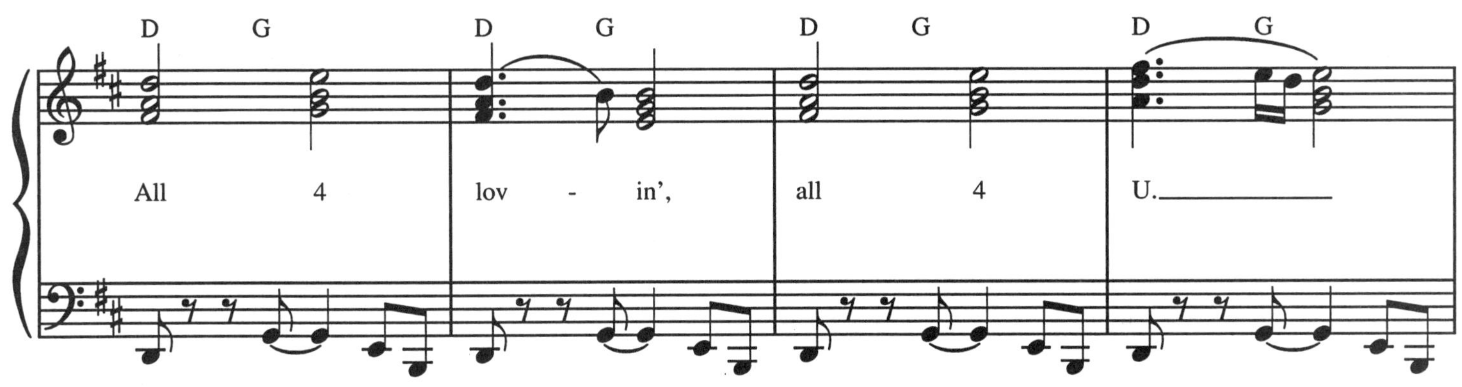
D
G
All 4 lov - in', all 4 U.

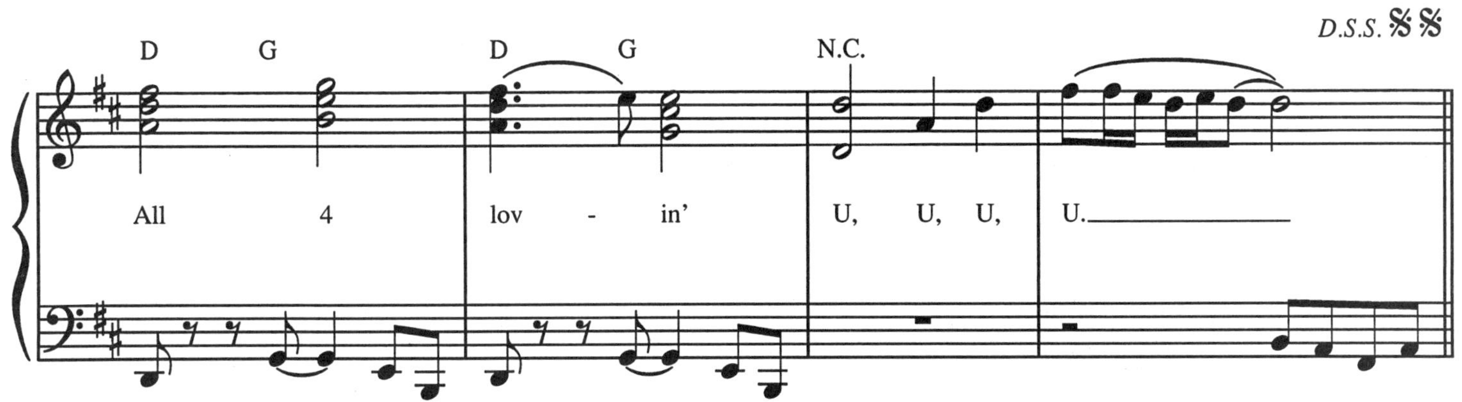
D.S.S.
D
G
N.C.
All 4 lov - in' U, U, U, U.

From the Original Motion Picture Soundtrack "THE THREE MUSKETEERS"

ALL FOR LOVE

Written by
BRYAN ADAMS, ROBERT JOHN "MUTT" LANGE
and MICHAEL KAMEN

Slowly ♩ = 76
D
Dsus
Verse:
D
Bryan: 1. When it's love you give,
Sting: I'll be a man of good
mp
(with pedal)
Dsus
D
D/F♯
then love you'll live.
faith.
I'll make a stand, I won't blink.
I'll be the rock you can
3
G
D/A
build on,
be there when you're old,
to have and to

Verse:
A
D
Dsus
Rod:
hold. 2. When there's love in - side,
then there's a rea - son why.
Bryan: I swear I'll al - ways be strong.
Rod: then it's love you take.
(3.) Sting: I'll be the fire in your night.
D
D/F♯
G
Both: I'll be the world that pro - tects you
I'll prove to you we be - long.
All: I'll be there when you need me
I will de - fend I will fight.
D/A
A
Asus
A
from the wind and the rain, from the hurt and the pain.
when hon - or's at stake, this vow I will make:
cresc.

Chorus:
D Em7 D/F♯ N.C.
D/F♯
G
All: Let's make it
that it's
all for one, all for love.
mf
Em7
D/A
Let the one you hold be the one you want, the one you
A
D/F♯
G Bm A D/F♯
G
need. 'Cause when it's all for one, it's one for all. When there's
Em7
D/F♯
G
D/A
some - one that you know, then just let your feel - ings show and make it

1.
D.S. 𝄋
2.
G D/F♯ Em7 A
D
Dsus
D
all for one, all for love.
all,
Bryan: 3. When it's love you make,
dim.
mp
Bridge:
Bm
G
Em7 D/F♯ G A
Don't lay our love to rest, 'cause we could stand up to the test. We've got
Bm
D/F♯
G Asus A
ev - 'ry - thing and more than we had planned, more than the riv -
Bm
D/F♯
G
A
- ers that run the land, we've got it all in our hands.

1.
G
Em7
Dsus
D
(Instrumental solo . . .
Dsus
D
2.
Asus
A
N.C.
Now, it's
. . . end solo)
Chorus:
G
Em7
all for___ one, all for love.___
Let the one you hold be the one you___
D/A
A
D/F♯
G
Bm
A
D/F♯
want, the one you___ need. 'Cause when it's all for___ one, it's one for all.___

G
Em7
D/F♯
When there's some - one that you know, then just
G
D/A
G/B
D/F♯
let your feel - ings show. When there's some - one that you want, when there's
G
D/A
Em
N.C.
some - one that you need, let's make it all, all for one,
slower
a tempo
Gm7
Gm(maj7)
Gm/A
D
D(2)
and all for love.
mp
slower
a tempo
rit. e dim.
p

ALL I HAVE

Words and Music by
BETH NIELSEN CHAPMAN
and ERIC KAZ

G(2)
G
G/A
A7
D
D/F♯
Trust - ing you is
Right here with you is where my life
Gmaj7
A(2)
F♯m7
Bm7
Cmaj7
eas - y. 'cause I be - lieve in you.
has come to - geth - er, and where love has filled my heart.
Em7
G/A
A7
F♯m7
Bm7
Cmaj7
3
Em7
A7sus A7
There is noth - ing I would miss as long as we're in love like this.
You know I'd go an - y - where as long as I have you to care.
All
cresc.

Chorus:

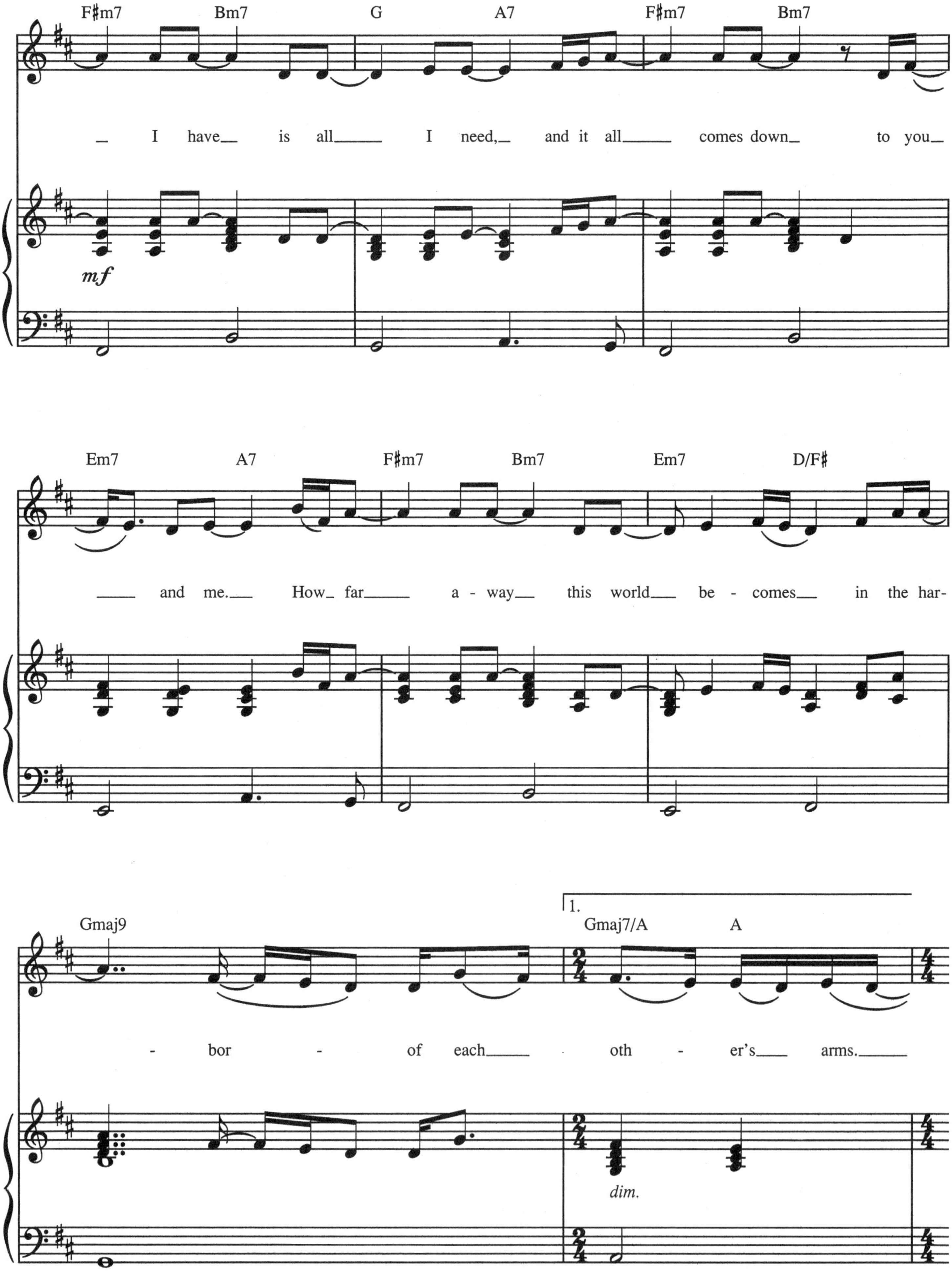

F♯m7 Bm7 G A7 F♯m7 Bm7
I have is all I need, and it all comes down to you
mf
Em7 A7 F♯m7 Bm7 Em7 D/F♯
and me. How far a - way this world be - comes in the har-
Gmaj9 1. Gmaj7/A A
- bor - of each oth - er's arms.
dim.

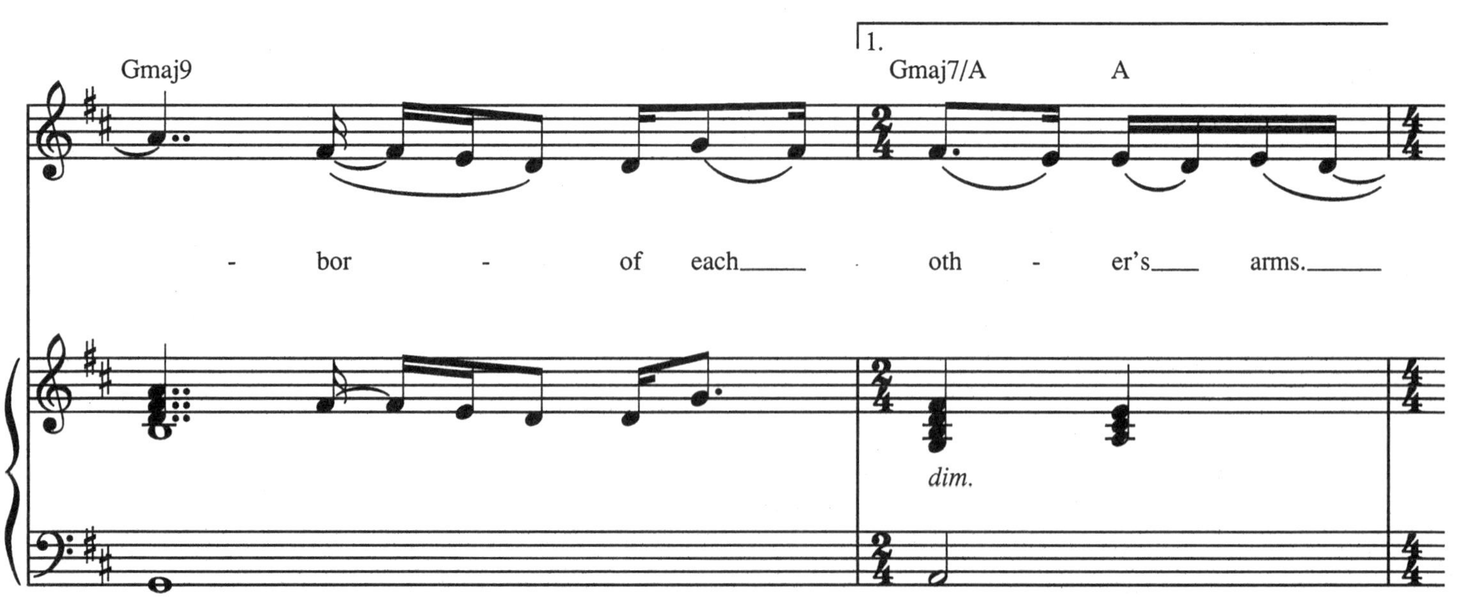

2.
D D/F♯ Gmaj9 A7sus Gmaj7/A A
— 2. I oth - er's_ arms.__
mp
Bridge:
D E7/G♯ F♯/A♯ Bm E/G♯
— Ooh,_ and with the love you bring,___ I nev - er want for
A Em7(4) D/F♯ G(2) A7sus A7
an - y-thing. I found___ what I've been search-ing for__ in you.

Gm7
Cm7
A♭
B♭7
All I have is all I need, and it all
Gm7
Cm7
Fm7
B♭7
comes down to you and me. How far
Gm7
Cm7
Fm7
E♭/G
a - way this world be - comes in the har -

1.
A♭maj9
A♭maj7/B♭
B♭
E♭
- bor of each oth - er's arms.
2.
A♭maj9
A♭maj7/B♭ B♭
E♭
E♭(2)/G
- bor of each oth - er's arms.
dim.
mp
A♭2
B♭
Gm7
Cm7
A♭
A♭maj7/B♭ B♭
E♭
poco rit. e dim
p

ALWAYS TOMORROW

Words and Music by
GLORIA ESTEFAN

Gm7
C
F/C
C
Make love, make mu - sic, make a - mends.
Try
Gm7
C
Csus
B♭
Am7
to make a dif - f'rence, try to love, try to un-der-stand.
In-stead of just giv-ing
Gm7
C7sus
up, I'd use the pow-er at my com-mand.
But there's al - ways to -
cresc.
Chorus:
B♭maj7
Am7
mor - row
to start o - ver a - gain.
mf
To Coda
Gm7
Things will nev - er stay the same,
the on - ly one sure thing is change.

1.
Gm7/C
B♭maj7
F
D.S. 𝄋
That's why there's al - ways to - mor - row.
dim.
2. I guess it
mp
2.
Gm7/C
To next strain
3.
Gm7/C
D.S. 𝄋𝄋 al Coda
That's why there's al - ways to-mor -
cresc.
That's why there's al - ways to -
E♭(2)
F
row
f
be-fore your last set-ting sun.
E♭(2)
And ev-'ry-thing your heart has longed for and yet to be won.
F
3
Yes, there's al - ways, al - ways, al -

Verse 2:
I guess it took a little time, for me to see
The reason I was born into this world
And what I'd have to go through.
For I've finally realized that I could be
Infinitely better than before, definitely stronger.
I'll face whatever comes my way,
Savor each moment of the day,
Love as many people as I can along the way.
Help someone who's giving up, if it's
Just to raise my eyes and pray.
(To Chorus:)

ANGEL

Words and Music by
JON SECADA and
MIGUEL A. MOREJON

C
G/B
Am7
give
me the
morn - ing.
C/G
F
C/E
Shar - ing an - oth - er day
with
you
is all I
Chorus:
Dm7
G
Am
want to know.
cresc.
And ba - by, I,
mf
Em7
F
C
G
I've tried to for - get you,
but the
light of your eyes
still
Am
Em7
F
To Coda
shines;
you shine like an
an - gel,
a

1.
C
G
C
Fmaj7
spir - it that won't let me go.
dim.
mp

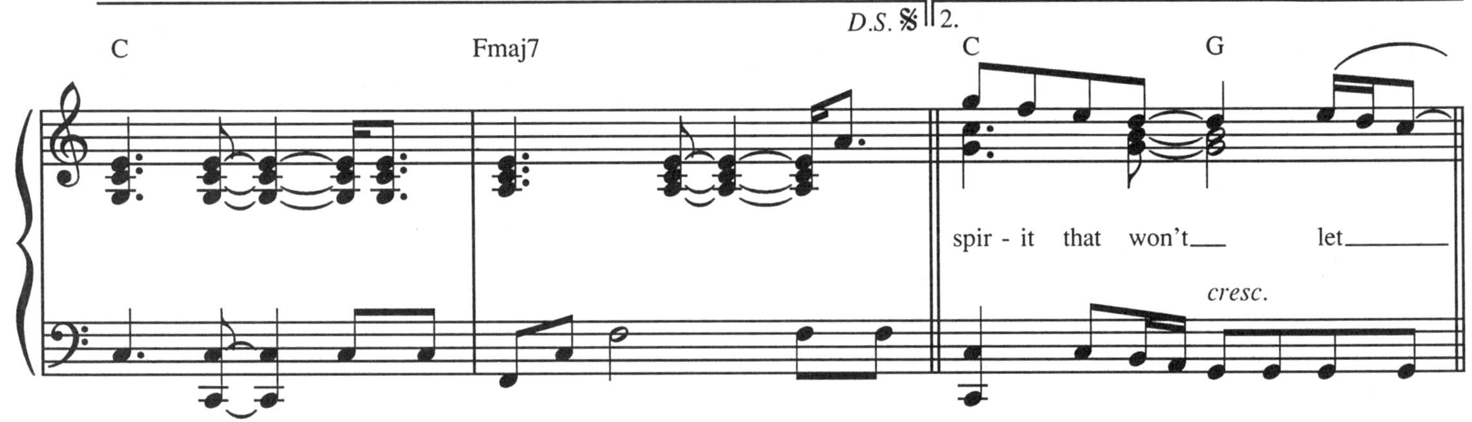
C
Fmaj7
D.S. 𝄋
2.
C
G
spir - it that won't let
cresc.

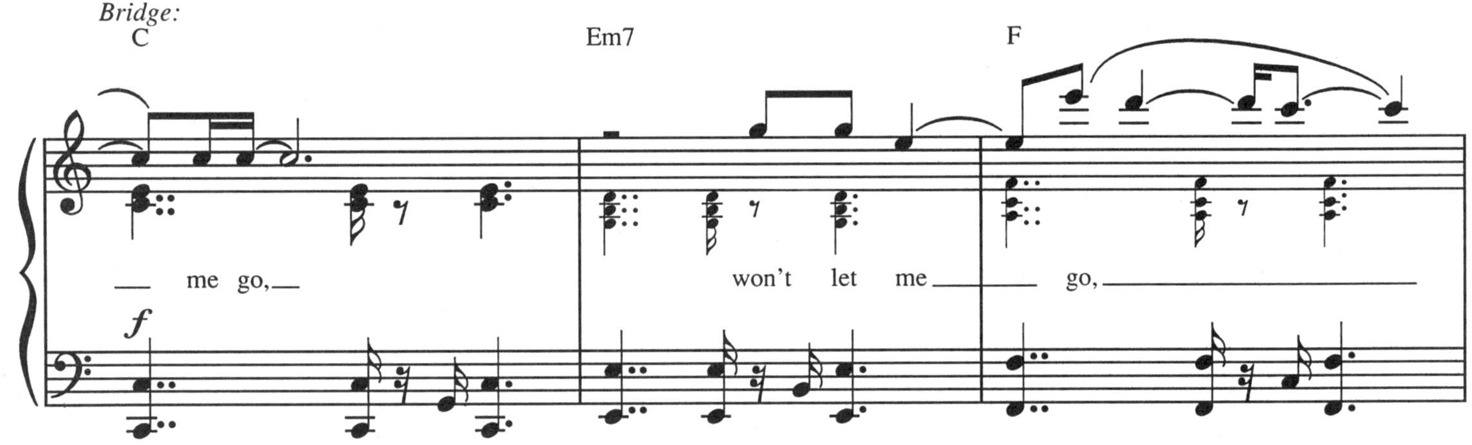
Bridge:
C
Em7
F
me go,
won't let me go,
f

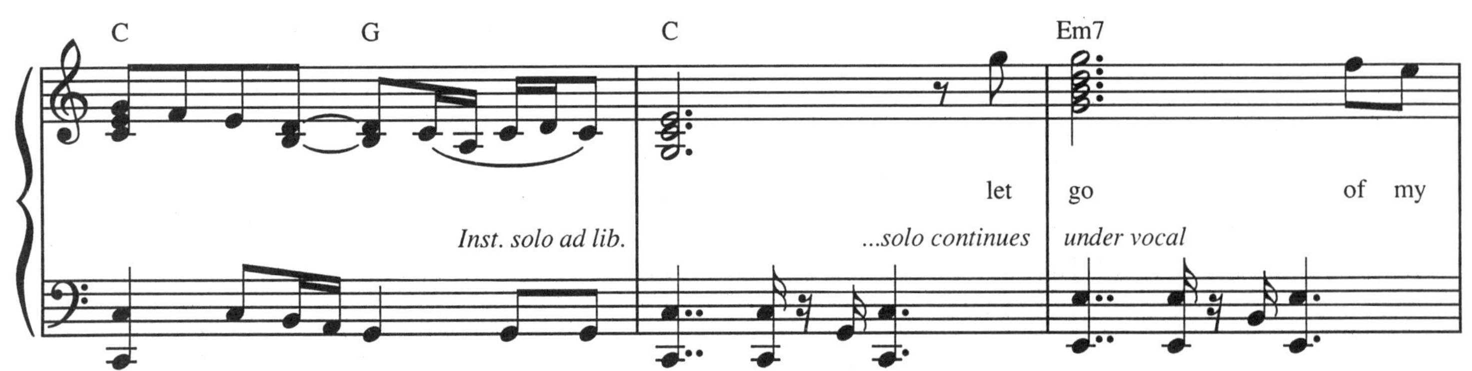
C
G
C
Em7
let go of my
Inst. solo ad lib.
...solo continues
under vocal

F C G Dm7

heart.

G Dm7 G D.S.S. 𝄋𝄋 al Coda

And ba-by I,

...end solo

𝄌 Coda

C G C

spir - it that won't let me go.

dim. *mp*

Fmaj7 C Fmaj7 C

dim. *p*

Verse 2:
And I, I didn't wanna tell you
Things I didn't wanna know myself,
I was afraid to show.
But you, you gave me a reason,
A reason to face the truth, oh yes you did,
To face the truth, face the truth, face the truth.
(To Chorus:)

From the Motion Picture "REALITY BITES"

BABY, I LOVE YOUR WAY

Words and Music by
PETER FRAMPTON

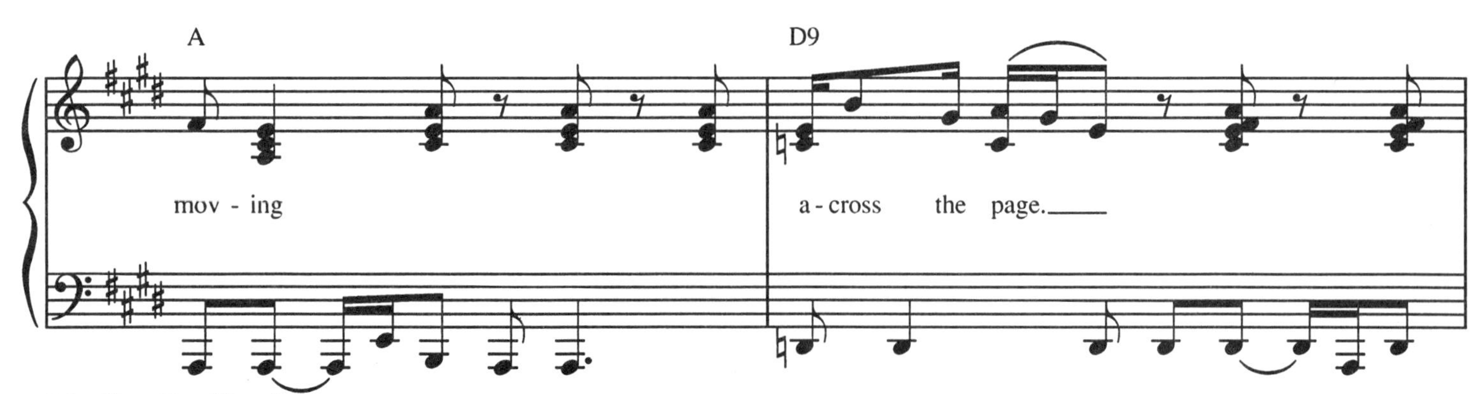

Baby, I Love Your Way - 4 - 1

E
G♯m7/D♯
C♯m
C♯m/B
Sud-den - ly, the day turns in - to night far a -
A
1.2.4.
D9
To Next Strain
way from the ci - ty. But don't
3.
F♯m7
D.S. 𝄋 al Coda
Bridge:
G♯m7
C♯m
. . . end solo)
hes - i - tate, 'cause your
F♯m7
To Coda 𝄌
A/B
B
love just won't wait.
Chorus:
E
B
F♯m
A
Ooh, ba - by, I love your way ev - 'ry day.

E
B
F♯m
A
I wan-na tell you I love_ your way___ ev-'ry day._

E
B
F♯m
A
D.S. 𝄋
I wan-na be with you night_ and day.___ 2. The

Coda
A/B
B♭/C
wait,___ just won't wait.___

Chorus:
F
C
Gm
B♭
Ooh, ba-by, I love_ your way___ ev-'ry day._

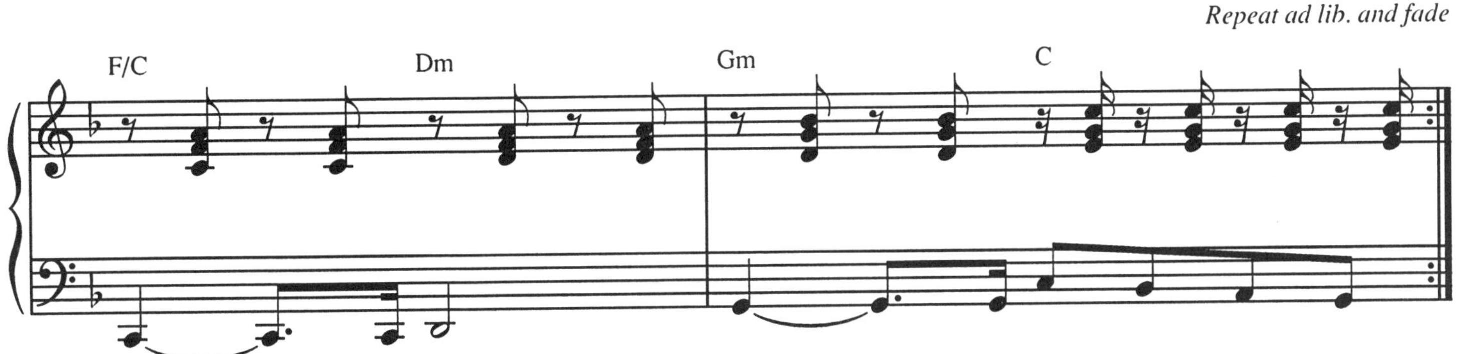

Verse 2:
The moon appears to shine and light the sky
With the help of some fireflies.
I wonder how they have the power to shine;
I can see them under the pine.
(To Bridge:)

Verse 3:
Instrumental solo

Verse 4:
I can see the sunset in your eyes,
Brown and gray and blue besides.
Clouds are stalking islands in the sun.
I wish I could buy one out of season.
(To Bridge:)

(THERE'LL NEVER BE) ANOTHER YOU

Words and Music by
LARRY WEIR

Fm7 B♭7 A♭7 Gm7 G7/B Cm7 B♭ A♭maj7 B♭/A♭ G7
spe - cial that I know who real-ly cares. But late some nights a voice cries
Cm7 F13 Fm7 B♭7 E♭ G7
through, re - mind-ing me there'll nev-er be an - oth-er you.
Bridge:
Cm7 F7 B♭maj7 E♭maj7
1. I can re - call all those win - ters and falls, nights of
2. (Instrumental solo . . .
A♭maj7 Am7(♭5) D7(♭9) D/G Gm D7/G G♯dim
love that I thought would be al - ways with us.
. . . end solo)
Cm7 F7 B♭maj7 E♭maj7
Writ - ing our plans on the beach in the sand, but they
If I could hold you a - gain for one night, it would

Abmaj7 Am7(b5)/D D7(b9) D/G Gm D7/G F#7(#5) Fm7 Abmaj7/Bb

fade___ through___ time___ in the wind and with you, oh. I think of
make___ my whole world___ come a - live a - gain,___ oh. I will sur -

Abmaj7 Ab/Bb Ebmaj7 Cm7 Fm7 Bb7 Ab7

you from time to time. Some-times I won - der___ if I ev - er cross your
vive and car - ry on. Once in a - while I___ hear an old fa - mil - iar

Gm7 G7/B Cm7 Bb Abmaj7 Bb/Ab G7 Cm7 F13

mind. But look - in' back is hard to do, 'cause it re -
song. It takes me back and makes me blue, re-mind-ing

Fm7 Bb7 | 1. Eb G7 *D.S.* 𝄋 | 2. Cm7 F9

minds me___ there won't be an - oth - er you, oh. you. Yes, I
me there'll___ nev - er be an - oth - er

molto rit.

Fm7 Bb7 Am7(b5) Abm(#7) Eb(2)/G Gb13 Fm9 Fb13(#11) Db13(#11) Ebmaj13(#11)

know___ there'll nev-er be___ an-oth-er you.

BABY, COME TO ME

Words and Music by
ROD TEMPERTON

Moderately
Am7
Dm7
Em7
mp
Am
D/A
Am7
D/A
Am
D/A
Am7
D/A
Am7
D/A
1. Think - in' back in time, when love was
2. (See additional lyrics)
Am7
D/A
F/G
G
on - ly in the mind, I re - a - lize

F/G G Am7 D/A Am7 D/A
ain't no sec - ond chance; you've got to hold on to ro - mance. Don't
F/G G F/G G Am7
let it slide. There's a
B♭maj7 Am7
spe - cial kind of mag - ic in the air when you
A♭maj7 G11 F/G G
find an - oth - er heart that needs to share. Ba - by,
cresc.

Chorus:

Cm7 Fm9 Ab/Bb Fm

come to me; let me put my arms a-round you. This was
(you.)

mf

Gm7 Ebmaj9 G7-9

meant to be, and I'm oh, so glad I found you. Need you

Cm7 Fm9 Ab/Bb Fm

ev - 'ry day; got to have your love a-round me. Ba - by,

Gm7 *To Coda* 1. Dm7 G7-9

al - ways stay, 'cause I can't go back to liv - in' with-out

D.S. al Coda
2.3. etc.
D.S.S. al Chorus repeat and fade
Cm
Cm/B♭
B♭
Dm7
G7-9
you.
can't go back to liv - in' with-out
descresc.
Coda
Dm7
G7-9
Csus
can't go back to liv - in' with-out you.
C
A♭maj7
The night can get
Cm7
A♭/B♭
cold; there's a chill to ev-'ry eve - ning

Ebmaj7
Bbm7
Fm9
when you're all a - lone. Don't talk an - y - more, 'cause you
D.S.S. al 2nd ending
Abmaj7
G11
G
know that I'll be here to keep you warm. Ba - by,

2. Spendin' ev'ry dime to keep you
Talkin' on the line;
That's how it was, and
All those walks together
Out in any kind of weather,
Just because.
There's a brand new way of
Looking at your life, when you
Know that love is standing by your side.

To Chorus:

BECAUSE THE NIGHT

Words and Music by
PATTI SMITH and BRUCE SPRINGSTEEN

A Bm G A Bm
fire I breathe. Love is a ban - quet on which we feed.
guised as lust, here in our bed un - til the morn-ing comes.
G A D A Bm G
Come on now, try and un - der - stand the way I feel un - der
mf
A D G A C
your com - mand. Take my hand as the sun de - scends. They can't hurt you now,
Bm F♯
can't hurt you now, can't hurt you now.
cresc.

Chorus:
Bm G A Bm G A Bm
Be-cause the night be - longs to lov - ers. Be-cause the night be - longs to us.
f
G A Bm G A Bm
1. D.C.
Be-cause the night be - longs to lov - ers. Be-cause the night be - longs to us.
dim.
2.
A Bm G A D A Bm G
longs to us.
dim.
mf (Instrumental solo . . .
A D G A G

D A D A
With love we sleep; with doubt the vi - cious cir - cle
. . . end solo)
Bm A D A Bm A D
turns and turns. With - out you, oh I can - not live, for - give, the
A D G D G Bm
yearn - ing, burn-ing, I be - lieve in time, too real to feel. So, take me now,
cresc.
D G F♯
take me now, take me now.
f

Bm G A Bm G A Bm
Be-cause the night be - longs to lov - ers. Be-cause the night be - longs to us.
(Vocal 1st time only)
G A Bm G A Bm
1.
Be-cause the night be - longs to lov - ers. Be-cause the night be - longs to us.
2.
G A Bm G A Bm
dim.
p
Bm G A Bm A B2
1.
2.

BETTER DAYS

Words and Music by
BRUCE SPRINGSTEEN

Bm

-row to come, or that train___ to come roar-in' 'round the_ bend.___ I got a

Em

new suit of clothes,_ a pret-ty red rose______ and a wom-an I can call__ my friend._

Chorus:

G D

___ These_ are bet-ter days,______ ba - by.

{ Yeah,_ there's bet-ter
{ These are

G D

days shin - ing through.______ }
bet - ter days,__ it's true.______ }

These_ are bet-ter days,______ ba - by,

1. D.S. 𝄋

Em G D A

bet - ter days____ with a girl_____ like you. 2. Well,
There's *(2nd time only)*

Verse 2:
Well, I took a piss at fortune's sweet kiss,
It's like eating caviar and dirt.
It's a sad, funny ending to find yourself pretending
A rich man in a poor man's shirt.
Now, my ass was draggin' when from a passin' gypsy wagon,
Your heart, like a diamond shone.
Tonight I'm layin' in your arms, carvin' lucky charms
Out of these hard luck bones.

Chorus 2:
These are better days, baby.
These are better days, it's true.
These are better days.
There's better days shining through.

Verse 3:
Now, a life of leisure and a pirate's treasure
Don't make much for tragedy.
But it's a sad man, my friend, who's livin' in his own skin
And can't stand the company.
Every fool's got a reason for feelin' sorry for himself
And turning his heart to stone.
Tonight, this fool's halfway to heaven and just a mile outta hell,
And I feel like I'm comin' home.
(To Chorus:)

THE BEST YEARS OF MY LIFE

Lyrics and Music by
WILL JENNINGS
and STEPHEN ALLEN DAVIS

C7sus C7 D7(♭9) Gm9

One fine day,

C6 Fmaj9 Am7/D D7(♭9 ♭13)

one fine night, you lov-ing me on and on and on.

Gm9 A7 A7(♭9 ♭13) Dm7

We took our love as far as love can go, ooh,

Dm7/G G13 B♭maj9 1. B♭/C C

ooh. You've giv-en me the best years of my

F(2) B♭(2)

life.

2.
B♭/C
C
B♭/C
C
Dm7
Dm7/G
G13
best years of my life.
B♭maj9
B♭/C
C
B♭/C
C
F(2)
You've giv-en me the best years of my life.
F/E♭
cresc.
Bridge:
D♭6
D♭2
mf
Bring on the storm,
B♭5/C
A♭/C
D♭6
D♭(2)
B♭5/C
A♭/C
we'll see it through.
We'll take it all,
all life can do.
Gm
Am
B♭/C
C/D
Right to the end,
we'll say, "Let's be - gin."
cresc.

Verse 2:
When I play my memories again.
I feel all the pleasure and the pain.
Love can hurt, love can heal.
Oh, how we hurt and healed ourselves again.

We took our souls as far as souls can go, ooh yeah.
You've given me the best years of my life.
You've given me the best years of my life.

BLACK VELVET

Words and Music by
CHRISTOPHER WARD and DAVID TYSON

Moderately slow bluesy shuffle
Vocal 2nd time only
N.C.
Em
mf
Mm.
Mm.
1.
2.
Mis - sis - sip - pi in the mid - dle of a dry spell.
Up in Mem - phis the mu - sic's like a heat wave.

Jim - mie Rod - gers on the Vic - trola up high.
"White Light - nin' " bound to drive you wild.
Ma-ma's danc - in' with ba - by on her shoul - der.
Ma-ma's ba - by is in the heart of ev - 'ry school girl.
The sun is set - tin' like mo - las - ses in the sky.
"Love Me Ten - der" leaves 'em cry - in' in the aisle.
B7sus
B7
A7sus
A7
The boy could sing; knew how to move ev - 'ry - thing.
The way he moved it was a sin so sweet and true.

G7sus
G7
Dsus
Al - ways want - ing more.
He'd leave you long - ing for . . .
Am9
Chorus:
D
Black vel - vet and that lit - tle boy smile.
Am9
F
C
Black vel - vet {with / and} that slow south - ern style.
Am9
D
A new re - li - gion that - 'll bring you to your knees.

1.
C7
B7sus
Em
Black vel - vet, if you please.
2.
C7
B7sus
Black vel - vet, if you
Em
please.
Bridge:
Am
Ev-'ry word of ev-'ry song
B7
Em7
that he sang was for you.

Am
F
In a flash he was gone it hap - pened so
C
B7
Em7
soon.
What could you do?

Am7
Am9
Black vel - vet and that
D
lit - tle boy smile.
Am7
Am9
Black vel - vet in that
F
C
slow south-ern style.
Am7
Am9
A new re - li - gion that - 'll
D
bring you to your knees.
1.
C7
B7sus
Black vel - vet,

2.
Em
C7
B7sus
if you please.
Black vel - vet, if you
Em7
please.
If you please.
If you please.
If you please.
Mm.
1.
2.
Repeat ad lib. and fade
Mm.

CAN'T STOP THIS THING WE STARTED

Lyrics and Music by
BRYAN ADAMS and
R.J. LANGE

D/A
A
D/A
A
oth - er guys,
I can't fly,
but if
you wan - na stop me, ba - by,
don't ev - en try. I'm go-in' one
D
G/D
D
E
way,
your way.
A/E
E
D
G/D
D
Now, it's such a
strong way,
let's make it
E
F♯m7
Esus
Chorus:
D(2)
our way,
now, ba - by.
I can't stop this
E(2)
E/F♯
F♯m7
D
A
thing we start - ed.
You got-ta know
it's right.

To Coda
D(2)
E(2)
E/F♯
F♯m7
D
I can't stop this course we plot - ted, yeah.
A
D(2)
E(2)
This thing called love, we got it.
F♯m7
A
D(2)
No place for the brok - en heart - ed. I can't stop this
F♯m/E
E
Esus
E
D
thing we start - ed, no way. I'm go - ing
1.
D.S.
2.
E
A/E
E
your way.

B♭
E♭/B♭ B♭ E♭/B♭ B♭
F
Oh,
why take it
slow?

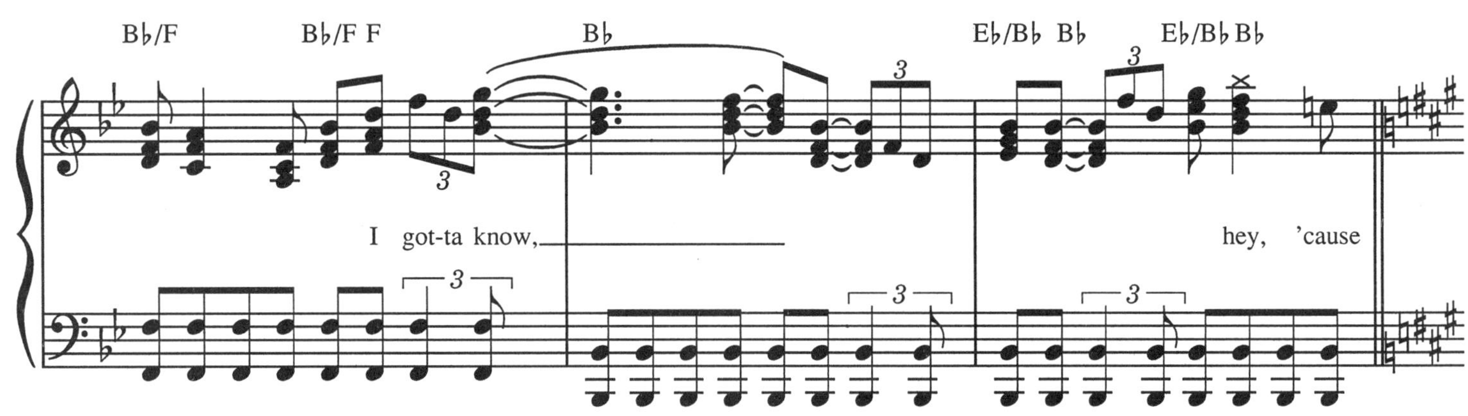
B♭/F B♭/F F
B♭
E♭/B♭ B♭ E♭/B♭ B♭
I got-ta know,
hey, 'cause

A
D
E
noth - ing can stop this
thing that we've got.
(Instrumental solo . . .

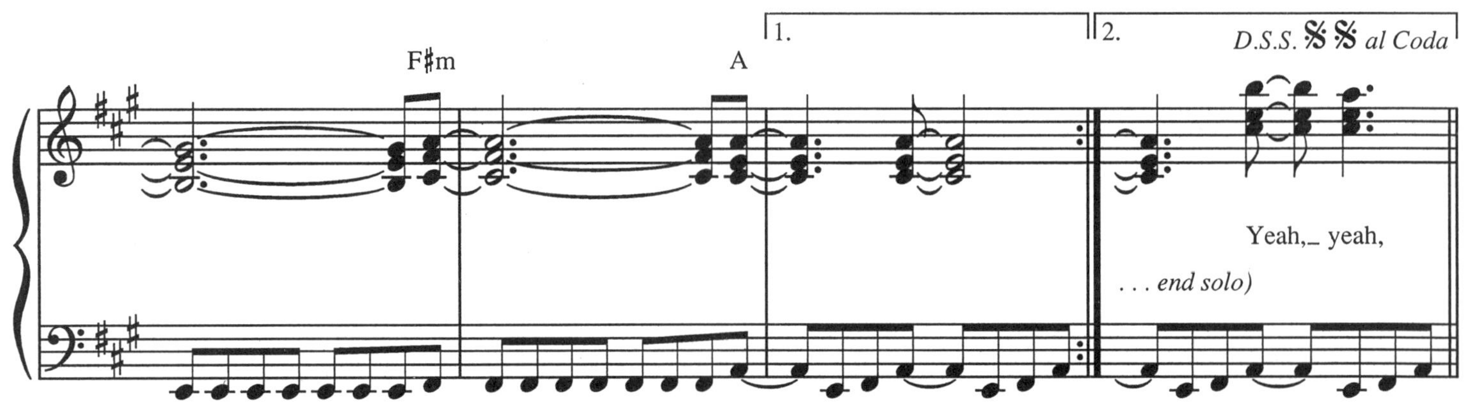
F♯m
A
1.
2.
D.S.S. 𝄋𝄋 al Coda
Yeah, yeah,
. . . end solo)

Coda
A
B♭
C
This thing called love, we got it.
F
B♭
D
Ain't no place for the brok - en heart - ed. I can't stop it.
E
D(2)
E(2)
I can't stop it. I can't stop this thing we start - ed.
E/F♯
F♯m7
D
A
D(2)
You got-ta know it's right. I can't stop this
Repeat ad lib. and fade
E(2)
E/F♯
F♯m7
D
A
course we plot - ted, yeah.

CAT'S IN THE CRADLE

Words and Music by
HARRY CHAPIN and SANDY CHAPIN

Moderately, with a 2 feel ♩ = 76
E♭5
mf

My

Verses 1 & 2:
E♭
D
G♭
F
A♭
G
child ar - rived__ just the oth - er day; he came to the world in the
son turned ten___ just the oth - er day. He said, "Thanks for the ball, Dad. Come

D
E♭
F
G♭
u - su - al way.__ But there were planes to catch__ and bills to pay.__
on, let's play.__ Can you teach me to throw?"_ I said, "Not to - day.__ I got a

G
D
C
C/B
A♭
E♭
D♭
D♭/C
He learned to walk while I was a - way. And he was talk - in' 'for I knew it. And
lot to do." He said, "That's o - kay." And he walked a - way, but his

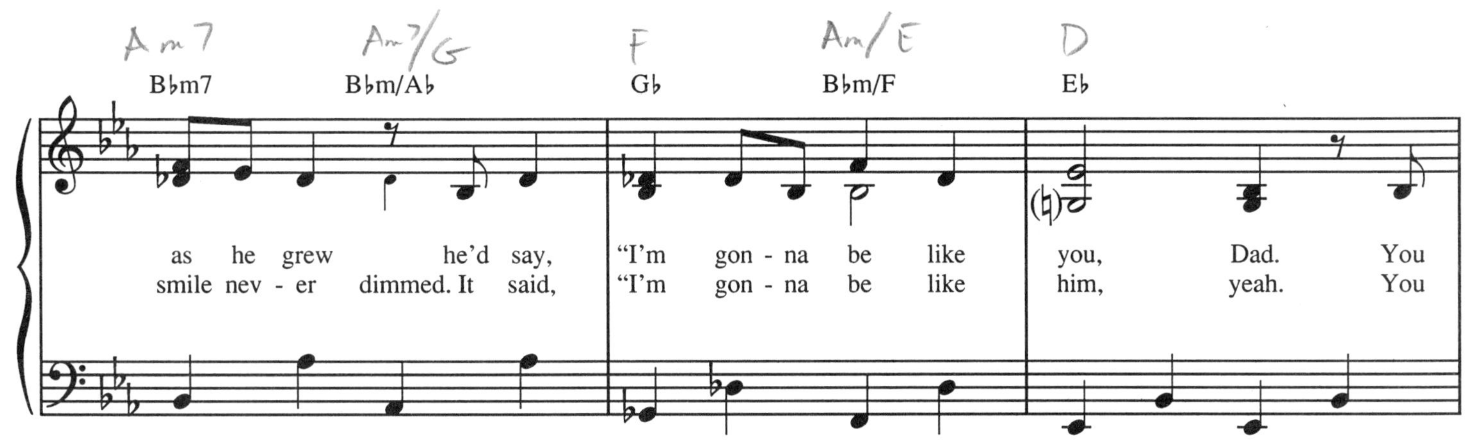
Am7
Am7/G
F
Am/E
D
B♭m7
B♭m/A♭
G♭
B♭m/F
E♭
as he grew he'd say, "I'm gon - na be like you, Dad. You
smile nev - er dimmed. It said, "I'm gon - na be like him, yeah. You

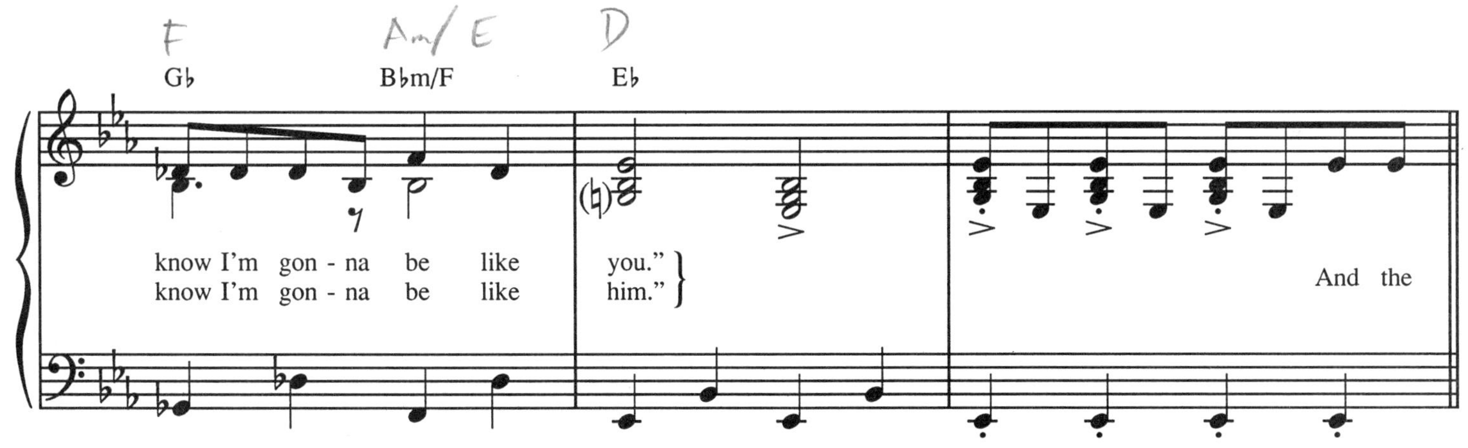
F
Am/E
D
G♭
B♭m/F
E♭
know I'm gon - na be like you."
know I'm gon - na be like him."
And the

D
C
F
Chorus:
E♭
D♭
G♭
cat's in the cra - dle and the sil - ver spoon,_ lit - tle boy blue and the man_

A♭
E♭
D♭
in the moon.
"When you com - in' home,
1. 2. Dad?"
3. 4 Son?"
"I
don't know when, but

4th time to Coda II
G♭
B♭m/F
E♭
3rd time to Coda I
G♭
B♭m/F
we'll get to - geth - er then,
Son.
yeah.
Dad.
You
know we'll have a good time

E♭
E♭5
then."

1.
2.
My
Well, he

Verse 3:
E♭
G♭
A♭
came from col - lege just the oth - er day, so much like a man I just
E♭
G♭
had to say, "Son, I'm proud of you. Can you sit for a while?" He
A♭
E♭
D♭
D♭/C
shook his head and he said with a smile, "What I'd real - ly like, Dad, is to
B♭m7
B♭m/A♭
G♭
B♭m/F
E♭
D.S. 𝄋 al Coda I
bor-row the car keys. See you lat - er. Can I have them, please?" And the
Coda I
E♭
C♭
D♭
B♭m
E♭
then."

C♭
D♭ B♭m
E♭
I've
Verse 4:
E♭
long since re - tired, my
G♭
son's moved a - way.
A♭
I called him up just the
E♭
oth - er day.
I said, "I'd
like to see_ you if
G♭
you don't mind."_ He said, "I'd
A♭
love to, Dad,_ if I can
E♭
find the time._
You see, my
D♭
D♭/C
new job's a has - sle and the
B♭m7
B♭m/A♭
kids have the flu,_ but it's
G♭
B♭m/F
sure nice talk - in' to

E♭ G♭ B♭m/F E♭
you, Dad. It's been sure nice talk - in' to you." And as I
D♭ D♭/C B♭m7 B♭m/A♭ G♭ B♭m/F
hung up the phone it oc - curred to me, he'd grown up just like
mp
Tempo I
D.S. 𝄋 al Coda II
E♭5 G♭ B♭m/F E♭
me. My boy was just like me. And the
mf
Coda II
A little slower
E♭ G♭ B♭m/F E♭ E♭5
Dad, we're gon-na have a good time then."
rit.
a tempo
E♭

COMING OUT OF THE DARK

Words and Music by
GLORIA ESTEFAN, EMILIO ESTEFAN, JR.
and JON SECADA

Gospel rock ♩ = 66
N.C.
mp
with pedal
Verse:
(E(2))
N.C.
(D/E)
(E(2))
1. Why be a - fraid if I'm not a - lone? Life is nev - er
2. Start-ing a - gain is part of the plan, and I'll be so much
D/E
E
eas - y, the rest is un - known. And up till now for
strong - er hold - ing your hand. Step by step I'll

(D2/E)
(F♯m/A)
D/E (E/G♯) (F♯m) (E) E
me it's been hands a - gainst stone.
make it through, I know I can.
I spend each and ev - ery
It may not make it
D/E E/D A/C♯ Amaj7 A/B
mo - ment search - ing for what to be - lieve.
eas - i - er, but I have felt you near all the way.
Com-ing out of the
Chorus:
E E7 A/E Am6/E
dark I fin - 'lly see the light, now, and it's shin - ing on me.

E
C♯m7
A(2)
A/B
Com-ing out of the
E
E7
dark,
I know the love that saved
1.
A/E
Am6/E
me, you're
shar - ing with me.
E
D2/E
E

D.S. 𝄋
2.
To Next Strain
3.4.etc.
D2/E
N.C.
A/E
A/B
A/E
Am6/E
me,__ you're shar-ing with me.____
me__you're shar - ing, you're shar-
(For
Repeat ad lib. and fade
E
C♯m7
A(2)
A/B
- ing with me,
shar - ing with me,__
shar-ing with me,__ shar-ing with me.
Bridge:
A
E/G♯
F♯m7 E/G♯
F♯m/A Amaj7/B
For-ev - er____
stand on the rock of your love.____
ev - er and ev - er,
stand on__ the__ rock.
For -

A
E/G♯
F♯m7
A/B
B♭7(♭5)
Ev - er,
ev - er,
ooh.
Can't no-bod - y
stop me! Watch me!
ev - er
and ev - er,
ooh.
For-
A
E/G♯
F♯m7
E/G♯
F♯m/A
Amaj7/B
Ev - er
and ev - er
stand on the rock of your love
ev - er
and ev - er,
stand on the rock of your love.
E
E/D
A/C♯
A
A/B
D.S.S.
is all it takes
no mat-ter what we face.
Com-ing out of the

DO YOU BELIEVE IN US

Words and Music by
JON SECADA and
MIGUEL A. MOREJON

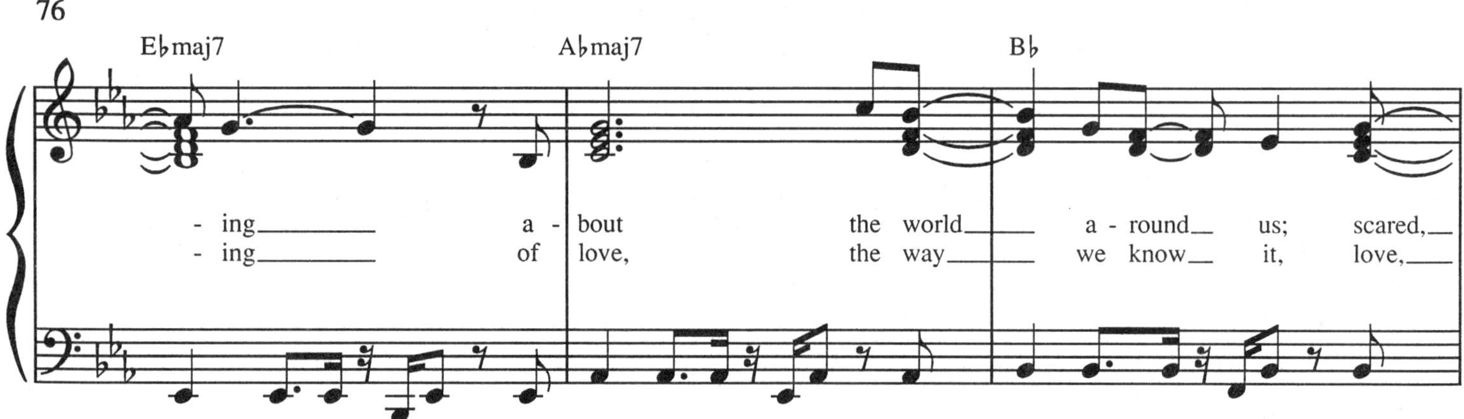

E♭maj7
A♭maj7
B♭
- ing a - bout the world a - round us; scared,
- ing of love, the way we know it, love,

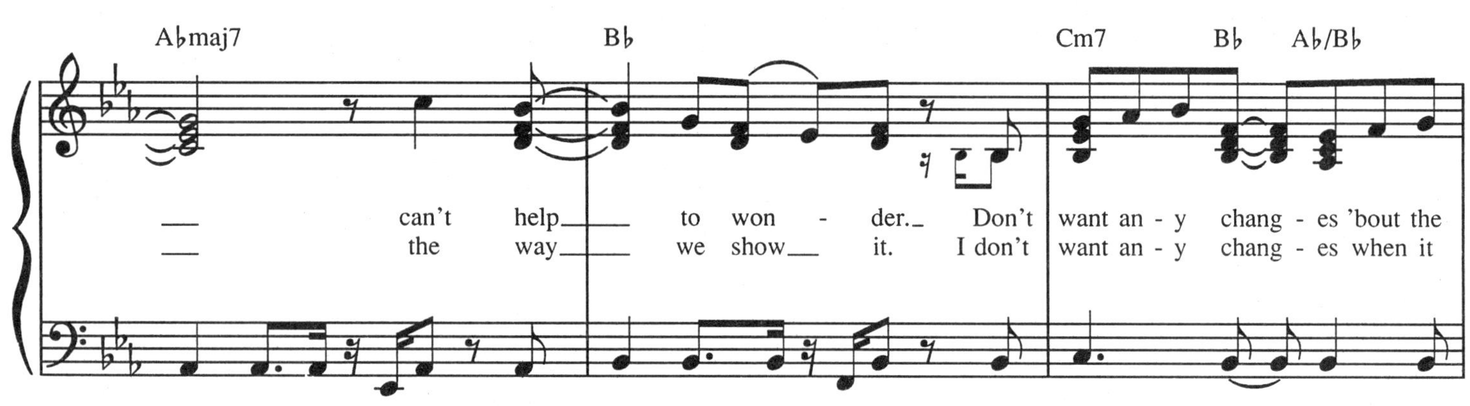

A♭maj7
B♭
Cm7
B♭
A♭/B♭
can't help to won - der. Don't want an - y chang - es 'bout the
the way we show it. I don't want an - y chang - es when it

B♭
A♭
Cm7
B♭
A♭
way we feel. Do you know what I mean?
comes to you. I like us the way it is. No

Cm7
B♭
A♭/B♭
B♭
A♭
B♭
Catch me, I'm fall - ing; say it's gon - na be al - right, it's gon-na
mat - ter what hap - pens, say it's gon - na be al - right, it's gon-na

Chorus:
E♭
B♭
be al - right.
be al - right.
cresc.
I know that we be - long; do you be -
f

Fm7
A♭
B♭
E♭
lieve in us? Just give it half a chance. Yes, our love will

B♭
Fm7
A♭
B♭
still be strong; girl, I be - lieve in us. I'll give you all I can.

E♭maj7/G
A♭(9)
E♭maj7/G
A♭(9)
E♭maj7/G
A♭(9)
mf

1.
D.S. 𝄋
2.
E♭
E♭m9
mp
F♯m7/B
Emaj9
mf
Amaj9
B
Amaj7
B
C♯m7
B
A/B
I don't want an - y chang - es un-less you
f
B
A
C♯m7
B
A
want them_ too._ For - ev - er ain't long_ e - nough,_ ba - by._

C♯m7
B
A/B
B
A
B
Noth-ing can change_ us; say it's gon - na_ be_ al - right, it's gon-na

E
B
be al - right.___ I know that we be - long;_ do you be -
cresc.
ff

F♯m7
A
B
E
lieve in us? Just give it half a chance. Yes, our love___ will

Repeat ad lib. and fade
B
F♯m7
A
B
still be strong;_ girl, I be - lieve in us. I'll give you all I can.

THE CRYING GAME

Words and Music by
GEOFF STEPHENS

Rock ♩ = 100
N.C.
mf

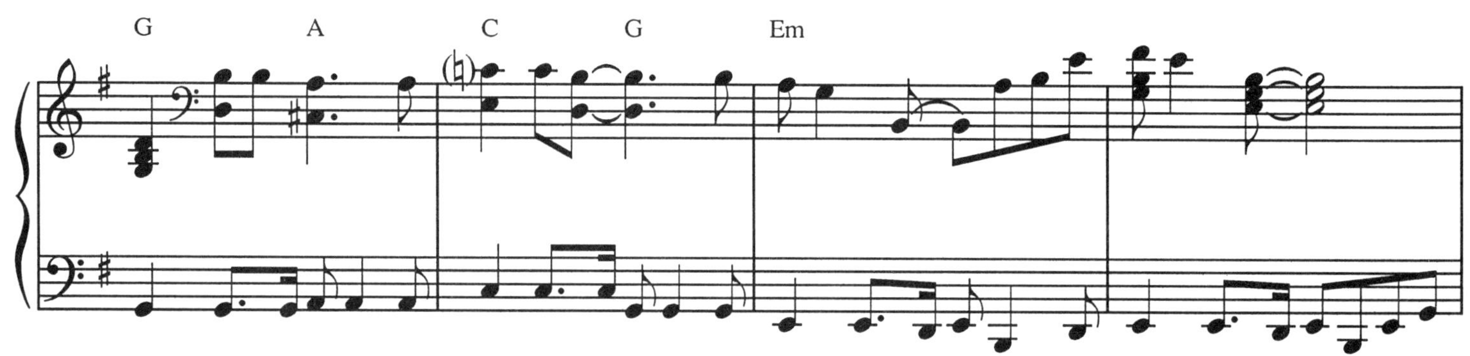
G
A
C
G
Em

Bm
C
Em

Verse:
G
A
C
G
Em
I know_ all there is to know_ a-bout the cry-ing game._
(Instrumental solo on D.S. . . .

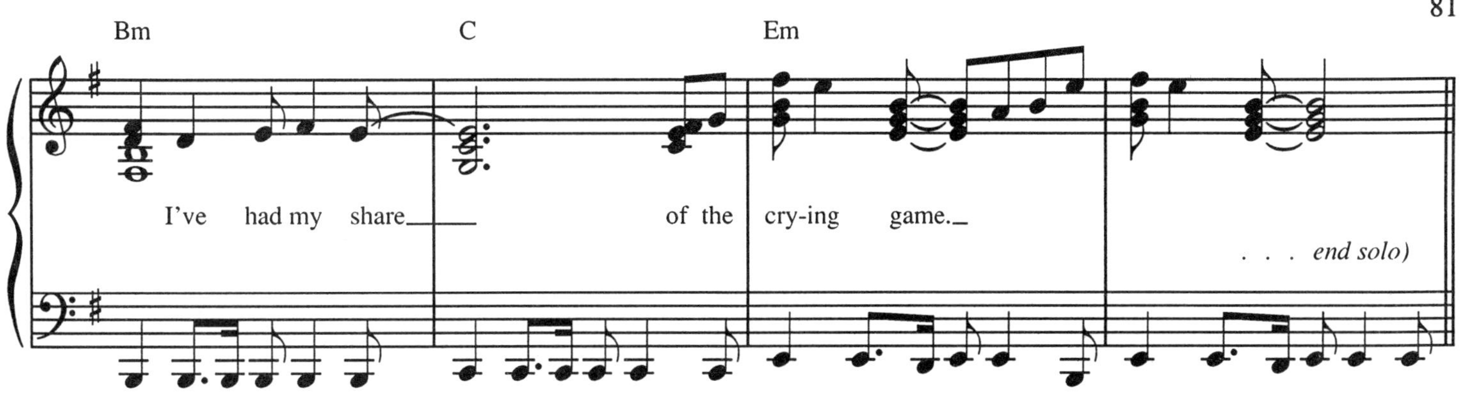
Bm
C
Em
I've had my share___ of the cry-ing game._
. . . end solo)

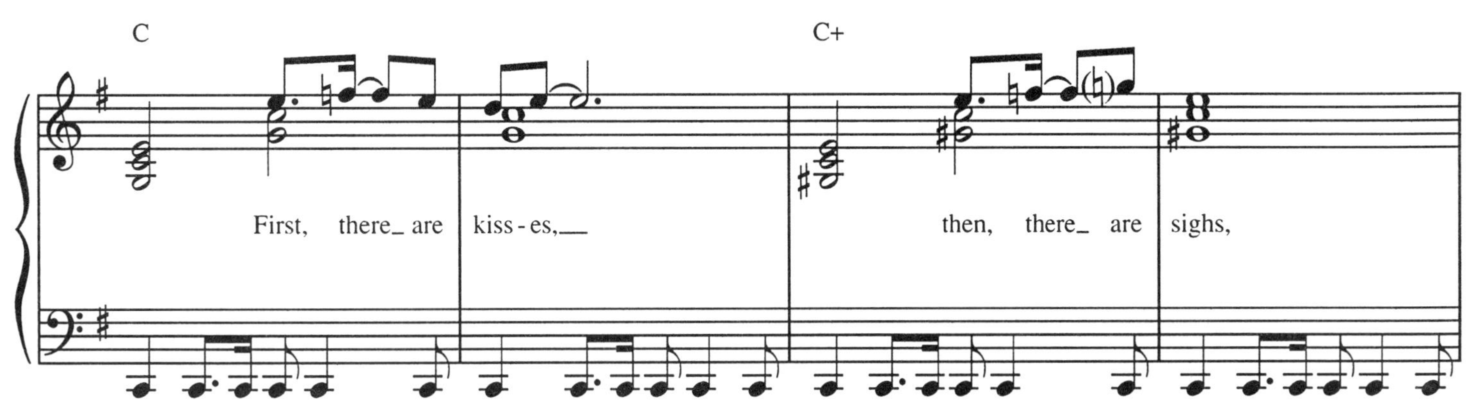
C
C+
First, there_ are kiss-es,___ then, there_ are sighs,

F
E♭
B♭
D
To Coda
and then, be-fore you know where_ you are, you're say-ing good-bye.________

N.C.
G
A
One day_ soon, I'm gon-na tell the moon_ a-bout the cry-ing game._

C
G
Em
Bm
And if he knows,

C
Em
C
may-be he'll ex - plain
why there are

C+
F
heart-aches,
why there are tears,
and what to do to

E♭
B♭
D
D.S. 𝄋 al Coda
stop feel - ing blue when love dis - ap - pears.

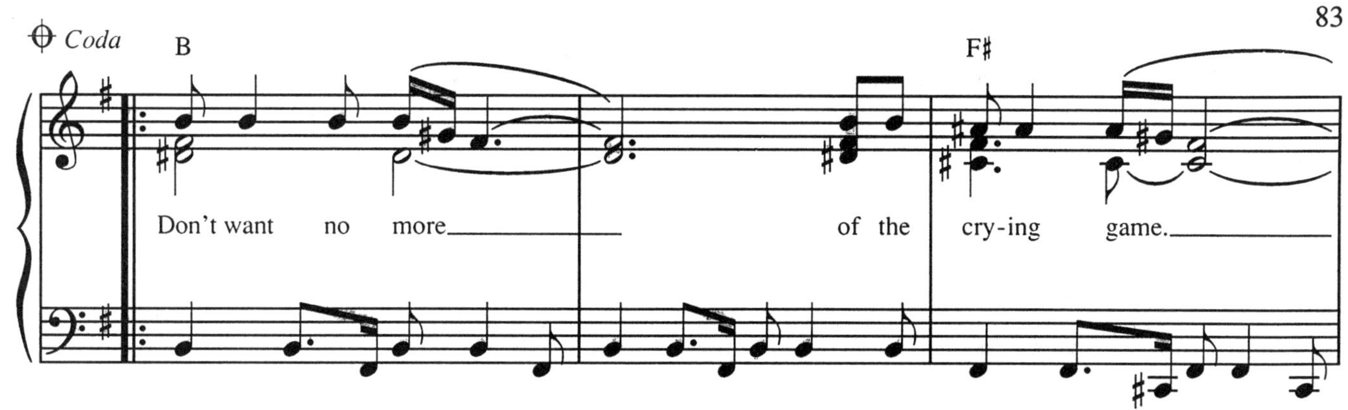
Coda
B
F♯
Don't want no more of the cry-ing game.

A
I don't want no more of the

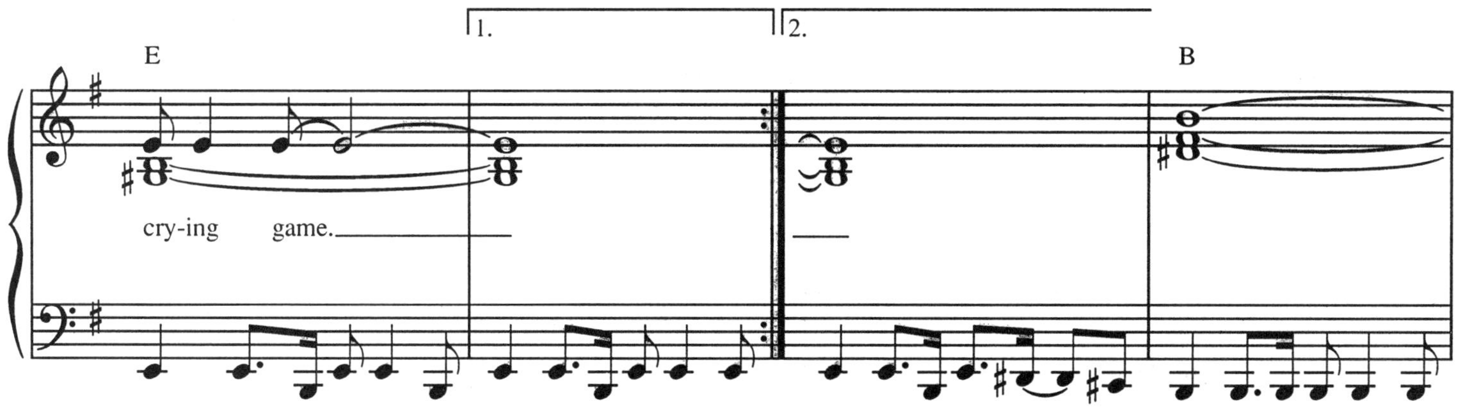
1.
2.
E
B
cry-ing game.

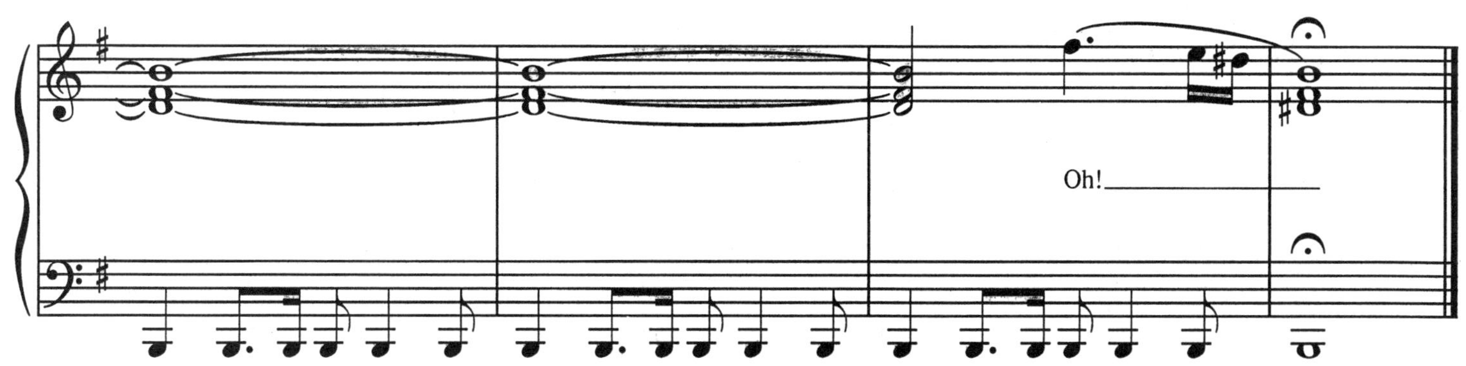
Oh!

CUTS BOTH WAYS

Words and Music by
GLORIA ESTEFAN

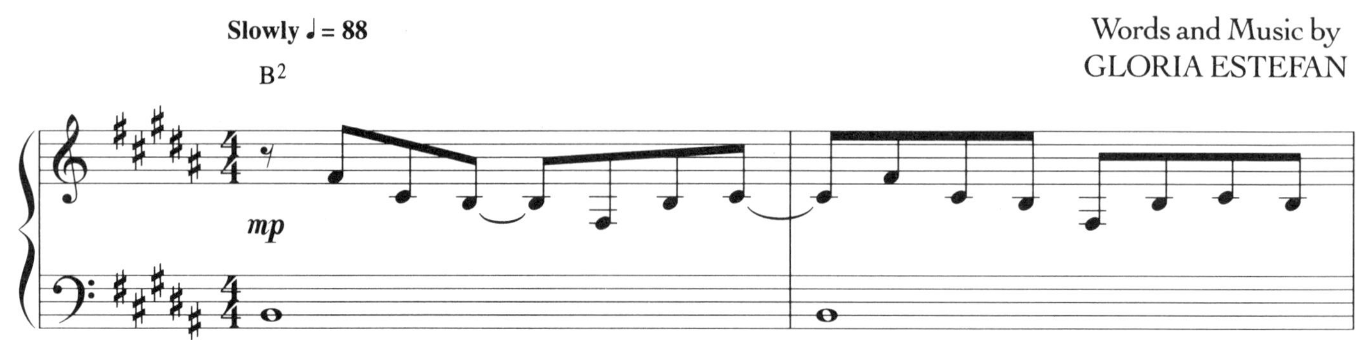

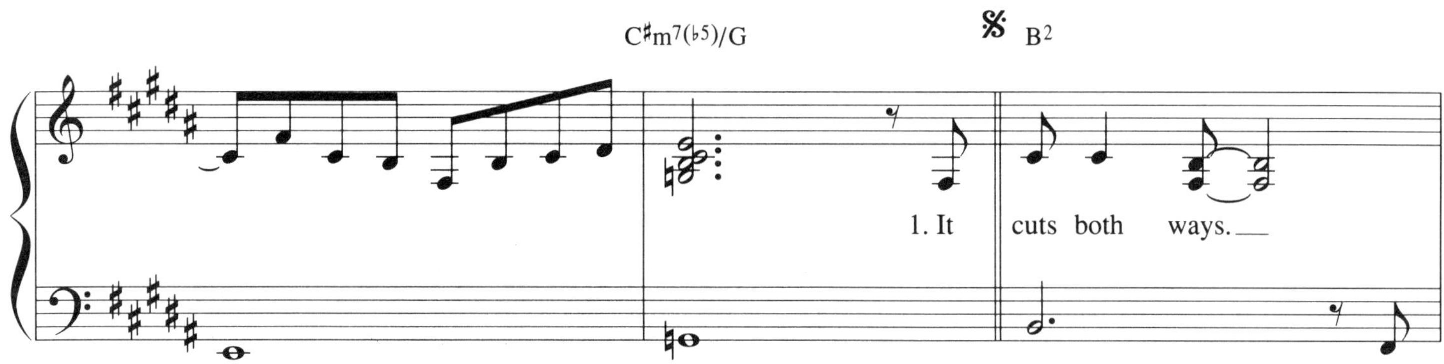

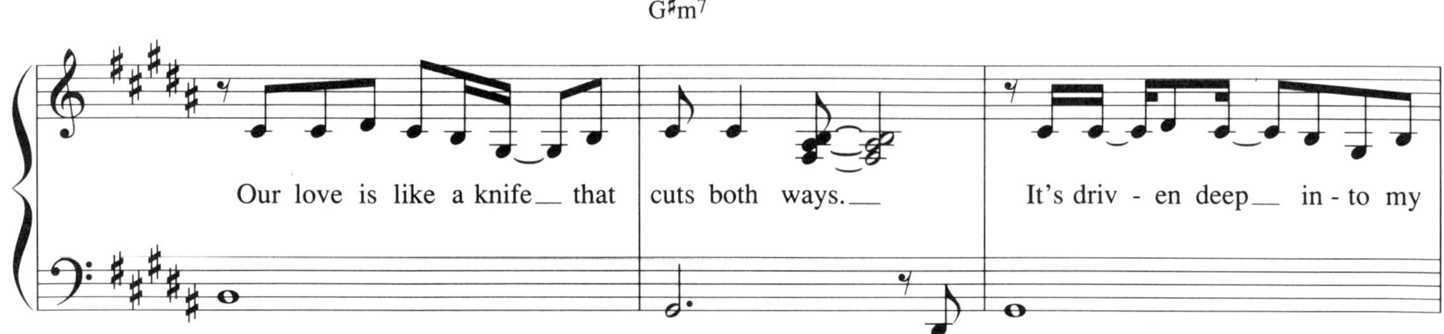

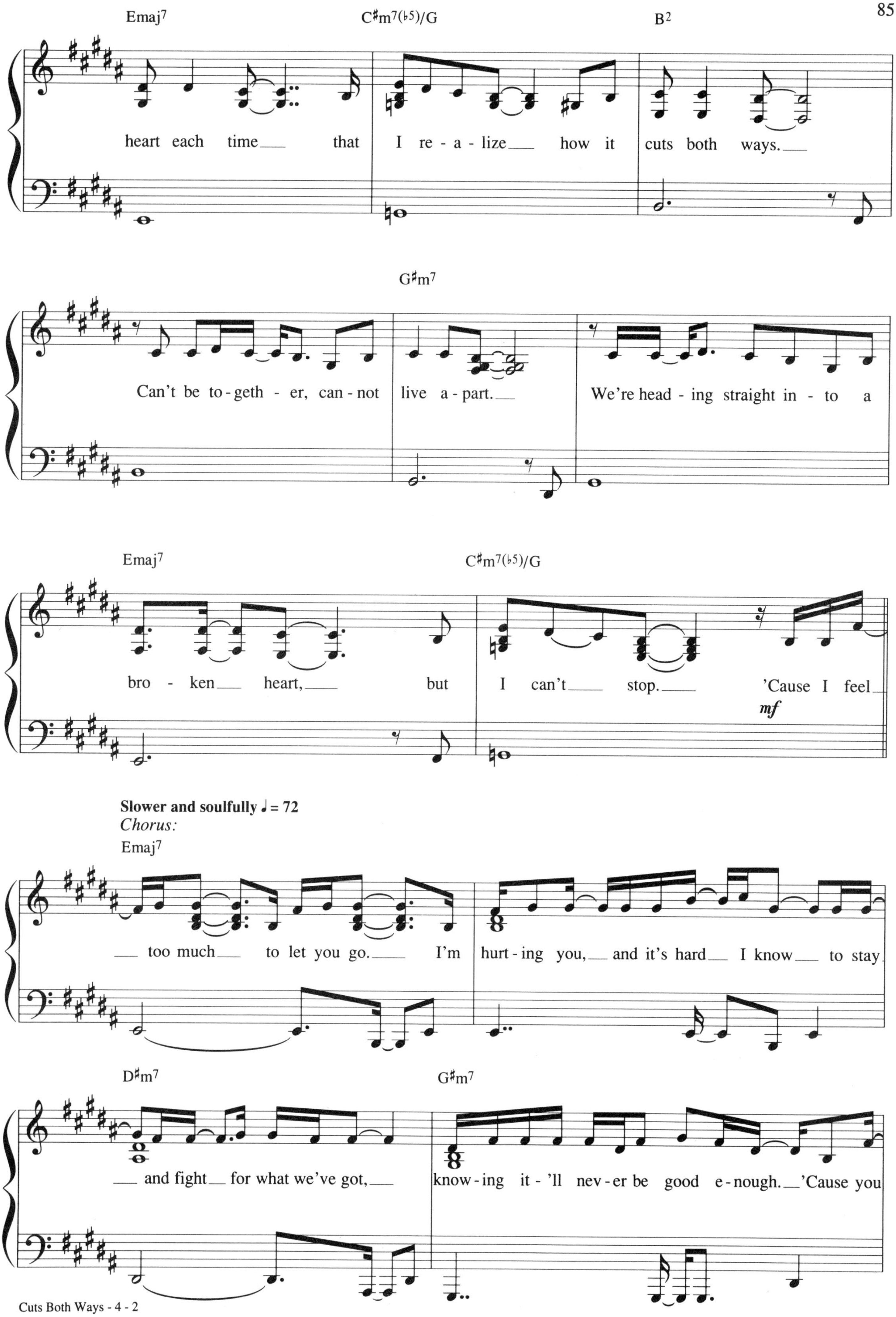

Emaj7 C♯m7(♭5)/G B2

heart each time that I re - a - lize how it cuts both ways.

G♯m7

Can't be to-geth - er, can - not live a - part. We're head - ing straight in - to a

Emaj7 C♯m7(♭5)/G

bro - ken heart, but I can't stop. 'Cause I feel

mf

Emaj7
and I are dan - ger - ous. We
want too much, and life ain't that way. Don't ask

D♯m7
1.
C♯m7
C♯m7(♭5)/G
for more, don't be a fool.
Have - n't we al - read - y bro - ken ev - ery rule?

D.S. 𝄋
Slowly ♩ = 88
2.
C♯m7
C♯m7(♭5)/G
2. It
dim.
mp
Have - n't we al - read - y bro - ken ev - ery rule?

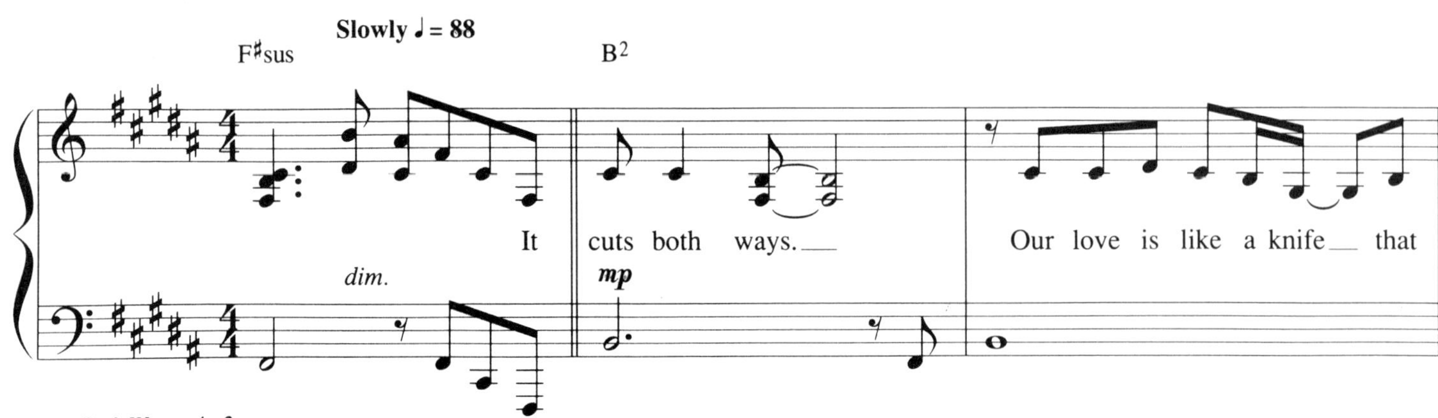
Slowly ♩ = 88
F♯sus
B2
It
cuts both ways.
Our love is like a knife that
dim.
mp

G♯m7
Emaj7
cuts both ways.
It's driv - en deep in - to my
heart each time I see we're

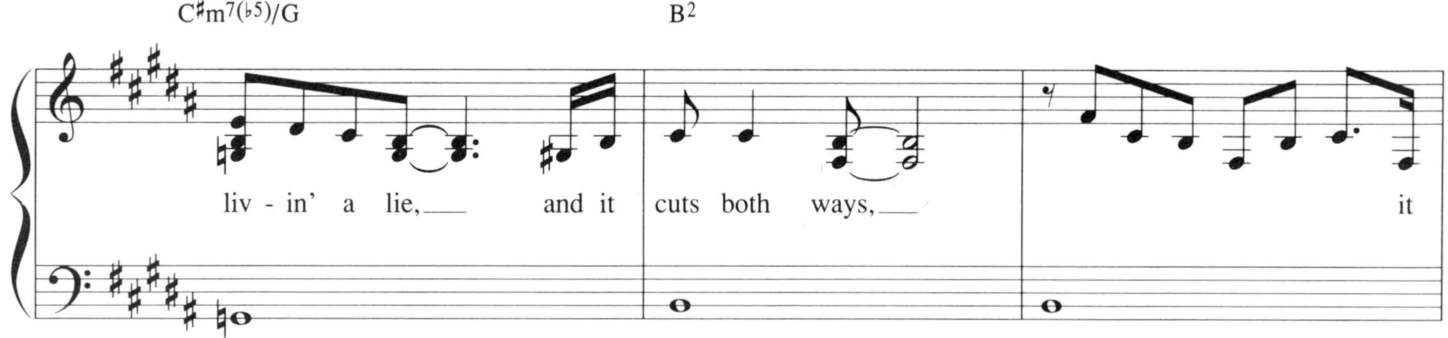
C♯m7(♭5)/G
B2
liv - in' a lie,
and it
cuts both ways,
it

G♯m7
Emaj7
cuts both ways.
Mm,
it
cuts both ways,

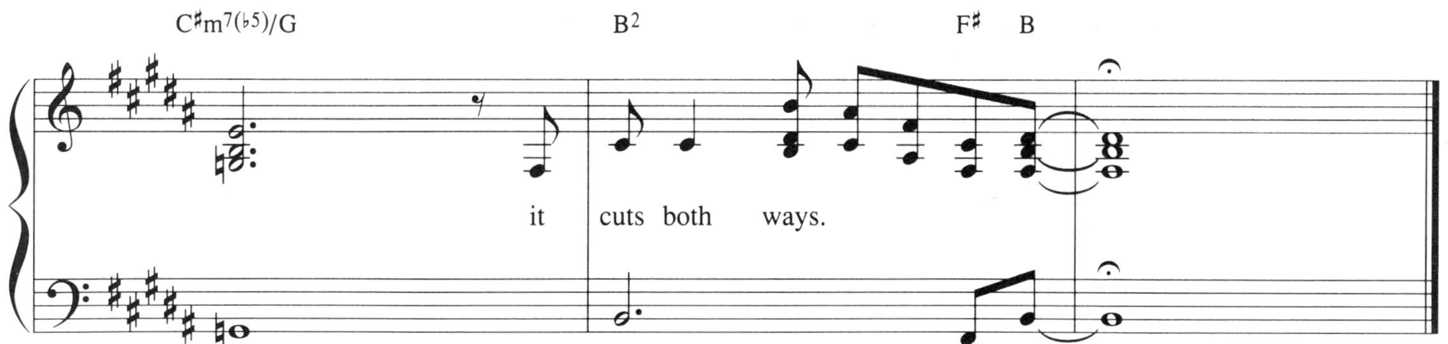
C♯m7(♭5)/G
B2
F♯
B
it
cuts both ways.

Verse 2:

It cuts both ways.
We're in too deep for sorry alibis.
Can't have regrets or even question why
We can't say goodbye,
Because it cuts both ways.
No more illusions of the love we make.
No sacrifice would ever be too great
If you would just stay.

(To Chorus:)

DO I HAVE TO SAY THE WORDS?

Lyrics and Music by
BRYAN ADAMS & JIM VALLANCE
& R.J. LANGE

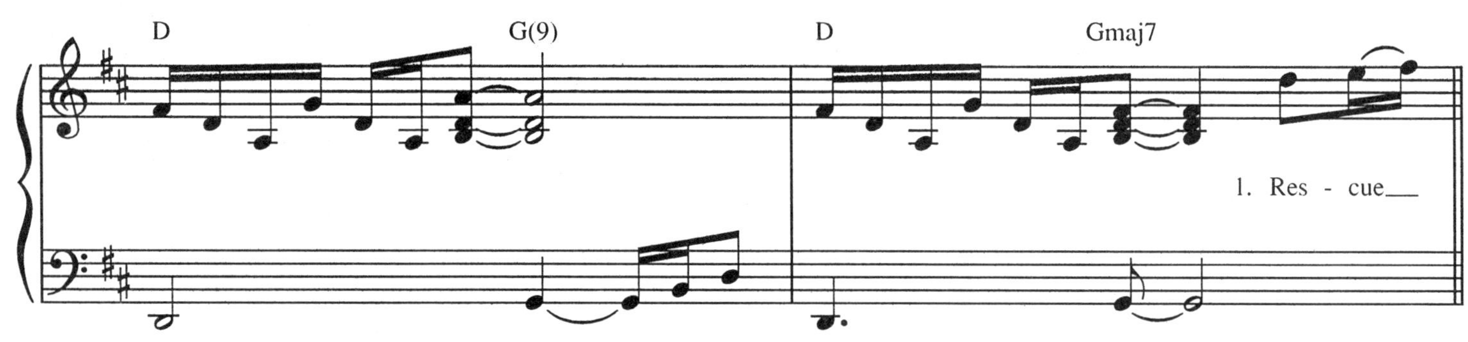

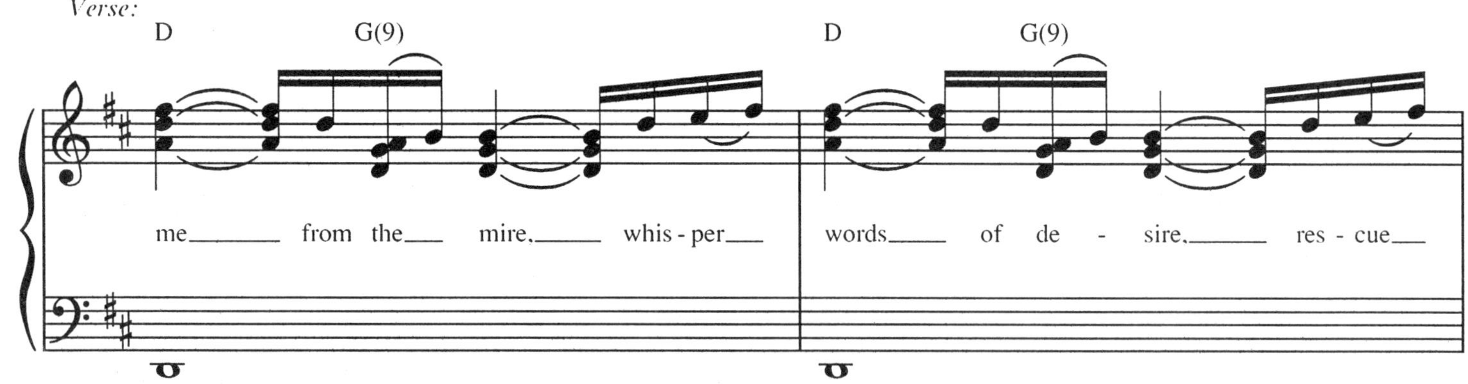

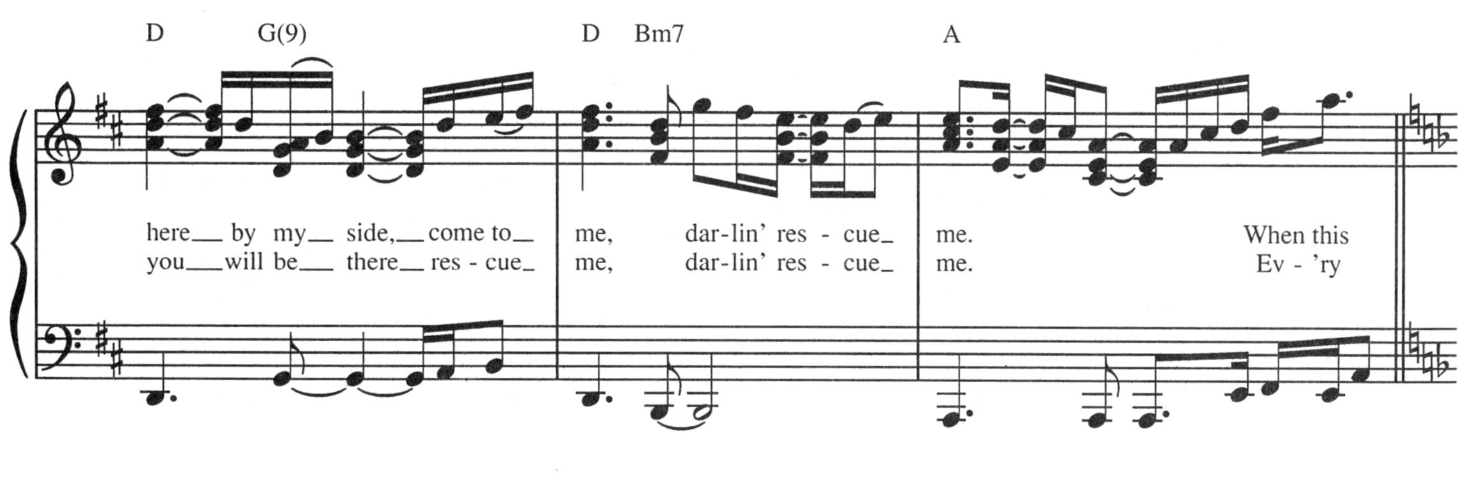
D G(9) D Bm7 A
here__ by my__ side,__ come to__ me, dar-lin' res - cue__ me. When this
you__ will be__ there__ res - cue__ me, dar-lin' res - cue__ me. Ev - 'ry

F B♭maj7 F B♭maj7
world's__ clos - ing__ in__ there's no__ need__ to pre - tend,__ set me__
dream__ that we__ share,__ ev - 'ry__ cross__ that we__ bear,__ come to__

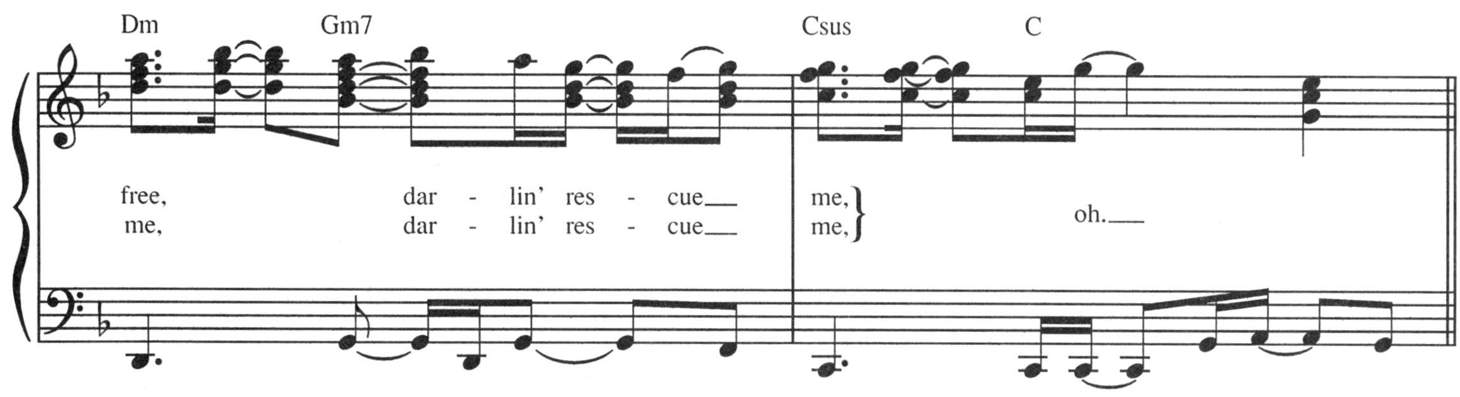
Dm Gm7 Csus C
free, dar - lin' res - cue__ me,
me, dar - lin' res - cue__ me,
oh.__

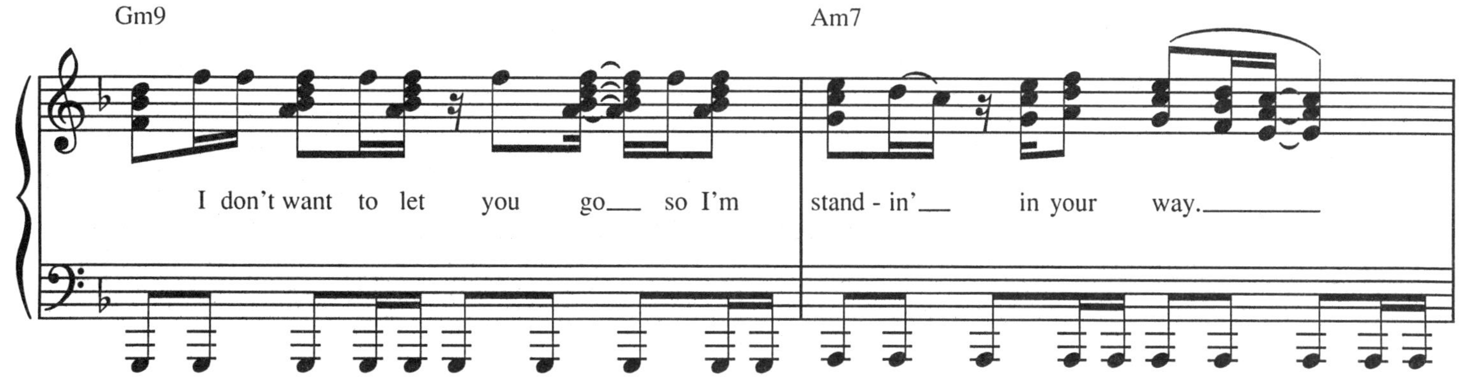
Gm9 Am7
I don't want to let you go__ so I'm stand - in'__ in your way.__

B♭
C
I never needed anyone like I'm
needin' you today.
Do I
N.C.
Chorus:
Dm
Gm
have to say the words?
Do I have to tell the truth?
C
F
B♭
Do I have to shout it out?
Gm
C
Dm
Do I have to say a prayer?
Must I prove to you
B♭
To Coda
C
how good we are together?
Do I have to say the words?

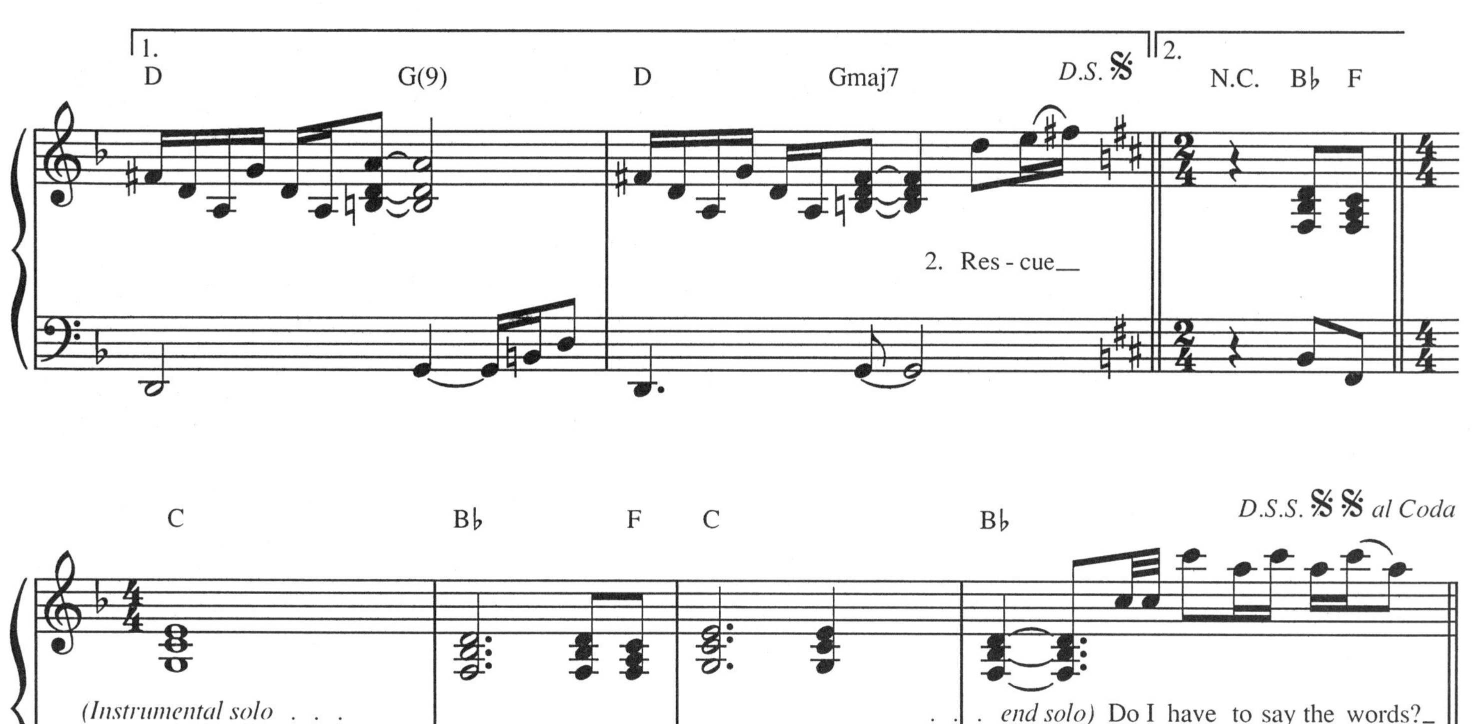
1.
D
G(9)
D
Gmaj7
D.S. 𝄋
2.
N.C.
B♭
F
2. Res - cue
C
B♭
F
C
B♭
D.S.S. 𝄋𝄋 al Coda
(Instrumental solo . . .
. . . end solo) Do I have to say the words?

Coda
C
N.C.
D
G(9)
- er?
Do I have to say the words?
(Ad lib. vocals)
(Instrumental solo 3rd time to end)

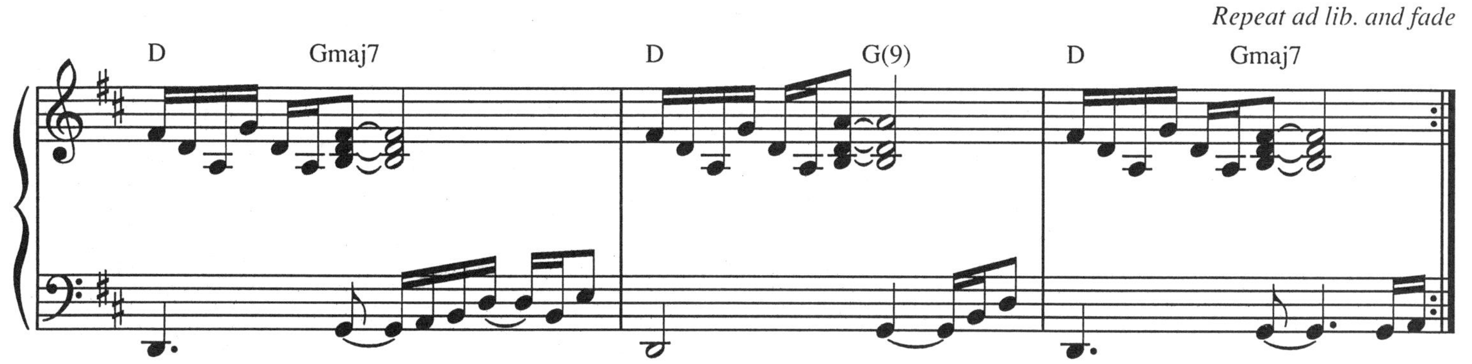
Repeat ad lib. and fade
D
Gmaj7
D
G(9)
D
Gmaj7

From the Motion Picture Soundtrack from Paramount Pictures' "BOOMERANG"

END OF THE ROAD

Words and Music by
BABYFACE, L.A. REID, DARYL SIMMONS

A♭
Gm7
Fm7
Fm7/B♭
How could you love me and leave me and never say good-bye? Well, I
Bridge:
Cm
Cm/B
E♭/B♭
Am7(♭5)
can't sleep at night with-out hold-ing you tight. Girl, each time I try I just break down and cry.
A♭maj7
Gm7
Fm7
Gm7
A♭maj7
A♭maj7/B♭
Pain in my head, oh, I'd rath-er be dead, spin-nin' a-round and a-round. Al-though we've
Chorus:
E♭
Fm/E♭
E♭
B♭/C
Cm7
B♭7
come to the end of the road, still I can't let you
A♭
E♭/G
Gm7
Fm7
A♭maj7/B♭
go. It's un-nat-ur-al. You be-long to me, I be-long to you.

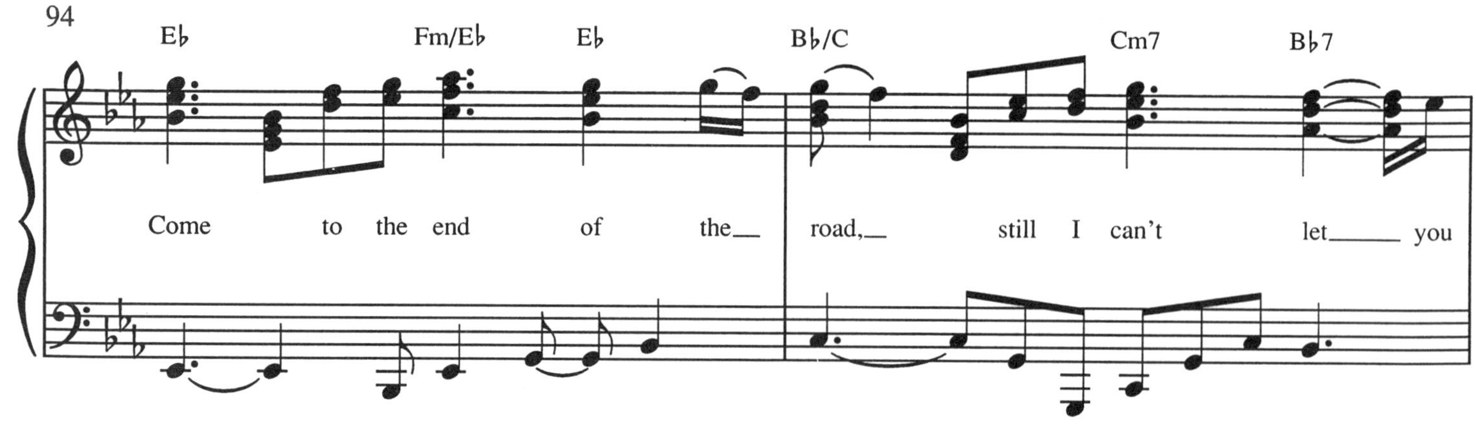

Verse 2:
Girl, I know you really love me, you just don't realize.
You've never been there before, it's only your first time.
Maybe I'll forgive you, mmm. . . maybe you'll try.
We should be happy together, forever, you and I.

Bridge 2:
Could you love me again like you loved me before?
This time, I want you to love me much more.
This time, instead just come back to my bed.
And baby, just don't let me down.

Verse 3, spoken:
Girl I'm here for you.
All those times at night when you just hurt me,
And just ran out with that other fellow,
Baby, I knew about it.
I just didn't care.
You just don't understand how much I love you, do you?
I'm here for you.
I'm not out to go out there and cheat all night just like you did, baby.
But that's alright, huh, I love you anyway.
And I'm still gonna be here for you 'til my dyin' day, baby.
Right now, I'm just in so much pain, baby,
'Cause you just won't come back to me, will you?
Just come back to me.

Bridge 3, spoken:
Yes, baby, my heart is lonely.
My heart hurts, baby, yes, I feel pain too.
Baby please . . .

EVERYTHING'S SO DIFFERENT WITHOUT YOU

Words and Music by
B. OCEAN and R. KELLY

Bbm(4)
Bbm
Ebm7
Gb/Ab
Gm7(b5)
Oh, I should-'ve
seen it in your eyes,
but I
didn't re-al-ize.
cresc.
Chorus:
Gbmaj7
Fm7
Abm7
G7(b5)
1.2.3. Thought that I could take
los - ing you, but I just can't make it. I
f
Gbmaj7
Fm7
Abm7
G7(b5)
know that I could win, but
be - ing a - lone just won't do.
To Coda
1.
Gbmaj7
Fm7
Ebm7
Gb/Ab
Ab
Be - ing on my own,
ev - 'ry - thing's so dif-f'rent with-out
D.S.
2.
To Next Strain
Db(2)
Fm7
Ebm7
Gb/Ab
Ab
Ebm7
Gb/Ab
Gm7(b5)
you.
ev - 'ry - thing's so dif-f'rent with-out

3. D.S.S. 𝄋𝄋 al Coda | Bridge:

Ebm7 Gb/Ab Gm7(b5) | Gbmaj7

ev - 'ry - thing's_ so dif - f'rent.___ Oh! | you. Thought that I___ could take_ the load_

Fm7 | Ebm7 Fm7 | Gb/Ab Gm7(b5) D.S.S. 𝄋𝄋

___ by my - self.___ | Now, I know_that I___ need | you and no one else.___

𝄌 Coda

Ebm7 Ab | Db(2) Fm7 | Ebm7 Gb/Ab

ev-'ry-thing's_ so dif - f'rent_ with-out | you. *dim.*

Db(2) Fm7 | Ebm7 Gb/Ab Ab | Db(2)

mf I said my heart_ would nev - er break.___ | *rit. e dim.* | *mp* *p*

Verse 2:
I made you think you were wrong,
I led you to believe in the lie.
While I was weak you were strong.
Oh, but now you see the change in me.
Won't you let me try?

I hope that you're reading my letter.
That I'm crying out to you in every line.
Tell me how could I have been so blind?
Now, I need you all the time.
To Chorus:

Chorus 4:
Oh, no, no, no, no, no.
It just won't do.
Being on my own,
Everything's so different without you.
I said my heart would never break.

THE MOST BEAUTIFUL GIRL IN THE WORLD

Composed by

The Most Beautiful Girl in the World - 5 - 1

F♯
C♯/F♯
D♯m7
C♯
Bmaj9
A♯m7
G♯m7/C♯
6fr.
4fr.
6fr.
When the day turns in - to the last day of all time, I can say I hope U are in these arms of mine.
get through days when I can't get through hours, oh no. I can try, but when I do I see U and I'm de - voured.
C♯/D♯
C♯/B

F♯
C♯/F♯
Bmaj9
C♯/B
And when the night
Who'd al - low
F♯
C♯/F♯
Bmaj9
D♯m7
C♯/D♯
6fr.
falls be - fore that day I will cry, I'll
a face 2 be as soft as a flower?
Bmaj9
C♯/B
F♯
C♯/F♯
Bmaj9
cry tears of joy, cause af - ter U, all one can do is die.
I can bow and feel proud in the face of this power.
F♯
C♯/F♯
D♯m7
6fr.
C♯
4fr.
Bmaj9
A♯m7
6fr.
G♯m7/C♯
Could U be

F♯
C♯/F♯
Bmaj9
F♯
C♯/F♯
the Most Beau - ti - ful Girl in the World?
Bmaj9
C♯
4fr.
F♯
C♯/F♯
Bmaj9
It's plain 2 see,
U're the rea - son that God made a girl.
F♯
C♯/F♯
D♯m7
6fr.
C♯
4fr.
Bmaj9
A♯m7
6fr.
G♯m7/C♯
1.
How can I
2.
D♯m9
11fr.
D♯m6/9
10fr.
D♯m9
11fr.
(Spoken): And if the stars ever fell one by one from the sky,
I know Mars could not be 2 far

D♯m6/9
10fr.
Bmaj9
A♯m9
6fr.
D♯m7
6fr.
C♯
4fr.
Bmaj9
A♯m7
6fr.
G♯m7/C♯
behind. Cuz baby, this kind of beauty has got no reason 2 be shy, this kind of beauty is the kind that comes from inside.
Repeat and fade
F♯
C♯/F♯
Bmaj9
Could U be the Most Beau - ti - ful Girl in the World?
F♯
C♯/F♯
Bmaj9
C♯
4fr.
F♯
C♯/F♯
It's plain 2 see, U're the rea -
Bmaj9
F♯
C♯/F♯
Bmaj9
C♯
4fr.
son that God made a girl.
Could U be

FREE FALLIN'

Words and Music by
TOM PETTY and JEFF LYNNE

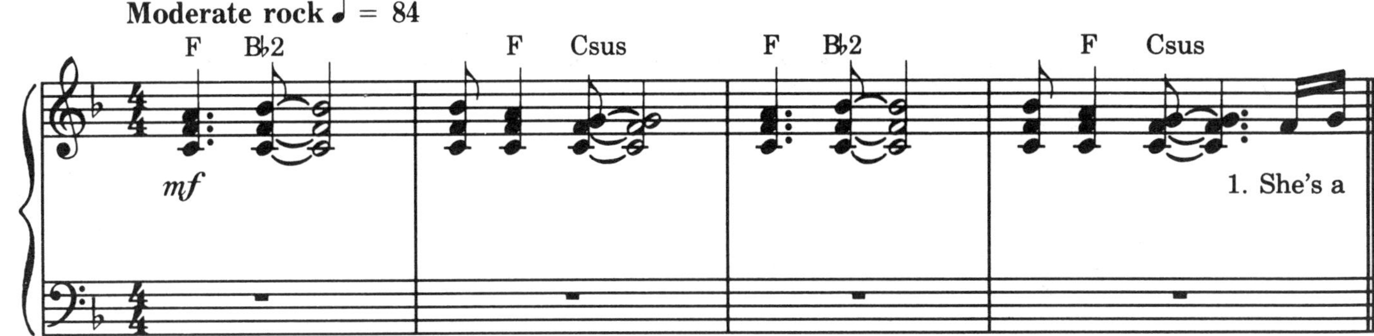

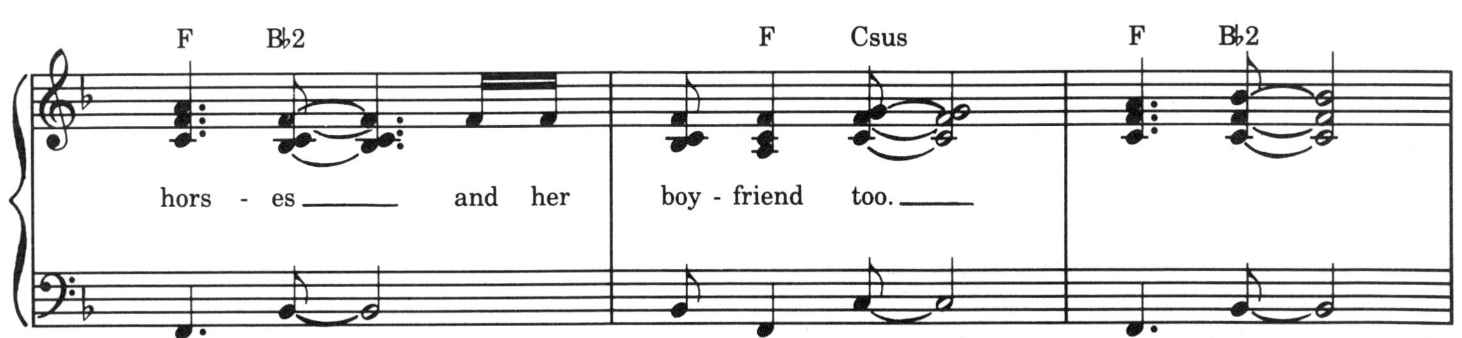

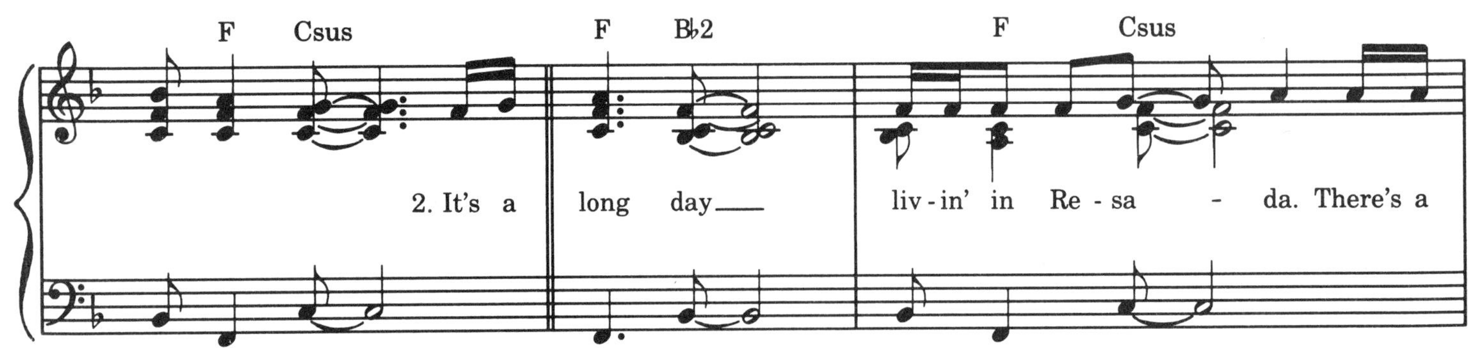
F
Csus
F
B♭2
F
Csus
2. It's a
long
day
liv - in' in
Re - sa
- da. There's a

F
B♭2
F
Csus
F
B♭2
free - way
run-nin' through the
yard.
And I'm a
bad
boy
'cause I

F
Csus
F
B♭2
F
Csus
don't e - ven
miss
her. I'm a
bad
boy
for
break-in' her
heart.
And I'm

Chorus:
F
B♭2
F
Csus
F
B♭2
free,
f
free
fall - in'.

Verse 3:
All the vampires walkin' through the valley
Move west down Ventura boulevard.
And all the bad boys are standing in the shadows.
And the good girls are home with broken hearts.
(To Chorus:)

Verse 4:
Wanna glide down over Mulholland.
I wanna write her name in the sky.
I wanna free fall out into nothin'.
Gonna leave this world for awhile.
(To Chorus:)

FROM A DISTANCE

Lyrics and Music by
JULIE GOLD

G D/G G Cmaj7 D Em
flight. From a dis-tance there is har - mo-ny, and it
cresc.
mf
C G/B G/D D C G/B C G/B
To Coda
ech-oes through the land. It's the voice of hope, it's the voice of peace. It's the
dim.
mp
C D
1.
G D/G C/G G
voice of ev - ery man.
D.S.
2.
Bridge:
C G/B D
G D/G G G/B G/C C6 D
2. From a man. God is watch-ing us. God is
cresc.
mf
D7/G G D/F♯ Em Em7 Am7 C/D D G
watch-ing us. God is watch-ing us from a dis - tance.
dim.
mp

G
G/B
C
D
Em7
G/B
C
G/B
Am
Em/G
D/F♯
D
G
D/F♯
C/E
G/D
cresc.
D.S. 𝄋 al Coda
C
Am
Em
D
Em
D/F♯
N.C.
mf
3. From a
mp
Coda
C
D7
D/E
Em
D/E
Em
Bm/D
heart of ev - ery man. It's the
cresc.
mf
C
G/B
C
G/B
3
C
D7
hope of hopes, it's the love of loves. This is the song of ev ery

Verse 2:
From a distance, we all have enough,
And no one is in need.
There are no guns, no bombs, no diseases,
No hungry mouths to feed.
From a distance, we are instruments
Marching in a common band;
Playing songs of hope, playing songs of peace,
They're the songs of every man.
(To Bridge:)

Verse 3:
From a distance, you look like my friend
Even though we are at war.
From a distance I just cannot comprehend
What all this fighting is for.
From a distance there is harmony
And it echos through the land.
It's the hope of hopes, it's the love of loves.
It's the heart of every man.

GEORGIA ON MY MIND

Lyrics by
STUART GORRELL

Music by
HOAGY CARMICHAEL

E G♯7(♭13) G♯7 C♯m Cm Bm E7
Geor-gia, I'm in Geor-gia, a song of
(Instrumental solo 2nd time . . . .
A A♯dim7 E/B D13(♯11) C♯7 F♯7 A/B
you comes as sweet and clear as moon-light through the
E A13 Emaj9 G♯7 C♯m A/C♯
pines. Oth-er arms,
. . . . end solo)
cresc.
f
C♯m6 A7 G♯7(♭13) C♯m A/C♯ C♯m7 F♯7
they reach out to me. Oth-er eyes smile ten-der-ly.
C♯m A/C♯ C♯m7 D♯7(♭13) G♯m7 (G9) C♯7(♭9)
Still in peace-ful dreams I see the road leads back to

F#9
F#m7/B
E
D#m7(b5)
G#7
you.
Geor-gia,
sweet Geor - gia,
C#m
E7/B
A#m7(b5)
Am7
Am6
E
D13(#11)
C#7
no peace I
find.
Just an
old sweet song
1.
D.S.
F#9
A/B
D9(#11)
C#9
F#9
A/B
keeps Geor-gia on my
mind.
Geor - gia on my mind.
2.
D9(#11)
C#9
F#m9
E/G#
A
A#dim
mind.
Just an
old sweet, sweet, sweet
A/B
E
E7/G#
A
A#dim7
E/B
F
E
E7(#9)
song, keeps Geor-gia for-ev-er on my
mind.
mp

From the TriStar Motion Picture "PHILADELPHIA"

HAVE YOU EVER SEEN THE RAIN?

Written by
J.C. FOGERTY

Moderate rock ♩ = 120
Gm
E♭
B♭
mf

N.C.
B♭
N.C.

Verse:
B♭
1. Some-one told me long a - go,
there's a calm be - fore

F
the storm. I know it;
it's been com - ing for

B♭
some time.
When it's o - ver, so

they say,
it'-ll rain a sun - ny day. I know

F
B♭
it,
shin-in' down like wa - ter.

Chorus:
E♭
F
I wan-na know, have you

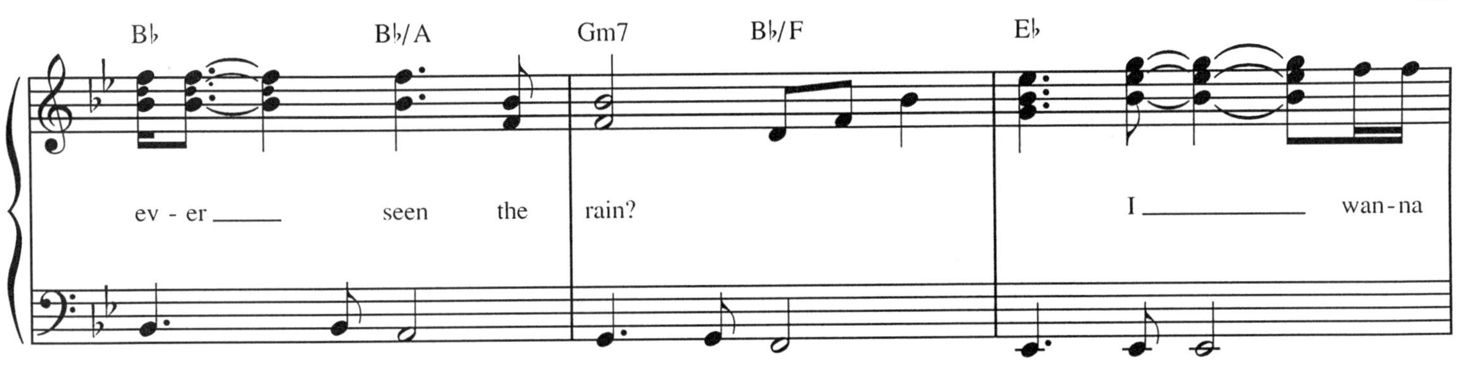
B♭
B♭/A
Gm7
B♭/F
E♭
ev - er ___ seen the rain? I ___ wan-na

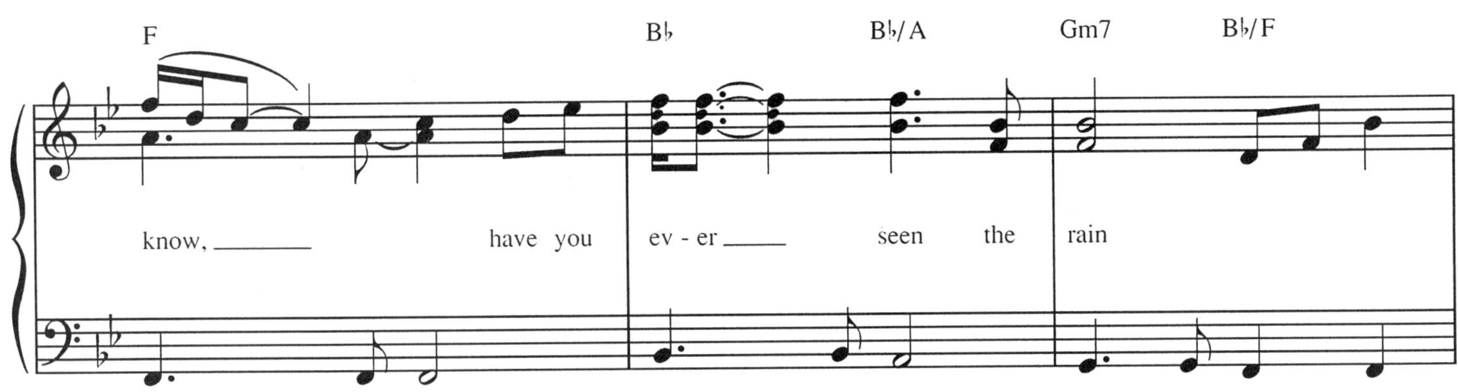
F
B♭
B♭/A
Gm7
B♭/F
know, ___ have you ev - er ___ seen the rain

E♭
F7sus
B♭
com - in' down ___ on a sun - ny day? ___

1.
N.C.
D.S. 𝄋
2.
3.
N.C.
B♭

Verse 2:
Yesterday and days before, sun is cold and rain is warm.
I know it; been that way for all my time.
'Til forever, long ago, through the circle, fast and slow,
I know it; it can't stop, I wonder.
(To Chorus:)

Theme from Columbia Pictures Feature Film "HERO"

HEART OF A HERO

Words and Music by
LUTHER VANDROSS

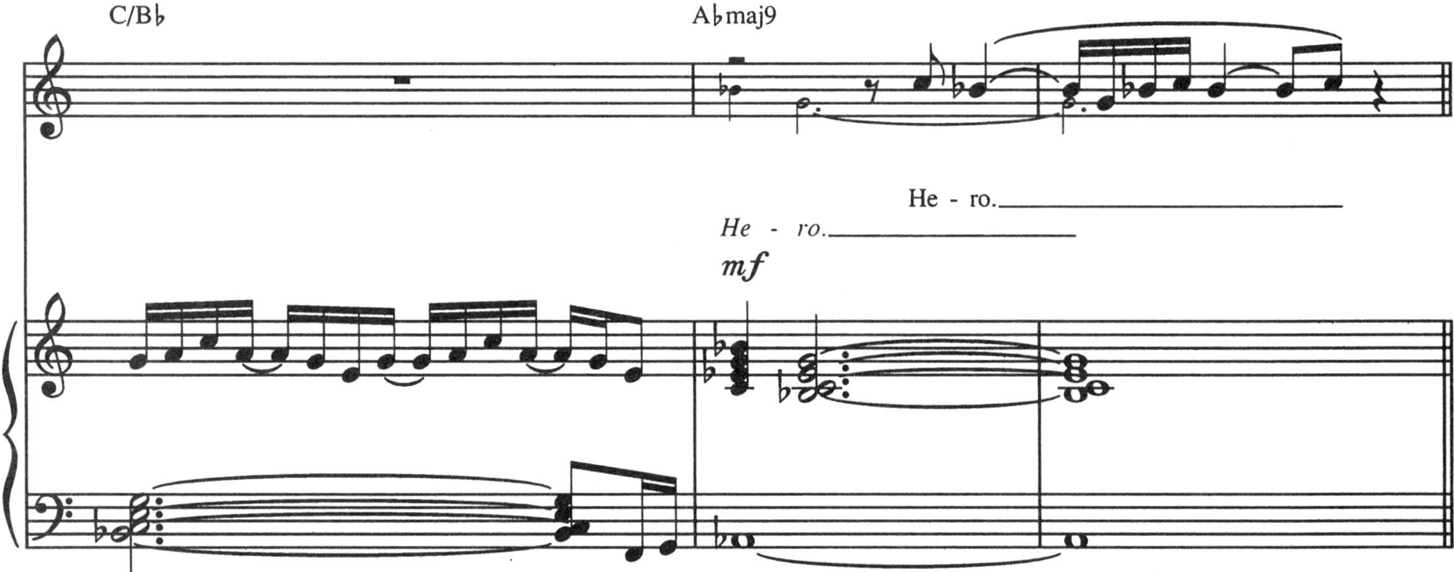

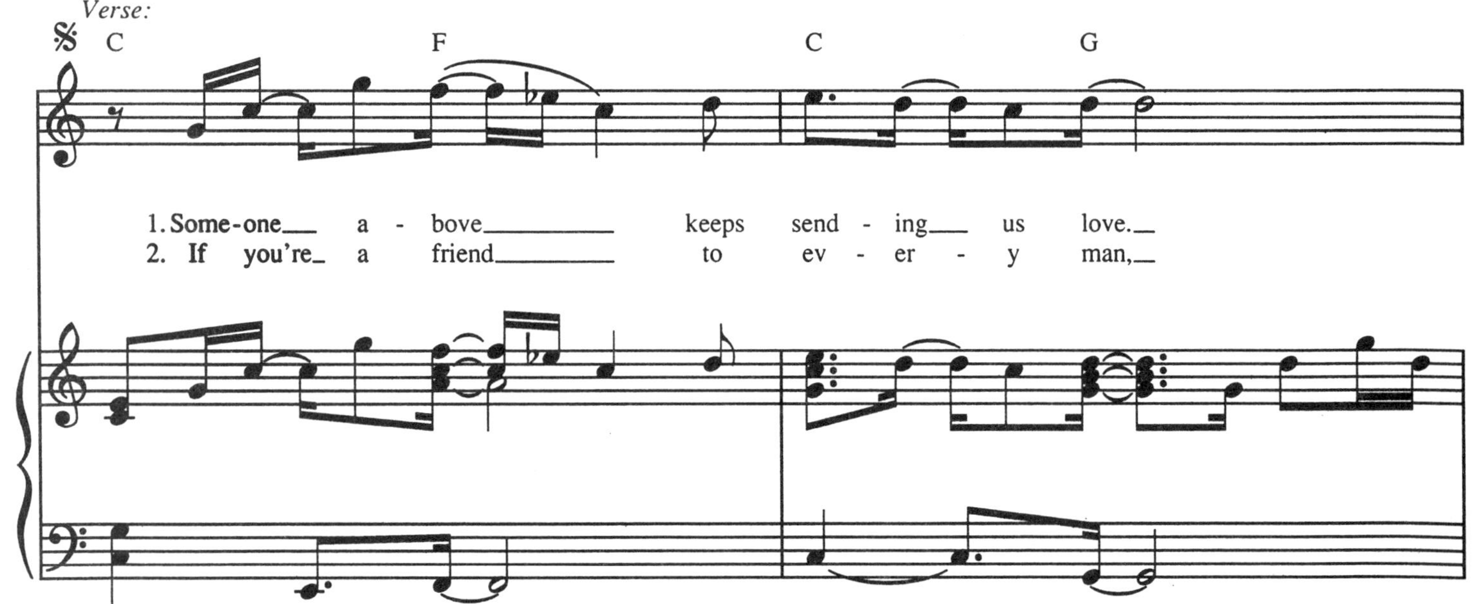

C
F
G
He wants_ us to___ love___ each oth - er.____ You see,
you're that__ much clos - er____ to heav - en.____ Heav - en knows__
C
F
C
G
the more__ we give,__ the bet - ter___ we live.__
__ the love__ we share,__ God wants us___ to care.__
C
F
G
Let's help__ the world_ of___ the fu - ture.__________ We're sing - ing,__
Think of___ the world_ we'll_ be get - ting.__________ Keep sing - ing,__
cresc.
cresc.

Chorus:

C F C Dm G C F
"Oh, hap - py day!_ Life is___ for us,___ but life with - out love_ is___ a ze-
"Oh, hap - py day!_ This world is___ for us,___ but a world with - out love_ is___ a ze-
f
f
G C F C Dm G
- ro."______ Sing_ it to-geth - er, "Oh, hap - py day!"_ I heard some-one say,_ "In -
- ro."___ There ain't_ noth-ing to it. "Oh, hap - py day!_ Give love to___some-one_ and
C B♭/C A♭/C C
side ev - 'ry heart_ is___ a he - ro.________ You're_ a he - ro."______________
you'll have_ the heart_ of___ a he - ro.________ You're_ a he - ro."______________

1.
D.S.
2.
Bridge:
Dm7
Some - times_ a he - ro does - n't
dim.
dim.
mf
dim.
mf
B♭maj7
Cmaj7
know he's_ a he - ro, and that's the beau - ty of___ shar-
Am7
Dm7
- ing love.___ And it does - n't___ take Su - per - man,_ just

B♭maj7
Dm7/G
plain or - di - nar - y peo - ple try - ing__ to give__ some - one__ a hand__
Em7/A
F♯m7/B
Chorus:
E
A
__________ if__ they can.__________ To - geth - er,__ "Oh, hap - py day!_ Thank
"Oh, hap - py day!_
cresc.
f
cresc.
f
E
F♯m
B
E
A
B
God for__ His love,_ 'cause life with_ no love_ is__ a ze - ro."__ Sing_ it to - geth - er,
Life is__ for us,_ but life with - out love_ is__ a ze - ro."__ Ev - er - y - bod - y sing,

E
A
E
F♯m7
B
E
D/E
C/E
"Oh, hap - py day! Send love to some-one and you'll have the heart of a he-
"Oh, hap - py day!" I heard some-one say, "In - side ev - 'ry heart is a he-
1.
2.
E
- ro."
ro.
You're a he - ro.
dim.
E/D
Cmaj9
He - ro."
He - ro.
p
mp
mf
dim. e rit.
mp

HERE AND NOW

Words and Music by
TERRY STEELE and
DAVID ELLIOTT

Slowly ♩ = 80
C(2)
D7sus
G
D/G
G
G(2)/B
C(2)
D7sus
p
with Pedal

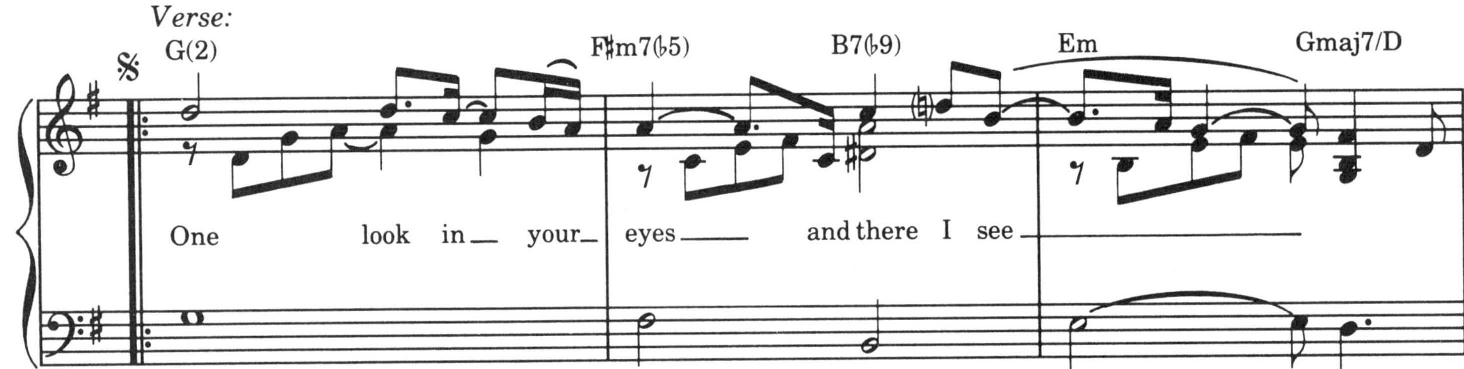
Verse:
G(2)
F♯m7(♭5)
B7(♭9)
Em
Gmaj7/D
One look in your eyes and there I see

C(2)
C/D
G(2)
D/G
G
F♯m7(♭5)
B7(♭9)
just what you mean to me. Here in my heart I be-lieve

Cmaj9
Bm7
Em7
D♯dim7
G/D
C(2)
your love is all I ev - er need.

1.
C G2/B D♯dim7 Em G2/B C(2) C/D
Hold-ing you close through the night, I need you.

2. 3.
Chorus:
F♯m7(♭5) A/B Bm7 Cmaj7 D/C D/F♯
cresc. Here and now, I prom-ise to love faith-ful-ly.
mf

G Bm7 C(2) F♯m7(♭5) A/B Bm7 Cmaj7
Faith - ful - ly. You're all I need. Here and now,

D/C D/F♯ G Bm7
I vow to be one with thee. You and me.

Cmaj9
To Coda
1.
C(2)
C/D
G
G(2)/B
Your love is all I need.

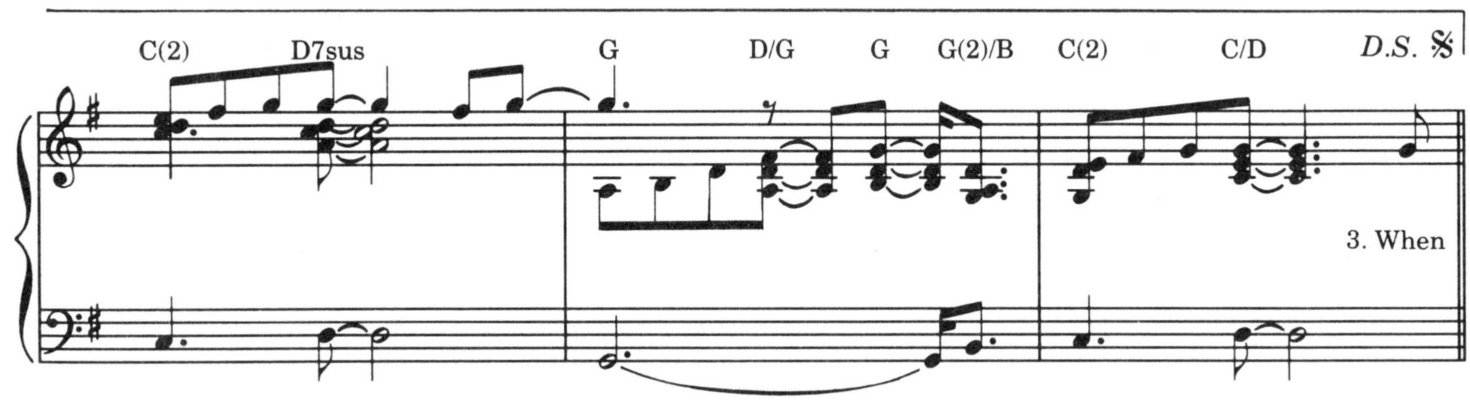
C(2)
D7sus
G
D/G
G
G(2)/B
C(2)
C/D
D.S.
3. When

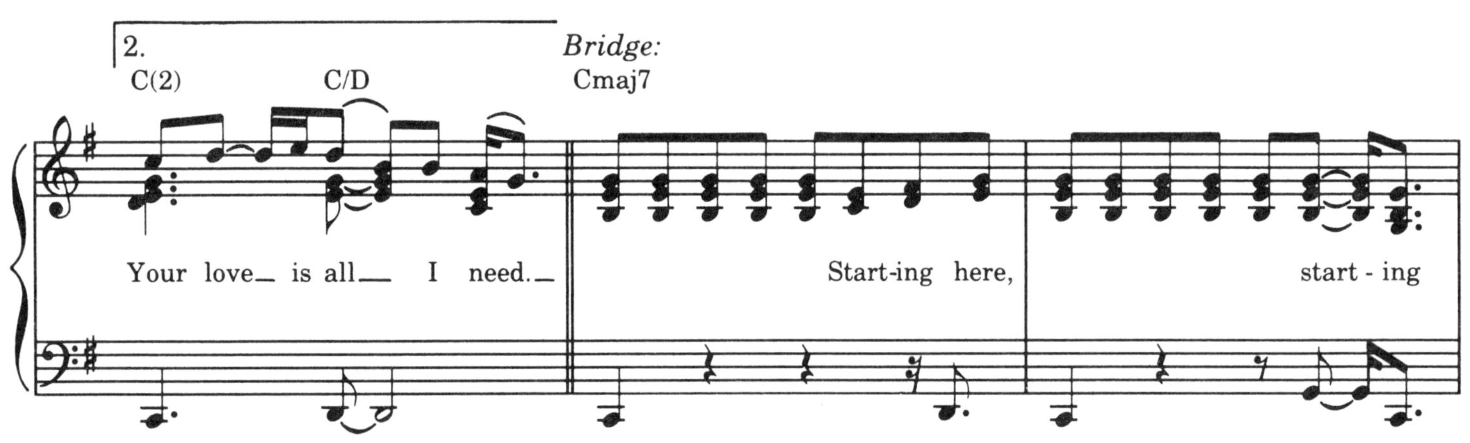
2.
C(2)
C/D
Bridge:
Cmaj7
Your love is all I need.
Start-ing here,
start - ing

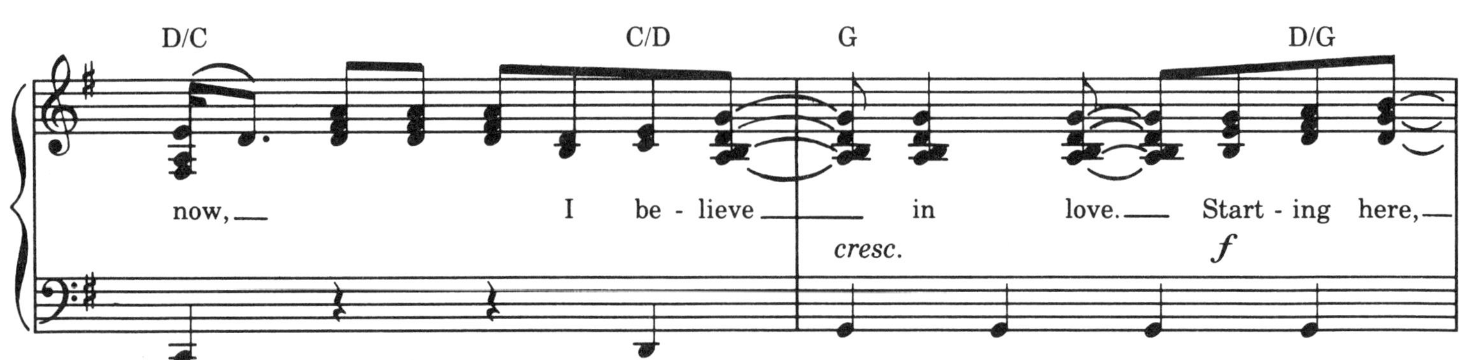
D/C
C/D
G
D/G
now,
I be - lieve
in
love.
Start - ing here,
cresc.
f

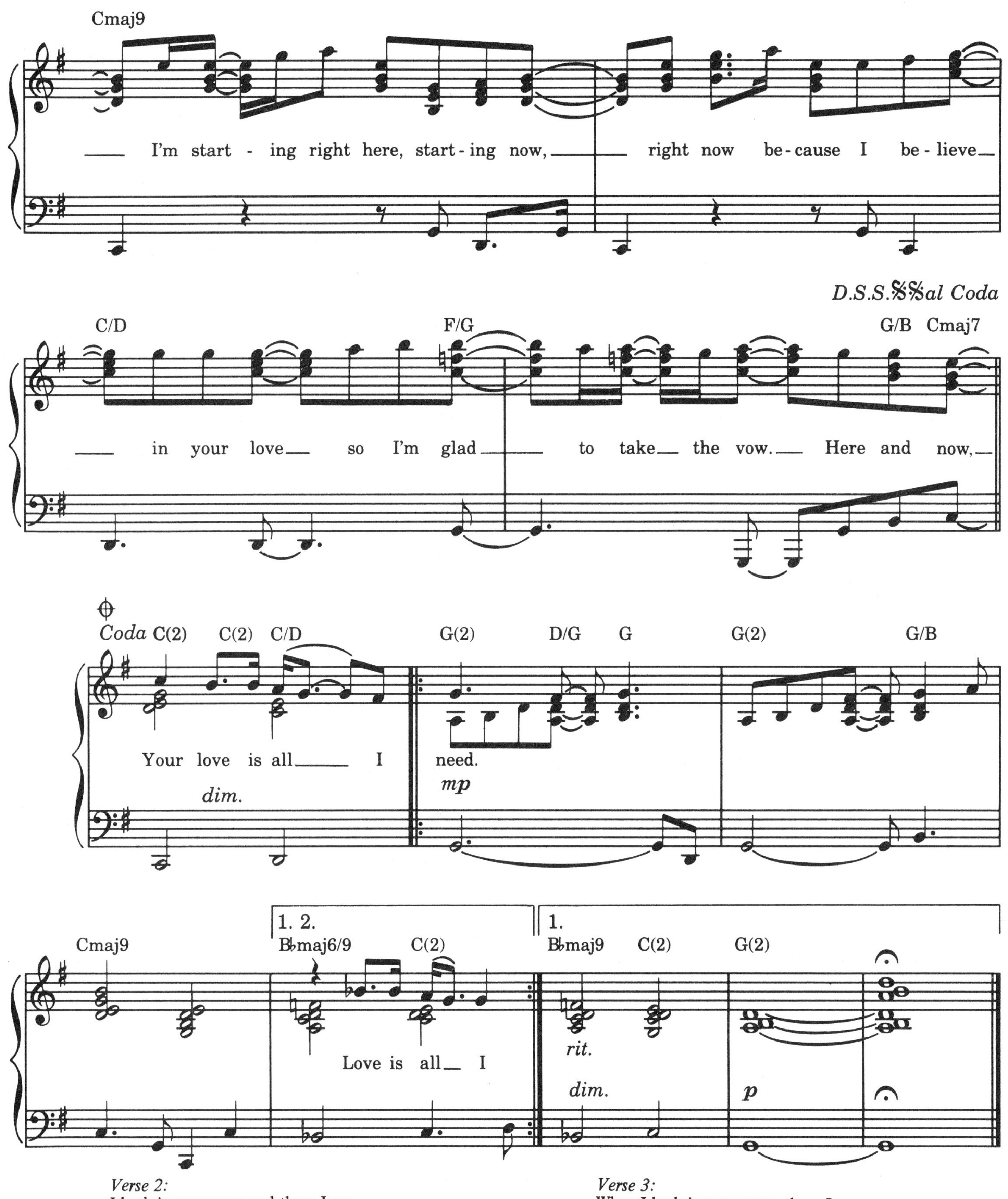

Verse 2:
I look in your eyes and there I see
What happiness really means.
The love that we share makes life so sweet,
Together we'll always be.
This pledge of love feels so right,
And ooh, I need you.
To Chorus:

Verse 3:
When I look in your eyes, there I see
All that a love should really be.
And I need you more and more each day,
Nothing can take your love away.
More than I dare to dream,
I need you.
To Chorus:

HERE WE ARE

Words and Music by
GLORIA ESTEFAN

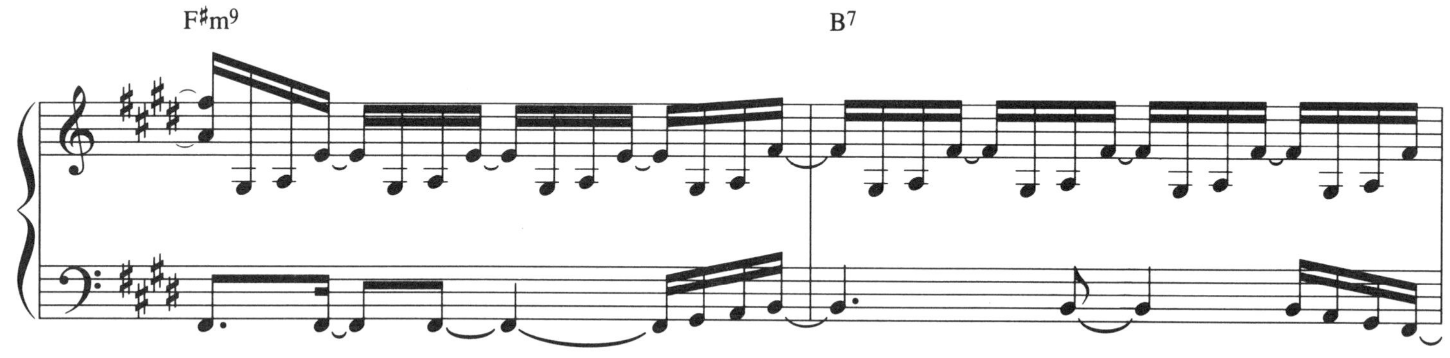

E
Emaj7
A/E
are face to face. We for - get time and
A2/E
E
place. Hold me now; don't let
Emaj7
A/E
go though it hurts, we both know.
A/B
B
Amaj7
The time we spend to - geth - er's gon - na fly.
G♯m7
Amaj7
and ev - ery - thing you do to me is gon - na feel so right.

G♯m7
C♯m
C♯m/B
Amaj7
Ba - by, when you're lov - ing me I feel like I could cry,
G♯m7
F♯m9
F♯m7/B
'cause there's noth - ing I can do
1.
F♯m9
to keep from lov - ing you.
B7
F♯m9
F♯m7/B
2. Here we
2.
E2
There's noth - ing I can
cresc.

Bridge:
Am9
B7
Emaj7
f
do; I'm help - less in ___ your arms. ___ Oh ba - by, what you
Cmaj7
Amaj9/B
Cmaj7
G/B
do; ___ I'm in love, ___ this is it. ___ There's no turn - ing back ___ this time.
Am7
Am7/D
No, no, no. ___ 3. Here ___ we
G
Gmaj7
C/G
are once ___ a - gain. But this time we're on - ly friends.
C2/G
G
Gmaj7
___ Fun - ny world; some - times lies ___ be - come the

C/G
C2/G
C/D
D
game when love's the prize. And though no
Am7/D
Bm7/D
one knows what's go - ing on in - side, all the love I feel
Cmaj7/D
Bm7/D
C/D
G7
for you is some - thing I should hide. When I have you close
Cmaj7
Bm7
to me the feel - ing's so sub - lime that there's
Am7
Am/D
noth - ing I can do to keep from lov - ing you.
mf

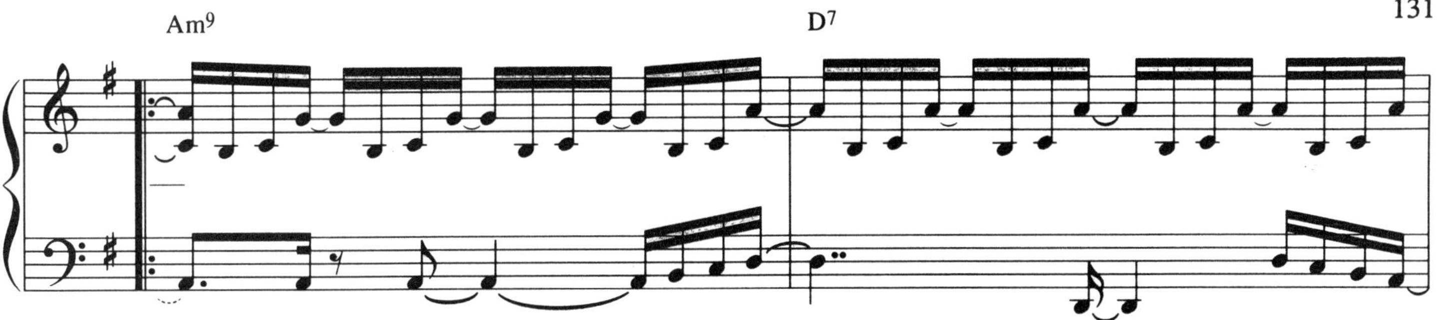
Am9
D7

Am9
D7
Repeat ad lib. and fade

Verse 2:

Here we are all alone;
Trembling hearts, beating strong;
Reaching out, a breathless kiss
I never thought could feel like this.
I want to stop the time from passing by.
I want to close my eyes and feel
Your lips are touching mine.
Baby, when you're close to me,
I want you more each time.
And there's nothing I can do
To keep from loving you.

(To Bridge:)

HOW 'BOUT US

Words and Music by
DANA WALDEN

1.
A
Dm/A
and if the fi - re's out we should both be gone.
too man - y lov - er's hearts
G9
Both:
To Next Strain
2.
Dm/A
Oh.
lose their dream.
(We won't lose it!)
cresc.
Chorus:
A
Both:
D/A
Some peo-ple are made for each oth - er;
some peo-ple can love one an-oth-er for life;
Dm/A
A
how 'bout
us?

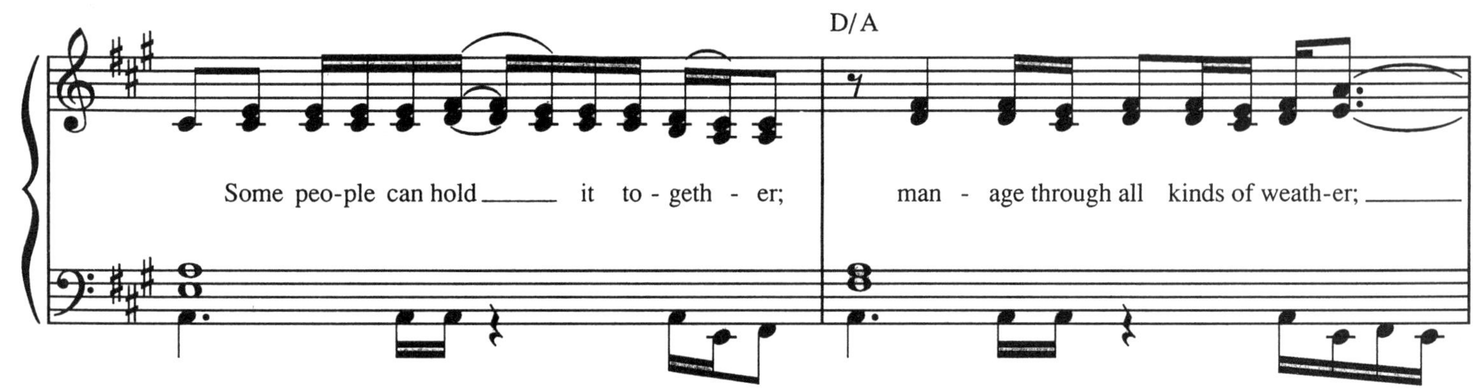
D/A
Some peo-ple can hold it to-geth - er;
man - age through all kinds of weath-er;

Dm/A
1.
A
Dm/A
Dm6/A
can
we?

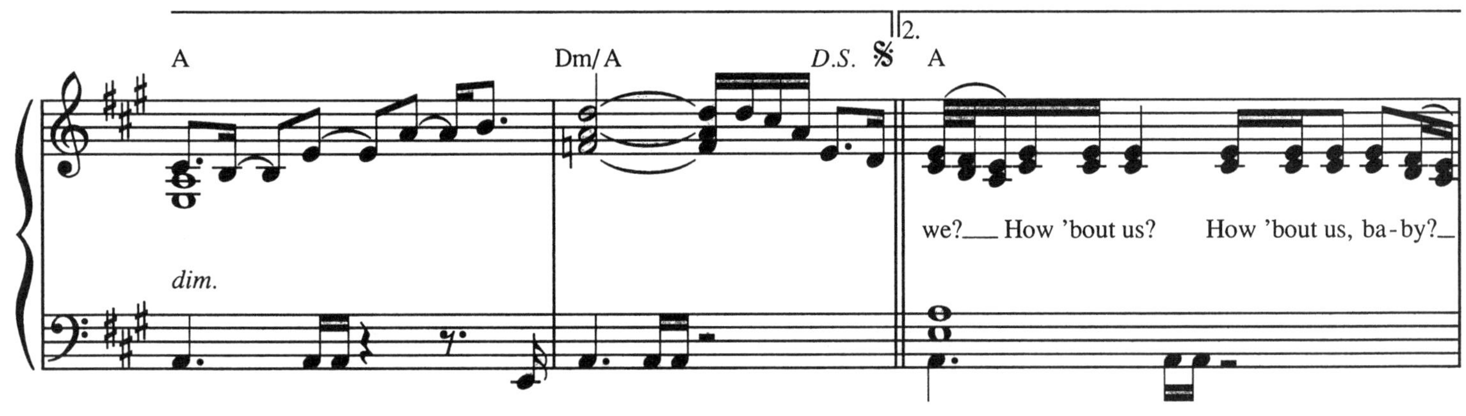
A
Dm/A
D.S. 𝄋
2.
A
we? How 'bout us? How 'bout us, ba-by?
dim.

Dm6/A
A
How 'bout us? How 'bout us, ba - by?
How 'bout us? How 'bout us, ba - by?

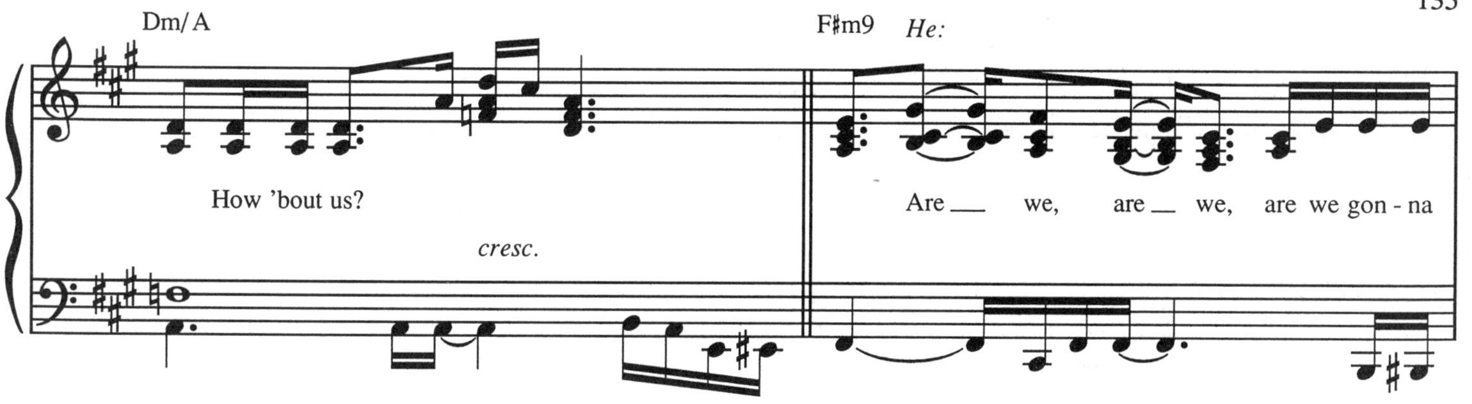
Dm/A
F♯m9
He:
How 'bout us?
cresc.
Are __ we, are __ we, are we gon - na

C♯m11
She:
He:
Both:
Em9
make it girl? _ I hope _ we can. Are we gon - na
drift, and drift, _ and drift, _ and drift, _ and

G9
C
drift to - geth - er? ______
Some peo-ple are made ___ for each oth - er;

F/C
Fm/C
some peo - ple can love _ one an - oth - er for life; ______ how 'bout

C
us?
Some peo-ple can hold it to-geth - er;

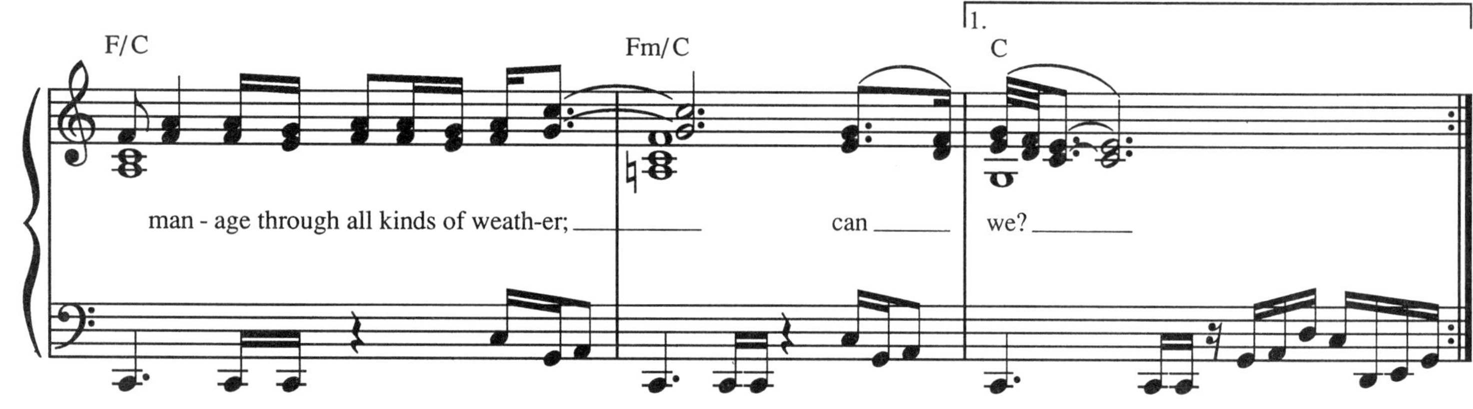
F/C
Fm/C
1.
C
man - age through all kinds of weath-er;
can
we?

2.
C
Fm/C
we?
How 'bout

C
Fm/C
Repeat ad lib. and fade
us?
How 'bout

HUMAN TOUCH

Words and Music by
BRUCE SPRINGSTEEN

F C G F C
mir - a - cles here.
Well, you can wait on your
bless-ings, my dar - lin', but
𝄋𝄋 Chorus:
F C G C/E F(2)
I got a deal for
you right here.
I ain't look - in' for
C F(2) C
pray - ers or pit - y.
I ain't com - in' 'round
search-in' for a crutch.
F(2) To Coda 𝄌 C F(2)
I just want
some-one to talk to
and a lit - tle of that
1.2.
To next strain
3.
D.S.S. 𝄋𝄋 al Coda
C G C/E F(2) C G C G C/E
hu-man touch.
Just a lit - tle of that
hu-man touch.
hu-man touch.

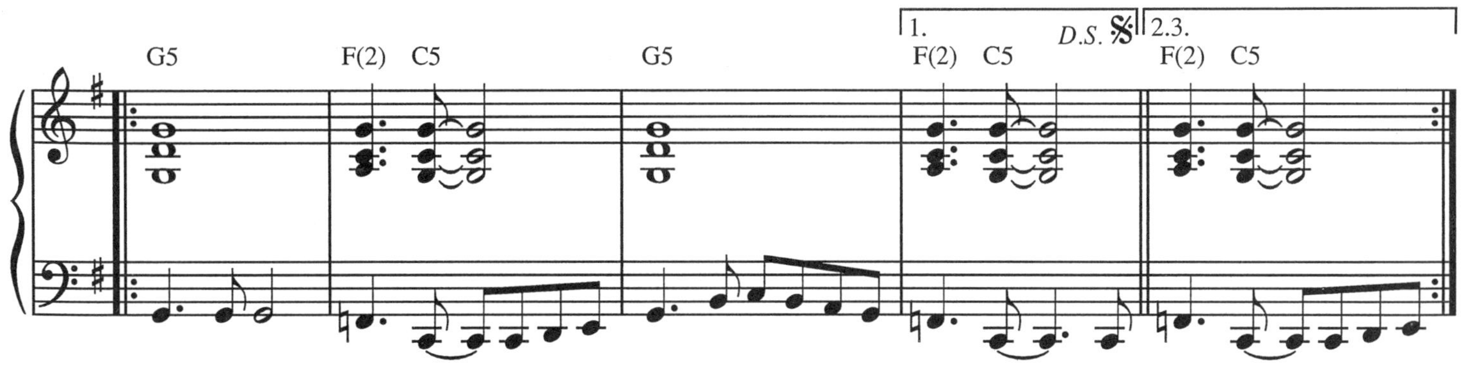

1.
D.S.
2.3.
G5
F(2) C5
G5
F(2) C5
F(2) C5

4.
F(2) C
Am
F C
G
Oh girl, that feel-ing of safe - ty you prize, well, it

Dm7
Am
F C
G
comes with a hard, hard price. You can't shut off the risk and the pain with-out

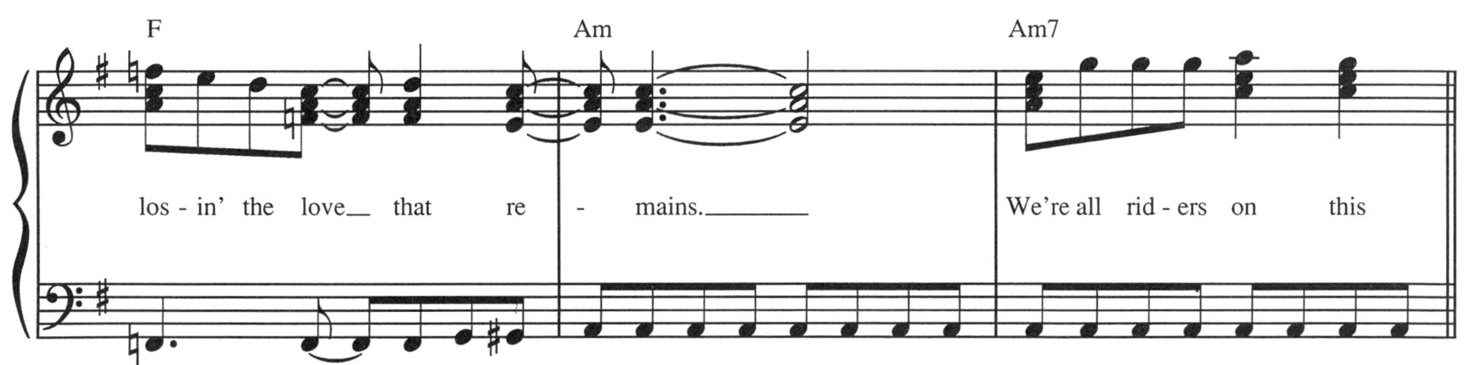

F
Am
Am7
los - in' the love that re - mains. We're all rid - ers on this

1.
2.
F(2)
C
F(2)
C
C
3
train._ (1st time only)
(Instrumental solo . . .
. . . end solo)
G5
F(2) C5
G5
1.
F(2) C5
2.
F(2) C5
D.S.
Coda
C
F(2)
feel you in my___ arms___
and share a lit - tle of that
Feel a lit - tle of that
Share a lit - tle of that
Give you a lit - tle of that
1.2.3.
C G C/E F(2) C G
hu - man touch._
hu - man touch._
hu - man touch._
hu - man touch._
Share a lit - tle of that
Feel a lit - tle of that
Feel a lit - tle of that
Give me a lit - tle of that
hu - man touch.______
hu - man touch.______
hu - man touch.______

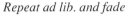

Verse 2:
Ain't no mercy on the streets of this town.
Ain't no bread from heavenly skies.
Ain't nobody drawin' wine from this blood,
It's just you and me, tonight.

Chorus 2:
Tell me, in a world without pity,
Do you think what I'm askin's too much?
I just want somethin' to hold on to
And a little of that human touch.
Just a little of that human touch.

Verse 3:
So you been broken, and you been hurt.
Well, show me somebody who ain't.
Yeah, I know I ain't nobody's bargain,
But hell, a little touch-up and a little paint . . .

Chorus 3:
You might need somethin' to hold on to
When all the answers, they don't amount to much.
Somebody that you can just talk to
And a little of that human touch.

Chorus 4:
Baby, in a world without pity,
Do you think what I'm askin's too much?
I just want to feel you in my arms
And share a little of that human touch . . .

I CAN SEE CLEARLY NOW

Words and Music by
JOHNNY NASH

To Coda
C
G
D
bright
sun-shin - y day.
(bright,
bright)
1.
C
G
It's gon-na be a bright,
bright
sun-shin - y day.
(bright,
bright)
D
2.
cresc.
Bridge:
F
C
Look all a - round,
there's noth-ing but
blue
sky.
mf
F
A
Look straight a - head,
there's noth-ing but
blue
sky.

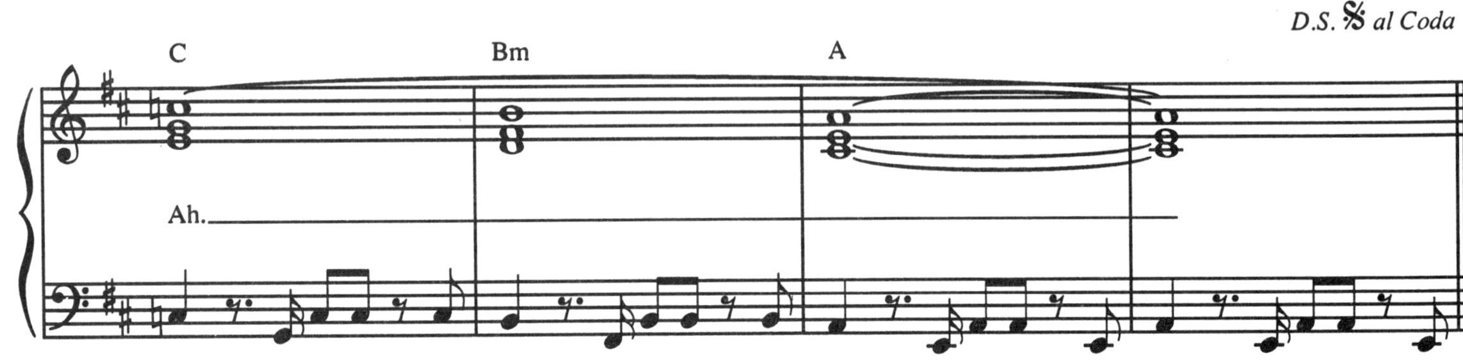

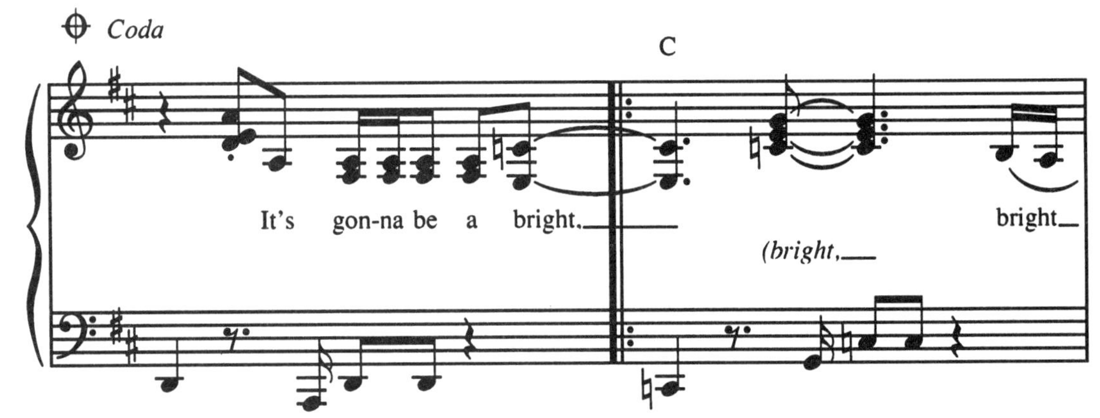

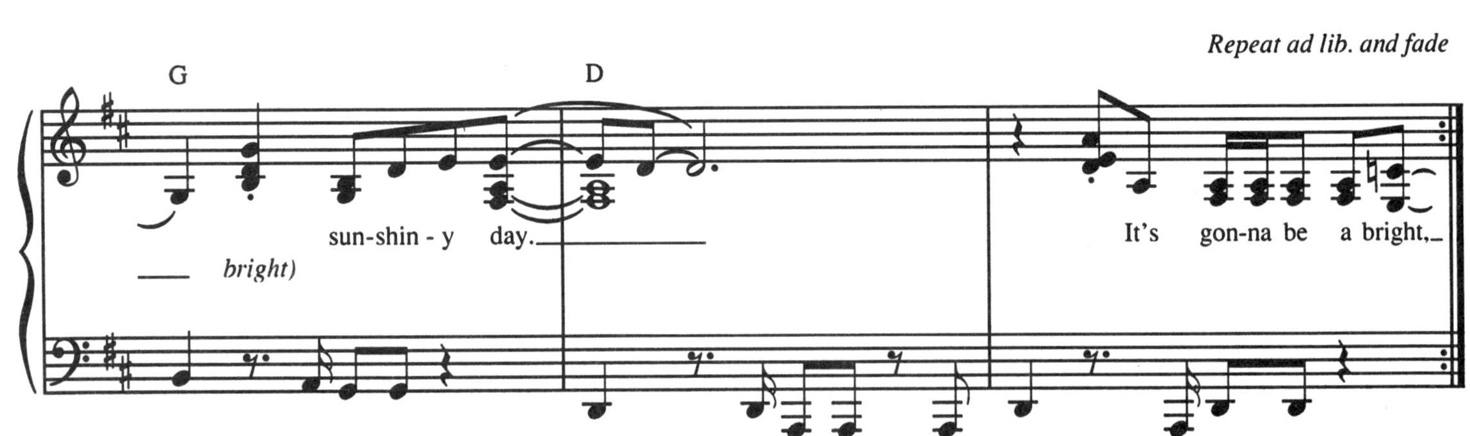

Verse 3:
I can see clearly now, the rain is gone.
I can see all obstacles in my way.
Here is that rainbow I've been praying for,
It's gonna be a bright, bright sunshiny day.
It's gonna be a bright, bright sunshiny day.

(EVERYTHING I DO) I DO IT FOR YOU

Lyrics and Music by
BRYAN ADAMS, R.J. LANGE
and M. KAMEN

Ebm
Db/F
Ebm/Gb
Db/F
Ebm
Db/F
tell me it's not worth try - in' for. You can't tell me it's not worth dy - in'
Ebm/Gb
Db/Ab
Ab5
for. You know it's true, ev-ery-thing I do, I do it for
Db2
Verse:
Db
you.
2. Look in-to your heart,
cresc.
mf
Ab/Db
Gb
Absus
Ab5
you will find there's noth - ing there to hide. Take me as I
Db
Ab/Db
Gb
am, take my life. I would give it all, I would

D♭ A♭ E♭m D♭ E♭m D♭/E♭

sac - ri - fice. Don't tell me it's not worth fight - ing for. I can't

E♭m D♭ E♭m D♭

help it, there's noth-ing I want more. You know it's true, ev-ery-thing I

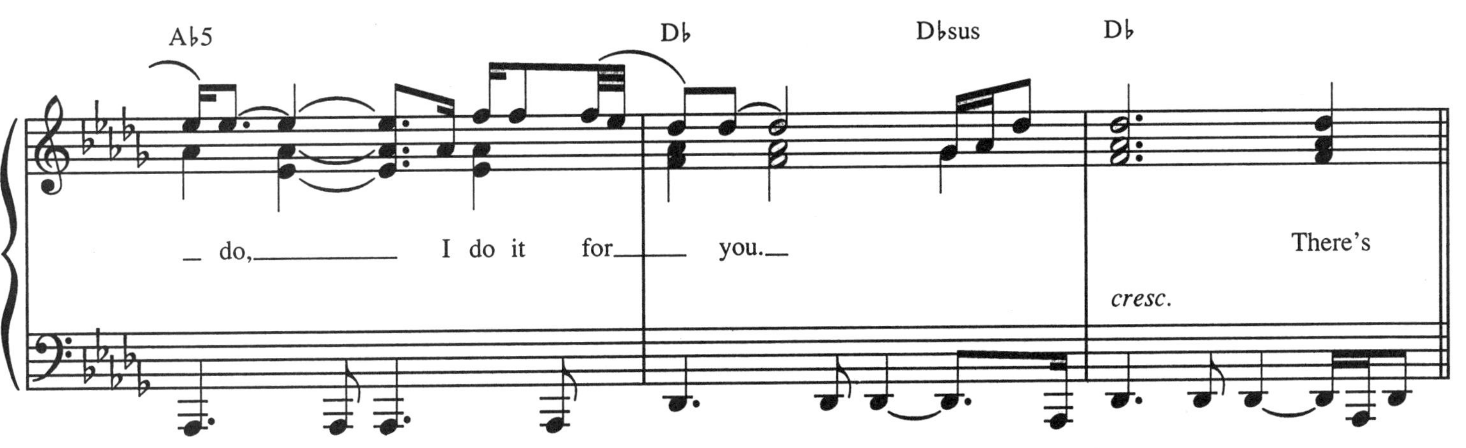

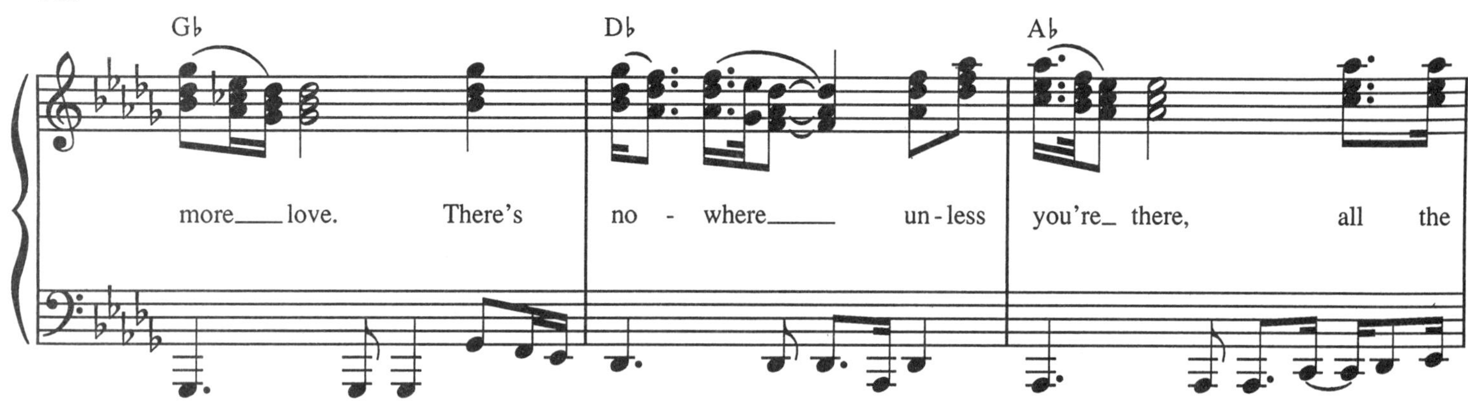
G♭
D♭
A♭
more love. There's
no - where un - less
you're there, all the

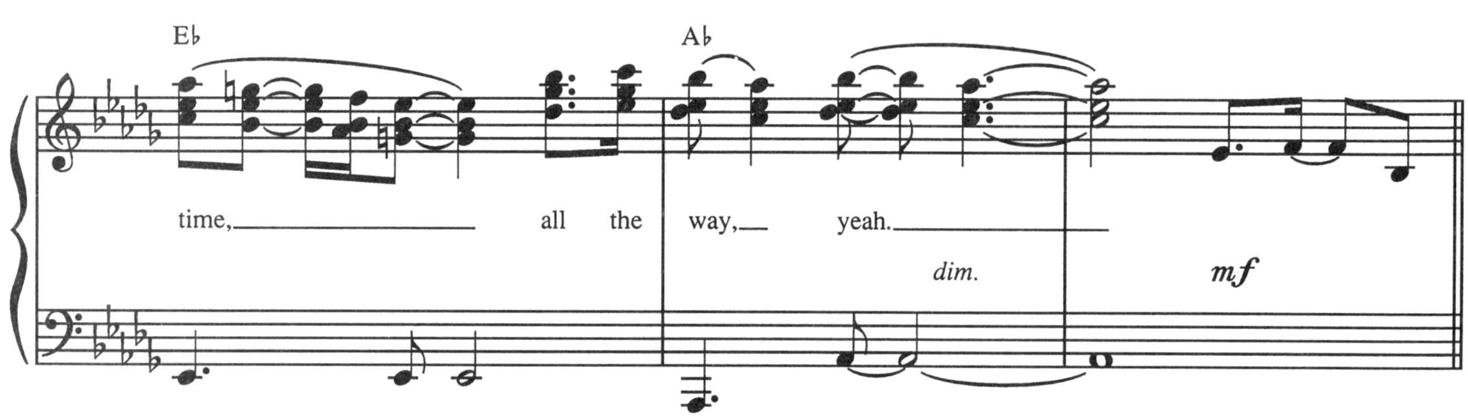
E♭
A♭
time, all the
way, yeah.
dim.
mf

G♭
D♭
D♭sus
(instrumental solo . . .

1.
2.
D♭
D♭
E♭m
Oh, you can't
tell me it's not worth try - in'
. . . end solo)

A♭ E♭m A♭ G♭/A♭

for. I can't help it, there's noth-ing I want more. Yeah, I would

cresc. ***f***

D♭ A♭ G♭

fight for you, I'd lie for you, walk the wire for you, yeah, I'd

I CAN'T MAKE YOU LOVE ME

Lyrics and Music by
MIKE REID and ALLEN SHAMBLIN

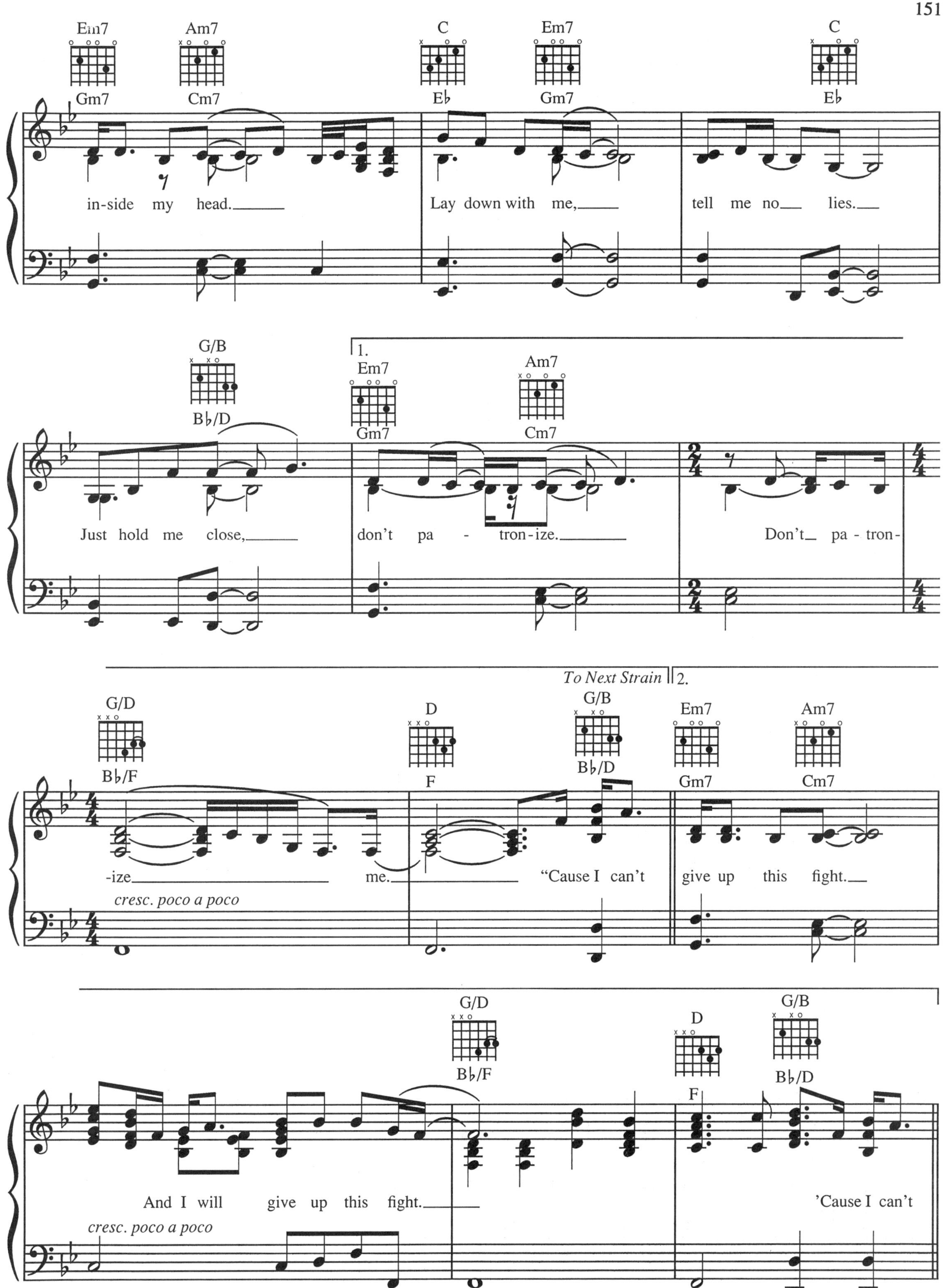

Em7
Am7
C
Em7
C
Gm7
Cm7
E♭
Gm7
E♭
in-side my head.
Lay down with me,
tell me no lies.
G/B
B♭/D
1.
Em7
Am7
Gm7
Cm7
Just hold me close,
don't pa - tron-ize.
Don't pa - tron-
To Next Strain
2.
G/D
B♭/F
D
F
G/B
B♭/D
Em7
Am7
Gm7
Cm7
-ize
me.
"Cause I can't
give up this fight.
cresc. poco a poco
G/D
B♭/F
D
F
G/B
B♭/D
And I will give up this fight.
'Cause I can't
cresc. poco a poco

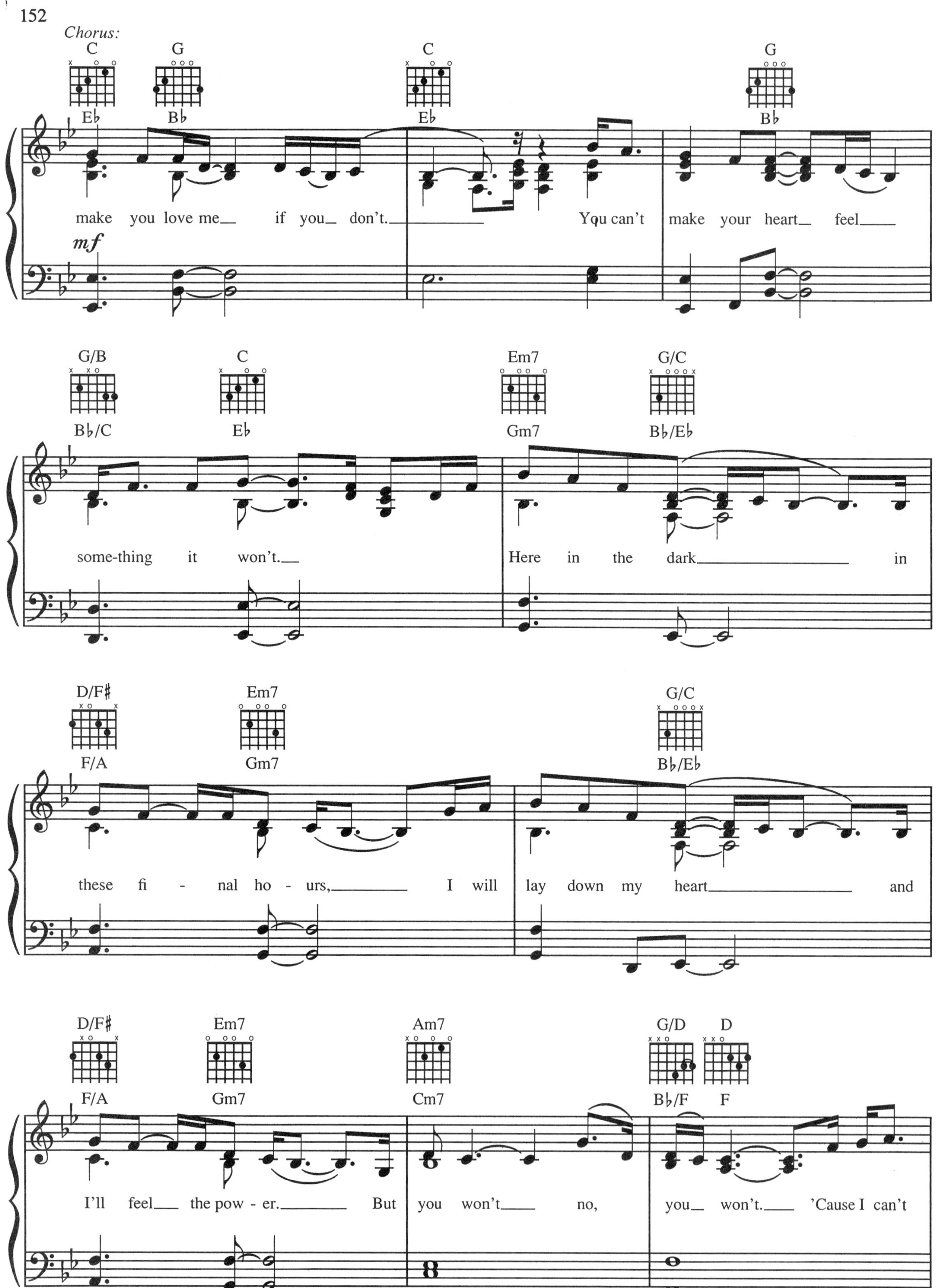
Chorus:
C G C G
E♭ B♭ E♭ B♭
make you love me if you don't. You can't make your heart feel
mf
G/B C Em7 G/C
B♭/C E♭ Gm7 B♭/E♭
some-thing it won't. Here in the dark in
D/F♯ Em7 G/C
F/A Gm7 B♭/E♭
these fi - nal ho - urs, I will lay down my heart and
D/F♯ Em7 Am7 G/D D
F/A Gm7 Cm7 B♭/F F
I'll feel the pow - er. But you won't no, you won't. 'Cause I can't

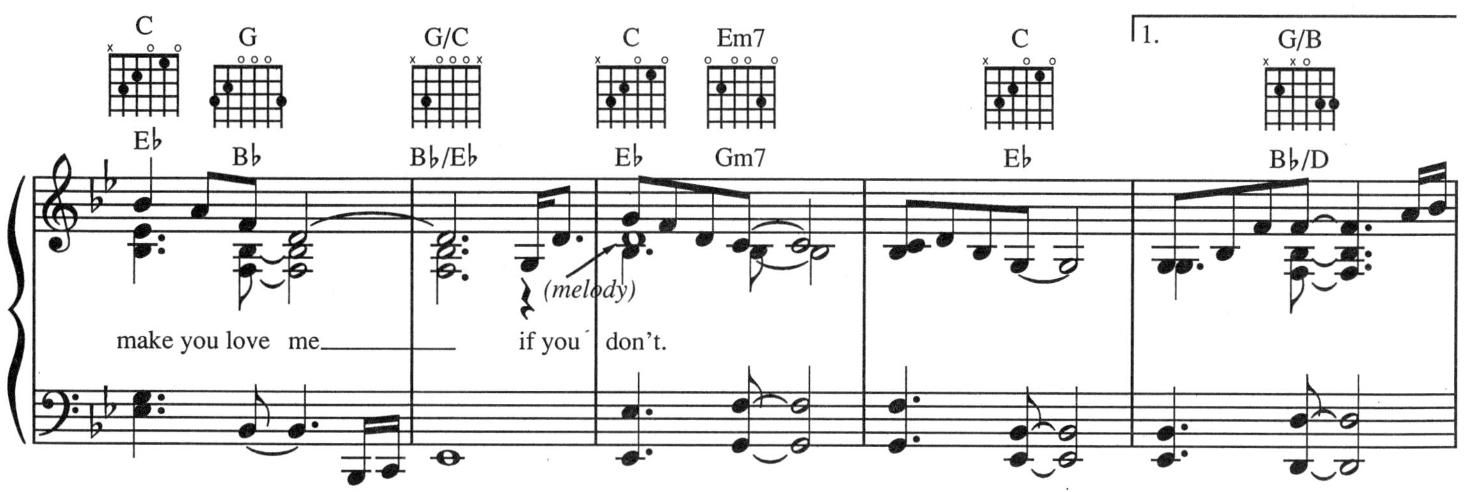

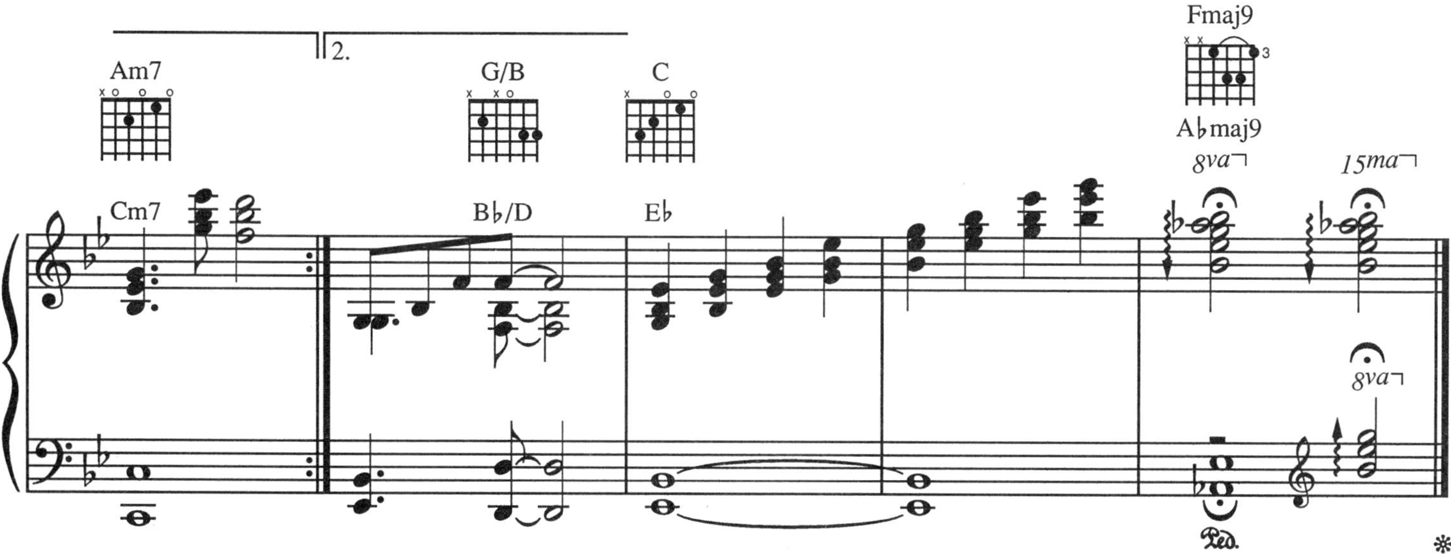

Verse 2:
I'll close my eyes, then I won't see
The love you don't feel when you're holdin' me.
Mornin' will come and I'll do what's right.
Just give me till then to give up this fight.
And I will give up this fight.
(To Chorus:)

I DON'T HAVE THE HEART

Words and Music by
JUD FRIEDMAN and
ALLAN RICH

A/G G(2) Em7 D(2)/F♯
fi-nal-ly found. ev - ery - thing you've want - ed and
bout you. I'm trying to say this as
E7/G♯ Asus A/C♯ D A/C♯ Bm F♯m/A
need-ed in me. I don't have the
gent-ly as I can 'cause I don't have the
cresc.
mf
Chorus:
G(2) D/F♯ G A(2)/C♯ G/B A/C♯
heart to hurt you, it's the last thing I want to do
To Coda
D D/F♯ A/E B/D F♯m/A G(2) D/F♯ G A(2)/C♯
But I don't have the heart to love you
1.
D.S.
G2/B G D(2) Gm/B♭ A7sus A7
not the way you want me to.

2.
Bridge:
D(2)
Em7
F♯7sus
You're so
trust - ing
and
F♯7
F♯7sus
F♯7
Bm7
Em7(♭5)/B♭
o - pen,
hop - ing that love will start.
But
D.S.S. 𝄋𝄋 al Coda
D/A
A7sus
A7
D/A
A7sus
A7
D
A/C♯
Bm
F♯m/A
I don't have the heart.
I don't have the heart.
I don't have the
Coda
A(2)/C♯
G/B
A/C♯
D
E
B/D♯
C♯m
G♯/B
you,
not the
way that you want me
to.
I don't have the
cresc.
f
Repeat ad. lib. and fade
Amaj7
B(2)/D♯
A(2)/C♯
B(2)/D♯
E
E/G♯
B/F♯
C♯m/E
G♯/B
heart.
Instrumental solo. . .
I don't have the

I DON'T WANNA CRY

Words and Music by
MARIAH CAREY and
NARADA MICHAEL WALDEN

F♯m
Bm
F♯m/A
B♮/G♯
ba - by look what we've be - come.
E
Bm
A
mf
We can make a mil-lion prom - is - es, but we still won't change.
E
Bm7/E
It is - n't right to stay to - geth - er when you on - ly bring each oth - er pain.
cresc.
Chorus:
A
E/G♯
f
I don't wan - na cry, don't wan - na cry.
G
Bm/F♯
F♯7/A♯
Noth-ing in the world could take us back to where we used to be. Though I've giv-

Bm A/C♯ D E F♯m
- en you_ my heart_ and soul,___ (giv-en you_ my heart_ and soul,) I must find_
Bm A/C♯ Dmaj9
_ a way_ of let - ting___ go, 'cause ba - by I___ don't wan - na
dim
F♯m Bm F♯m7/A B♭/G♯ F♯m
cry._
mp
1. D.S. 𝄋 2. Bridge:
Bm F♯m/C♯ C♯7sus Bm F♯m/C♯ C♯7sus E
All the mag - ic's gone,_ there's just a
cresc.
mf
Bm A/C♯ E
sha-dow of a mem - o - ry.___ Some-thing just_ went wrong._ We can't go

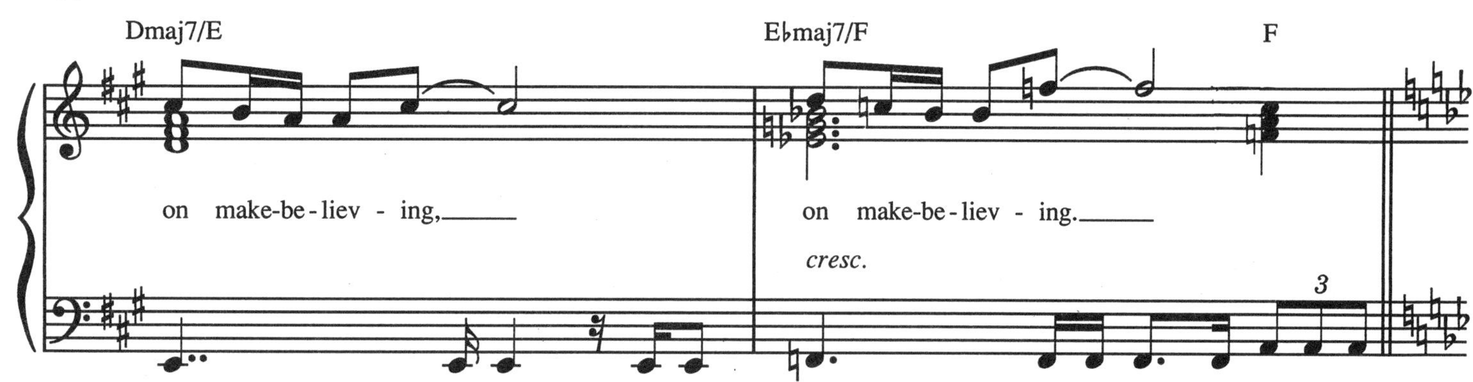
Dmaj7/E
Ebmaj7/F
F
on make-be-liev - ing,
on make-be-liev - ing.
cresc.
3

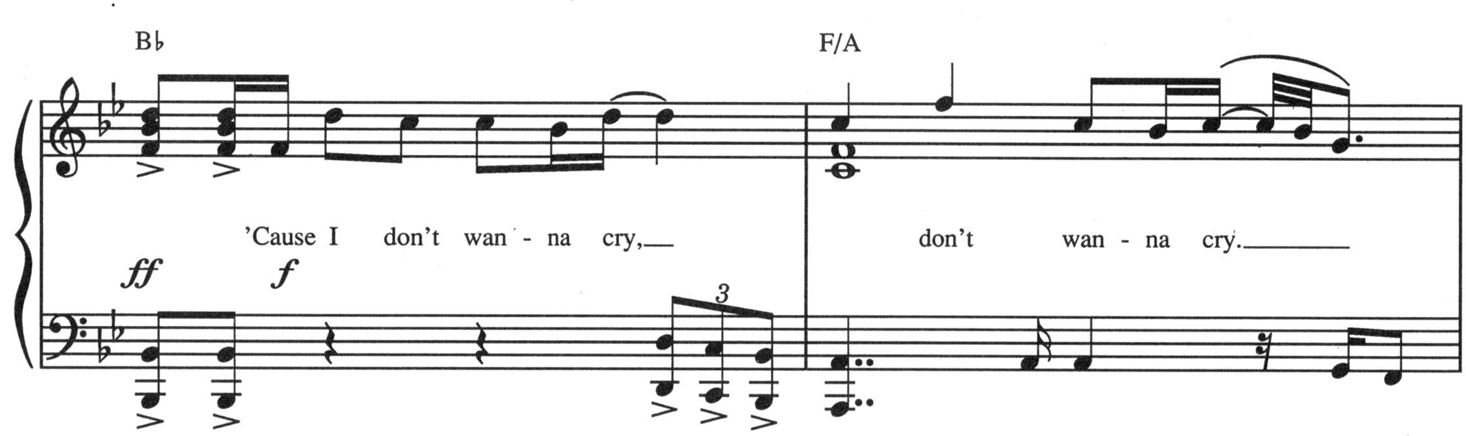
Bb
F/A
'Cause I don't wan - na cry,
don't wan - na cry.
ff
f
3

Ab
Cm/G
G7/B
Noth-ing in the world could take me back to
where we used to be. Though I've giv-

Cm
Bb/D
Eb
F
Gm
- en you my heart and soul,
(giv-en you my heart and soul,) said I've giv-

Verse 2:
Too far apart to bridge the distance,
But something keeps us hanging on and on.
Pretending not to know the difference,
Denying what we had is gone.
Every moment we're together,
It's just breaking me down.
I know we swear it was forever,
But it hurts too much to stay around.
(To Chorus:)

I DON'T WANNA FIGHT

Words and Music by
STEVE DUBERRY, LULU
and BILLY LAWRIE

D/F♯ Em7 D/F♯ D
It's not there an - y lon - ger, some-thing hap-pened some - where and we
Em7 D/F♯ G
both know why. But me, I'm get-ting stron - ger.
D/F♯ D Em7 Em7/A
We must stop pre-tend - ing, I can't live this lie.
Chorus:
D Em7
(1.2.) I don't care who's wrong or right. I don't real - ly wan - na
(3.) Oh ba - by, don't you know? No, I don't wan - na
part. (4.) (Instrumental solo)
Asus A G2 D
fight no more, too much talk - ing, babe. Let's sleep on it to -
hurt no more, this time, I'm walk - ing, babe. Don't care now who's to

To Coda
1.
Em7
Asus
A
G
night. I don't real - ly wan - na
blame. I don't real - ly wan - na
fight no more,
this is
this is
time for let - ting go.
D.S.
2.4.5.
D.S.S.
3.
To next strain
G2
D
tired of all these games.
time for let - ting go.
cresc.
6.
D.S.S. al Coda
Bridge:
Am7
Gsus
G
time for let - ting go.
Hang-ing on
to the past,
f
Dsus
D
C(2)
Am7
it on - ly stands in our way.
We have to grow for our

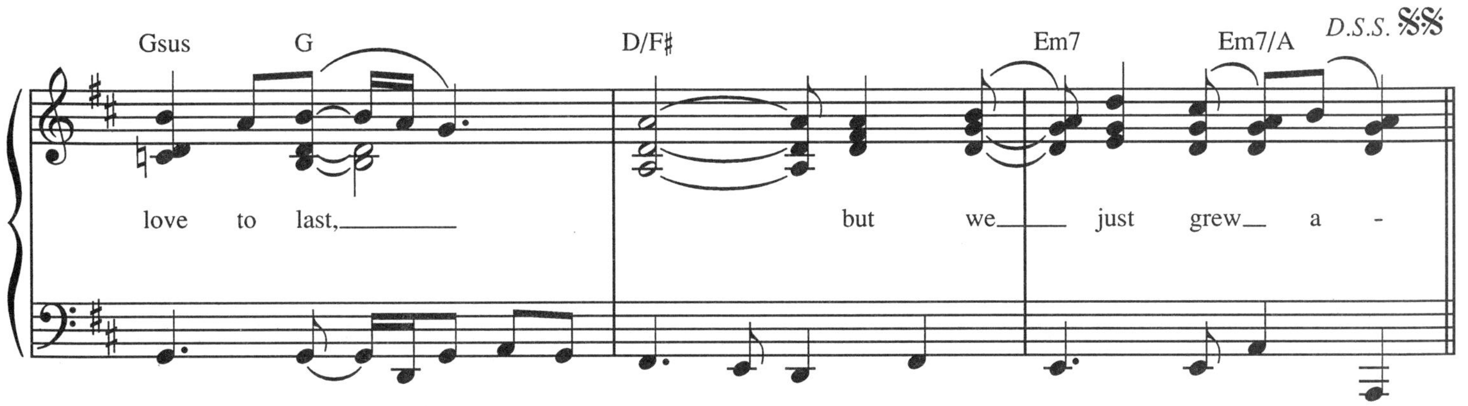

Verse 2:
I hear a whisper in the air
That simply doesn't bother me.
Can't you see that I don't care,
Or are you looking right through me?
It seems to me that lately,
You look at me the wrong way and I start to cry.
Could it be that maybe
This crazy situation is the reason why?
(To Chorus:)

Chorus 5:
Oh baby, don't you know?
No, I don't wanna hurt no more, too much talking, babe.
Don't care now who's to blame.
I don't really wanna fight no more, tired of all these games.

Chorus 6:
I don't care who's wrong or right.
I don't really wanna fight no more, this time I'm walking, babe.
Let's sleep on it tonight.
I don't wanna fight no more, this is time for letting go.

Chorus 7:
No, I don't wanna hurt no more.
Too much, hey, baby!
Don't care now who's to blame.
I don't really wanna fight no more, this is time for letting go.

I SEE YOUR SMILE

Words and Music by
JON SECADA and
MIGUEL A. MOREJON

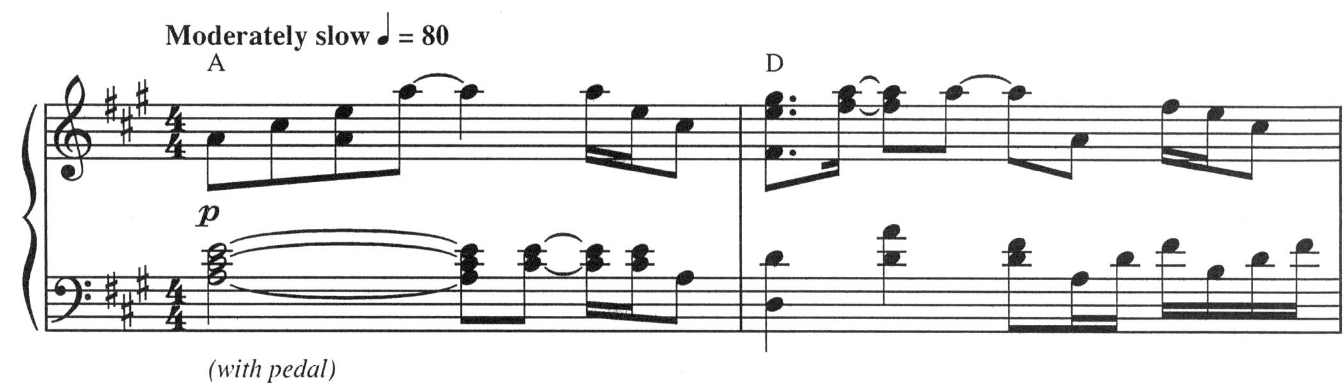
Moderately slow ♩ = 80
A
D
p
(with pedal)

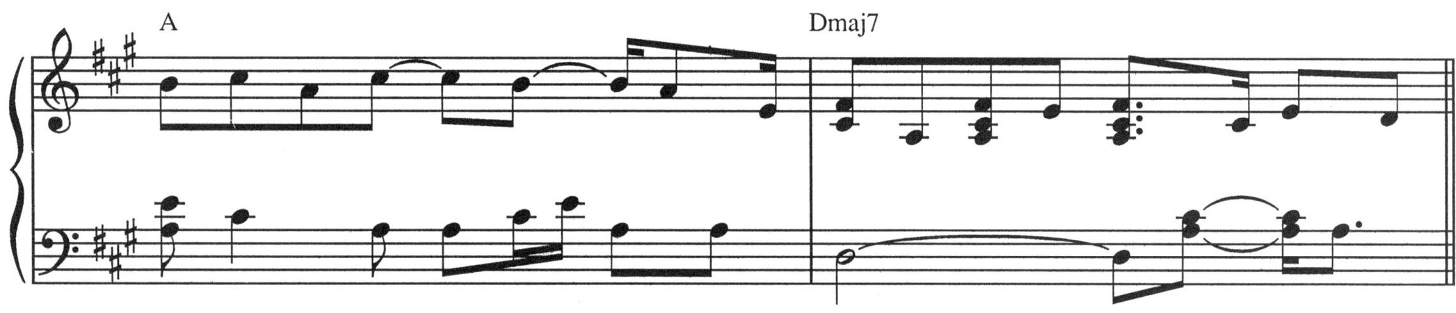
A
Dmaj7

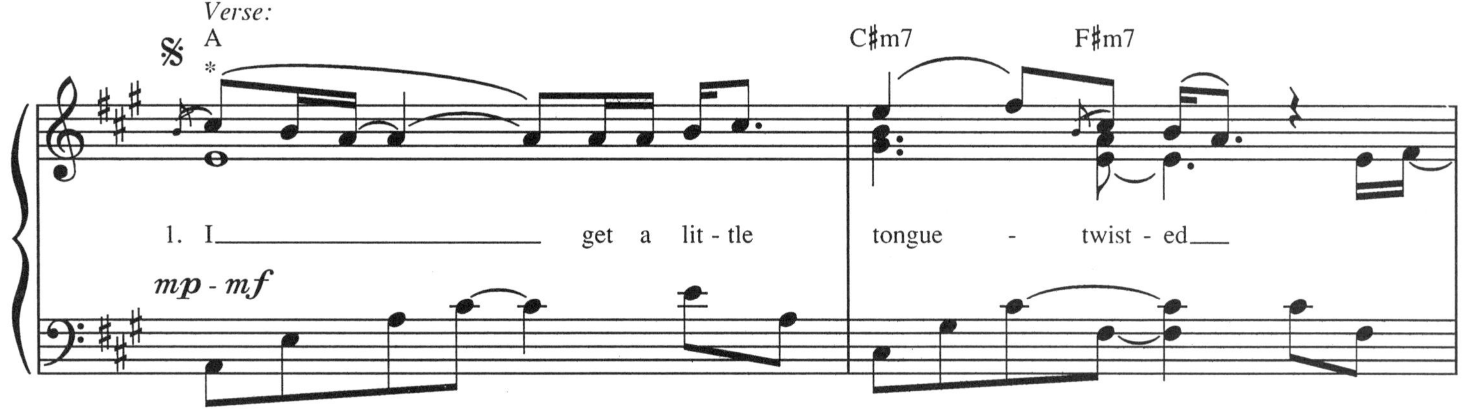
Verse:
A
C♯m7
F♯m7
1. I get a lit - tle
tongue - twist - ed
mp - mf

D
A
ev - 'ry time I talk to you when I
see you. And

*Melody is sung one octave lower.

C♯m7
F♯m7
I'm so glad that you just missed it,
D
E
Dmaj7
the way I stared to mem-o-rize your face,
to kiss you in my mind,
Amaj9
Dmaj7
E
love you all the time.
cresc.
Chorus 1 & 2:
A
Dmaj7
F♯m7
F♯m11
'Cause when I close my eyes,
I still can
mf-f
C♯m7
Dmaj9
A
Dmaj7
see your smile.
It's bright e-nough to light my life

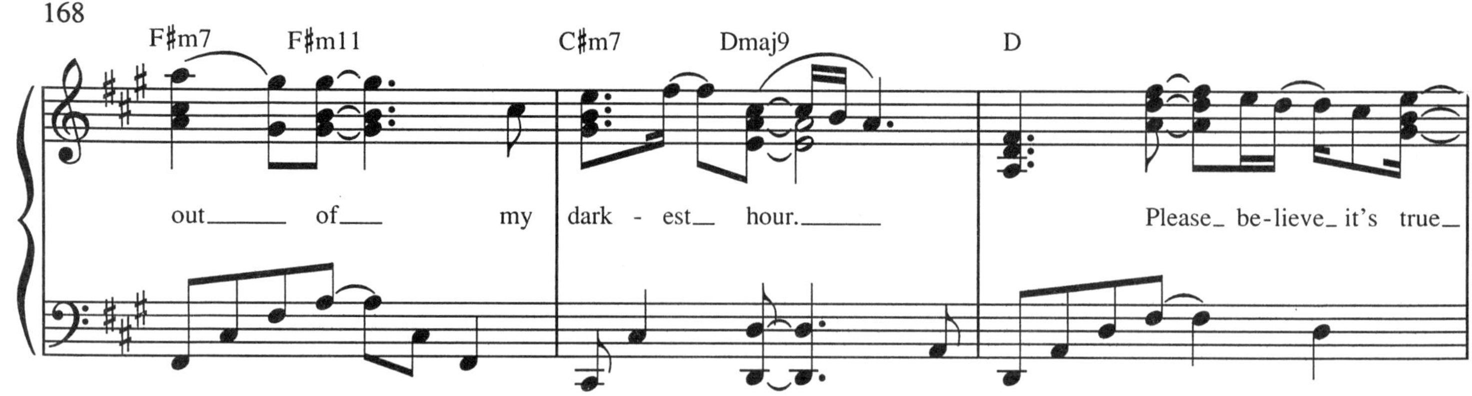
F♯m7
F♯m11
C♯m7
Dmaj9
D
out___ of___ my
dark - est__ hour.___
Please_ be-lieve_ it's true_

1.
D.S. 𝄋
E
D
E
___ when I tell___ you, "I___ love_ you."___

2.
D
E
___ you, "I___ love_ you."___
Woah,___ oh.___
cresc.
f

A
C♯m7
F♯m7
Dmaj9
E
___ (Instrumental solo ad lib. . .
. . . end solo)

Bridge:
Dmaj9
A
mf
I had to let you know just what would hap - pen.
Yes, I
Dmaj9
F♯m7
E
Dmaj7
had to let you know the truth.
cresc.
f
I know I've got to do
E
Dmaj7
E
this.
Would you hold my hand right through it?
Chorus 3 & 4:
A
Dmaj7
F♯m7
F♯m11
'Cause when I close my eyes,
I still can
C♯m7
Dmaj9
A
Dmaj7
see your smile.
It's bright e - nough to light my life

Verse 2:
I've taken too many chances,
Searching for the truth in love that's in my heart.
Tell me if I've made the wrong advances;
Tell me if I've made you feel ashamed.
'Cause I know I have to do this;
Would you hold my hand right through it?
(To Chorus:)

I WILL ALWAYS LOVE YOU

Words and Music by
DOLLY PARTON

D
A/C♯
3
Bm7
A/E Bm/E
You,
my darling, you.
Hmm.
2. Bitter -
Verses 2, 3, 4:
A
Bm/A
A
E/G♯
F♯m
C♯m/E
sweet
mem - o - ries
that is
all
I'm tak - ing
with
(Verse 3: Instrumental solo)
mf
D
E
A
E/A
A
E/G♯
me.
So, good - bye.
Please,
don't
cry.
We both
To Coda
1.
To Next Strain
2.
D.S. al Coda
F♯m
C♯m/E
Dmaj7
E
Dmaj7
E
know
I'm not what you,
you
need.
And I
4. I
. . . end solo)

Chorus:
A F♯m D E A F♯m
will_ al - ways_ love_ you. I
f
D E A D/A A C♯m/E Cm/E Bm/E
D.S. 𝄋
will_ al - ways_ love_ you.
Coda
Dmaj7 E N.C. B G♯m
love. And I
molto rit.
ff
a tempo
(Drums)

Emaj7
F♯
B
G♯m
C♯m7
F♯
will al - ways love you.
I will al - ways love
B
G♯m
Emaj7
F♯
B
G♯m
you.
I will al - ways love you.
I will al -
C♯m7
F♯
B
G♯m
Emaj7
F♯
- ways love you.
I will al - ways love
3

Verse 3: Instrumental solo

Verse 4:
I hope life treats you kind
And I hope you have all you've dreamed of.
And I wish to you, joy and happiness.
But above all this, I wish you love.
(To Chorus:)

IT'S SO HARD TO SAY GOODBYE TO YESTERDAY

Words and Music by
FREDDIE PERREN and CHRISTINE YARIAN

1.
Bsus
A6
Am6
E(2)
N.C.
to yes - ter - day.
2. I don't
2.
E(2)
N.C.
E
G♯7(♭9)
G♯7
And I'll
take with me the
mem - o - ries to
C♯m
C♯m/B
A
Am
E(2)
be my sun - shine af - ter the
rain. It's so
hard to say good - bye
Bsus
A6
Am6
E(2)
N.C.
to yes - ter - day.
And I'll

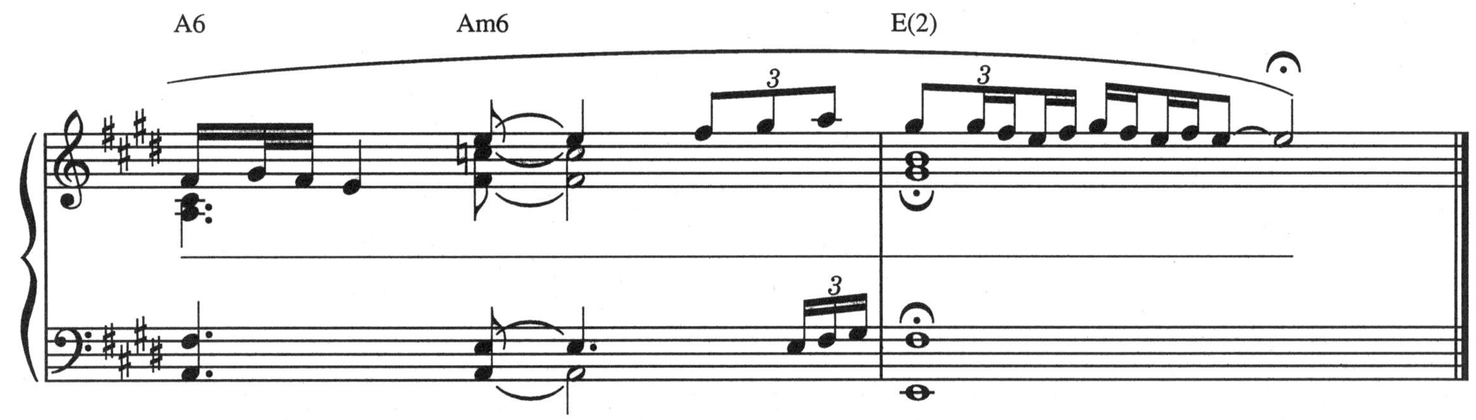

Verse 2:
I don't know where this road is going to lead.
All I know is where we've been and what we've been through.
If we get to see tomorrow, I hope it's worth all the pain.
It's so hard to say goodbye to yesterday.
(To Chorus:)

I'LL BE THERE

Words and Music by
BERRY GORDY, HAL DAVIS,
WILLIE HUTCH and BOB WEST

Verse:
F
C/E
Dm
Dm/C
2. I'll reach out my hand to you, I'll have faith in
mf
Am
B♭
F/A
Gm7
all you do. Just call my
B♭/C
F
name and I'll be there.
(I'll be there.)
B♭/F
F
Bridge:
A♭
E♭
I'll be there to com - fort you, I'll build my world
cresc.
f
B♭
F
of dreams a - round you, I'm so glad I found you, yeah.

A♭ E♭ B♭

I'll be there with a love so strong, I'll be your strength, you know I'll keep

1. To Next Strain 2.

B♭/C B♭/C

hold - in' on. hold - in' on. Oh!

dim. *dim.*

F *Verse:* C/E Dm Dm/C

3. Let me fill your heart with joy and laugh-ter, to-geth-er-ness,

mf

Am B♭ F/A Gm7

well, it's all I'm af - ter. Just call my

B♭/C 1. F B♭/F *D.S.* 𝄋

name and I'll be there.

(I'll be there.)

2.
F
Bb/F
Bb/C
be there.
(I'll be there.)
Don't you know, ba - by?
cresc.
f
Chorus:
F
C/E
Dm7
Dm/C
Yeah, yeah, I'll be there.
I'll be there.
Am7
Bb
F/A
Gm7
Bb/C
Just call my name and I'll
1.
F
Bb/F
Bb/C
be there.
(I'll be there.)
Ee-yeah, ee-yeah, ee-yeah!
2.
F
be there.
Just

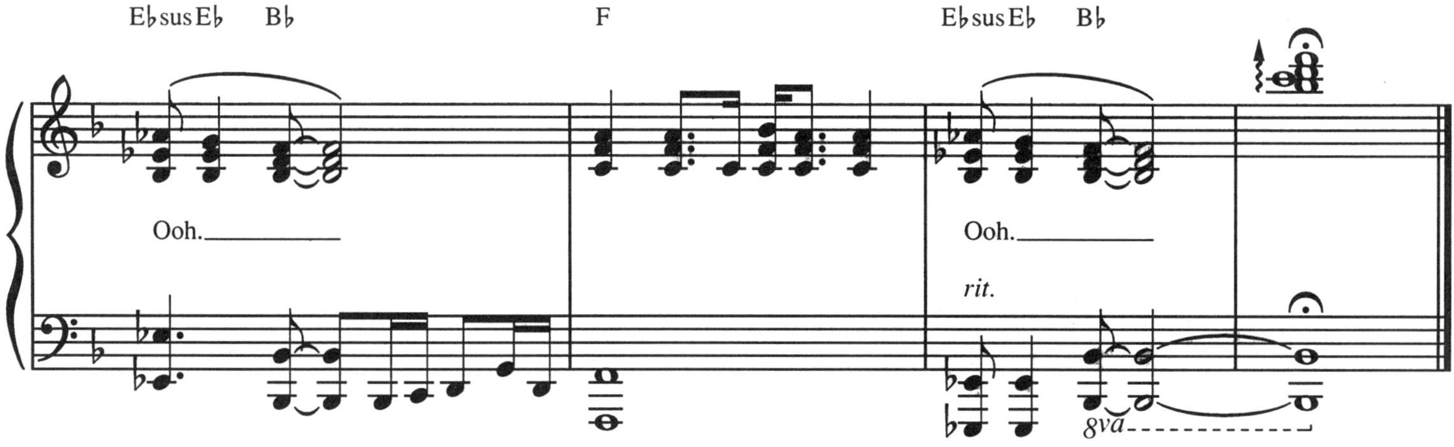

Verse 4:
I'll be there to protect you
With an unselfish love that respects you.
Just call my name and I'll be there.
(To Bridge:)

Verse 5:
If you should ever find someone new,
I know she'd better be good to you.
'Cause if she doesn't, then I'll be there.
(To Chorus:)

I'M EVERY WOMAN

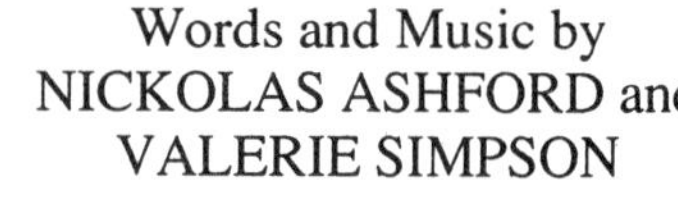
Words and Music by
NICKOLAS ASHFORD and
VALERIE SIMPSON

Slowly ♩ = 60

Abmaj9 Eb/G Cm7

mp

(with pedal)

Fm11 Ab/Bb Bbm7/Eb Eb Bbm7/Eb Eb/G Abmaj9

What-ev-er you want, what-ev-er you

Eb/G Cm7 Fm7 Ab/Bb

need, an - y - thing you want done, ba - by,

Bbm7/Eb Eb Db/Eb Eb Abmaj9 Eb/G

I'll do it nat-'ral - ly. 'Cause I'm ev-'ry wom-an, it's all in

Fm9 G7(b9) G7(#9 b13) N.C.

me. It's all in me, yeah,

cresc.

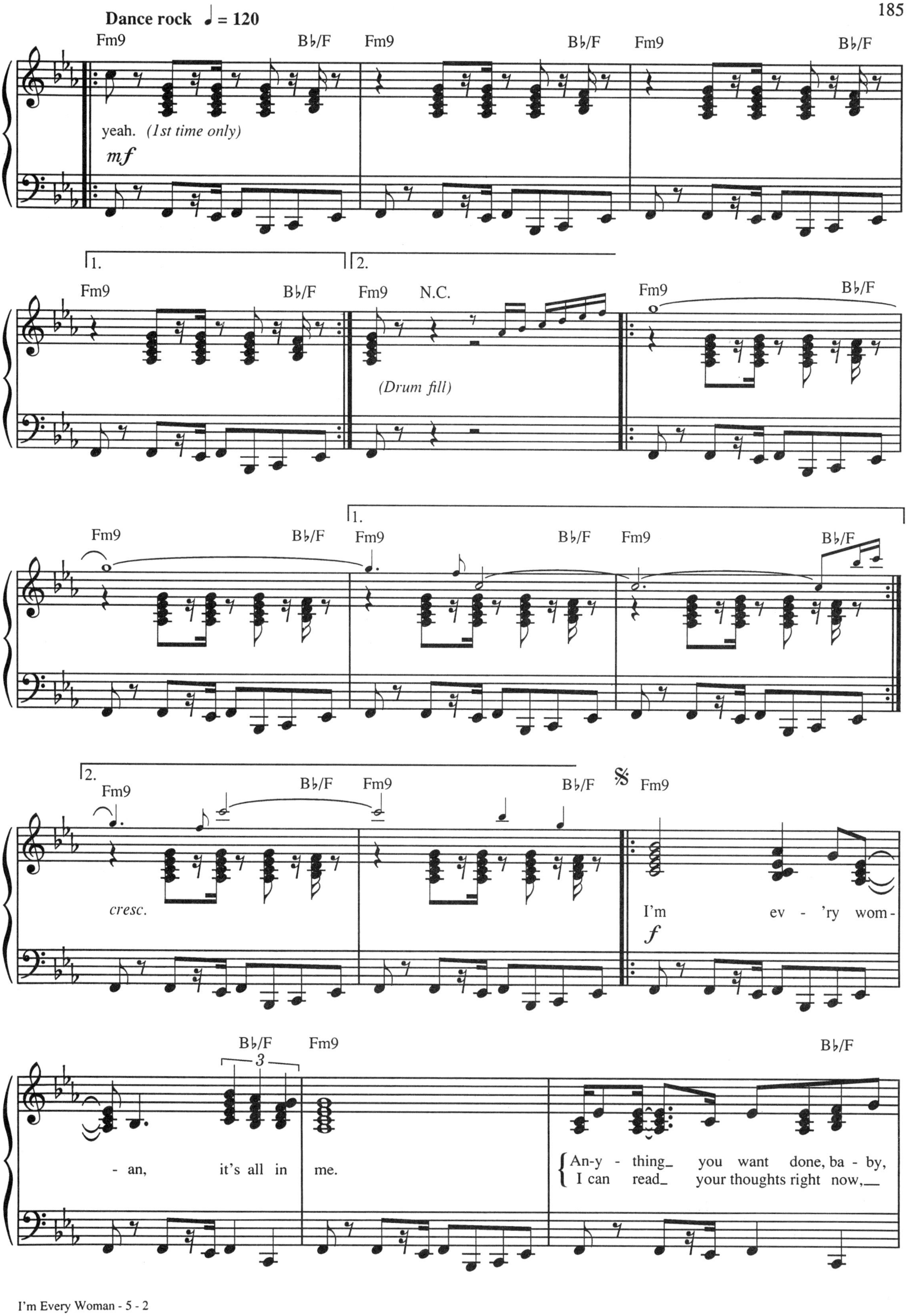

Dance rock ♩ = 120

Fm9 B♭/F Fm9 B♭/F Fm9 B♭/F

yeah. *(1st time only)*

mf

1. Fm9 B♭/F 2. Fm9 N.C. Fm9 B♭/F

(Drum fill)

Fm9 B♭/F 1. Fm9 B♭/F Fm9 B♭/F

2. Fm9 B♭/F Fm9 B♭/F 𝄋 Fm9

cresc.

I'm ev - 'ry wom -

f

- an, it's all in me.

B♭/F Fm9 B♭/F

An-y - thing_ you want done, ba - by,
I can read_ your thoughts right now,_

To Coda
1.
Fm9
Gm7
Cm7
I do it nat - 'ral - ly.
ev - 'ry one from A to Z.
C7(♭9 ♭13)
2.3.
Cm7
Gm7
Fm7
Cm7
Gm7
Fm7
To Next Strain
4.
Cm7
D.S. al Coda
C7(♭9 ♭13)
Verse:
Cm7
Gm7
Fm7
1. I can cast a spell
of se-crets you can't tell.
Cm7
Gm7
Fm7
Cm7
Gm7
Mix a spe - cial brew,
put fire in - side of you.
An-y - time you feel

Fm7
E♭maj9
C7(♭9 ♭13)
D.S. 𝄋
dan - ger or fear, then in - stant-ly, I will ap - pear. 'Cause
Coda
Cm7
Gm7
Fm7
Cm7
Gm7
Fm7
Cm7
I ain't brag - gin',
Fm9/C
Cm7
Fm9/C
'cause I'm the one. You just ask me, ooh, and it shall be
Cm7
Fm9
Cm7
done. And don't both - er to com - pare, I've got it!

Verse 2:
I can sense your needs like rain unto the seeds.
I can make a rhyme of confusion in your mind.
And when it comes down to some good old fashioned love,
I've got it, I've got it, I've got, got it, baby, baby! *(To Chorus:)*

I'M NOT IN LOVE

Words and Music by
ERIC STEWART and
GRAHAM GOULDMAN

Slow rock ♩ = 76

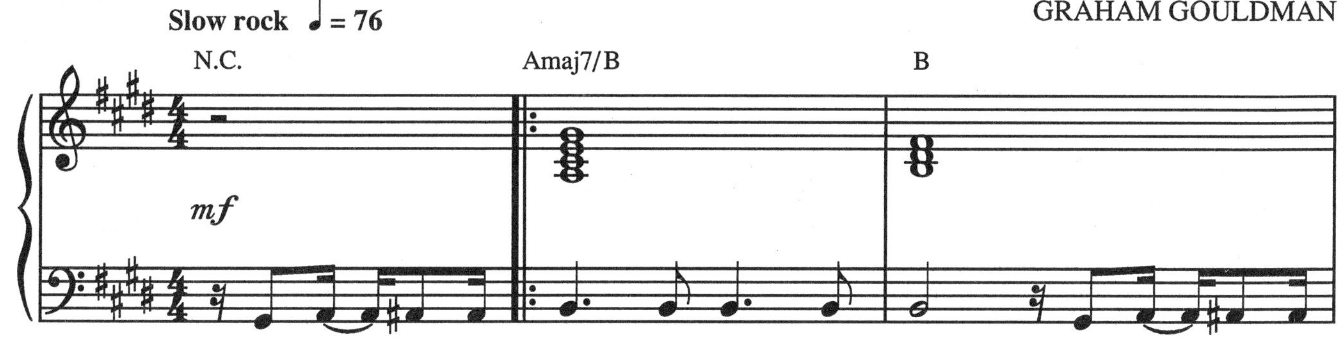

G♯m
G♯
C♯m
C♯m(4)
don't get me wrong, don't think you've got it made.

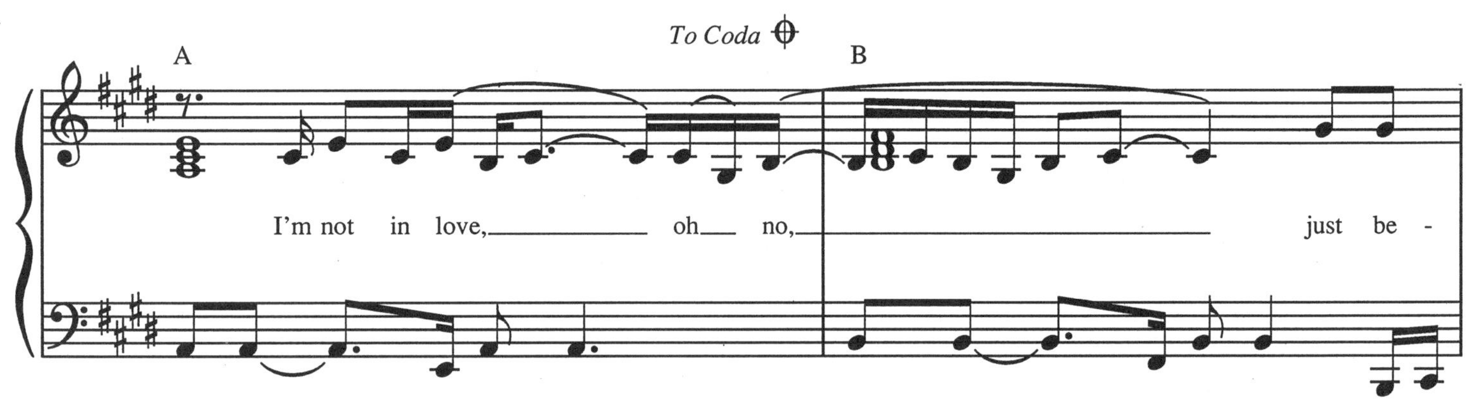
To Coda
A
B
I'm not in love, oh no, just be -

1.
2.3.
E
A/E
Em7
A/E
E
cause.
cause.
(There's something in the way
she makes me feel.)

Bridge:
Am7
D7
G
Em7
Am7
D7
Ooh, you'll wait a long time for me.
Ooh, you'll wait a long time.

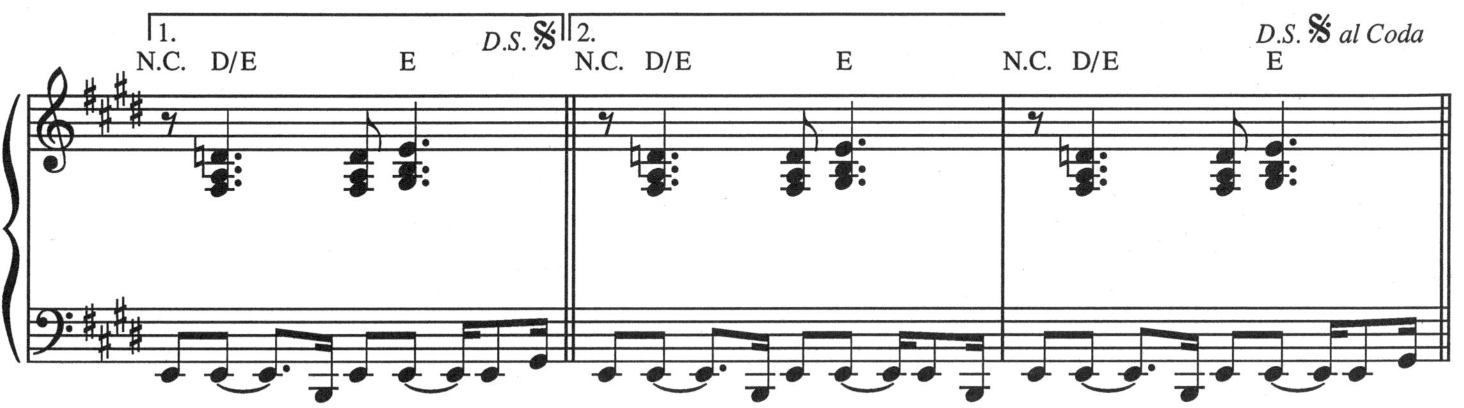

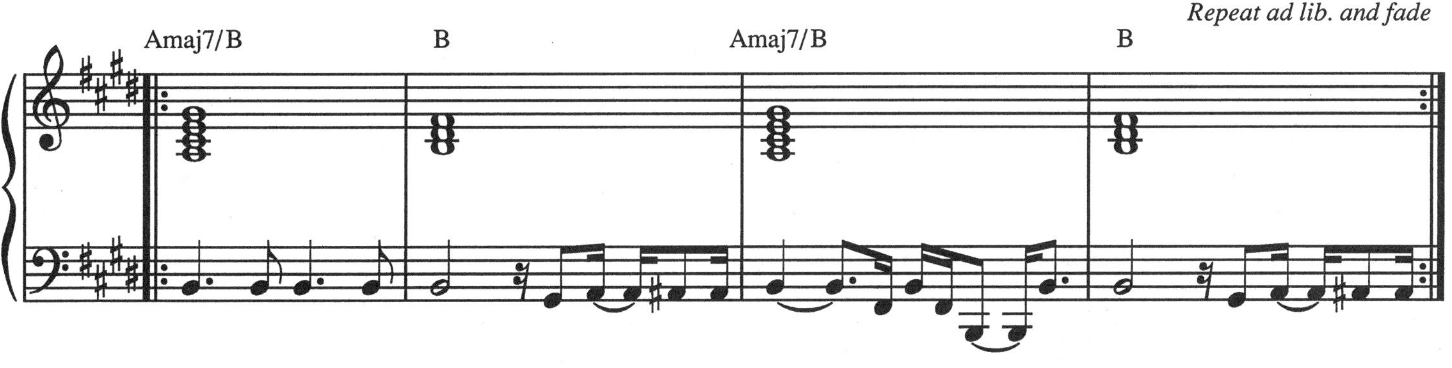

Verse 2:
I'd like to see you, but then again,
That doesn't mean you mean that much to me.
So, if I call you, don't make a fuss
Don't tell your friends about the two of us.
I'm not in love, no, no.

Verse 3: Instrumental Solo

Verse 4:
I keep you picture upon the wall,
It hides a messy stain that's lying there.
But, don't you ask me to give it back,
I know you know it doesn't mean that much to me.
I'm not in love,
I'm not in love.

I'M FREE

Words and Music by
JON SECADA and
MIGUEL A. MOREJON

Dm7
C
B♭
F
see be-yond my trou - bled_ mind,
a - fraid of what_ I'll find._ The
C
B♭/C
sto - ry of___ our lives,_ but there's_ to - mor - row.___ 'Cause I'm___
Chorus:
F
Am7
B♭
B♭/C
F
Am7
___ free, I'm___ free, and things are on - ly as im - por - tant as I
mf - f
B♭
B♭/C
F
Am7
Dm7
C
want them to be.___ We'll have___ a breath of sun-shine when the rain goes_ a - way,_ I___
1.
D.C.
B♭
B♭/C
___ pray,___ I___ pray.

2.
3.
To Next Strain
4.5.etc.
Repeat ad lib. and fade
B♭/C
B♭/C
B♭/C
pray. I'm
pray. ba - by.
pray. I'm

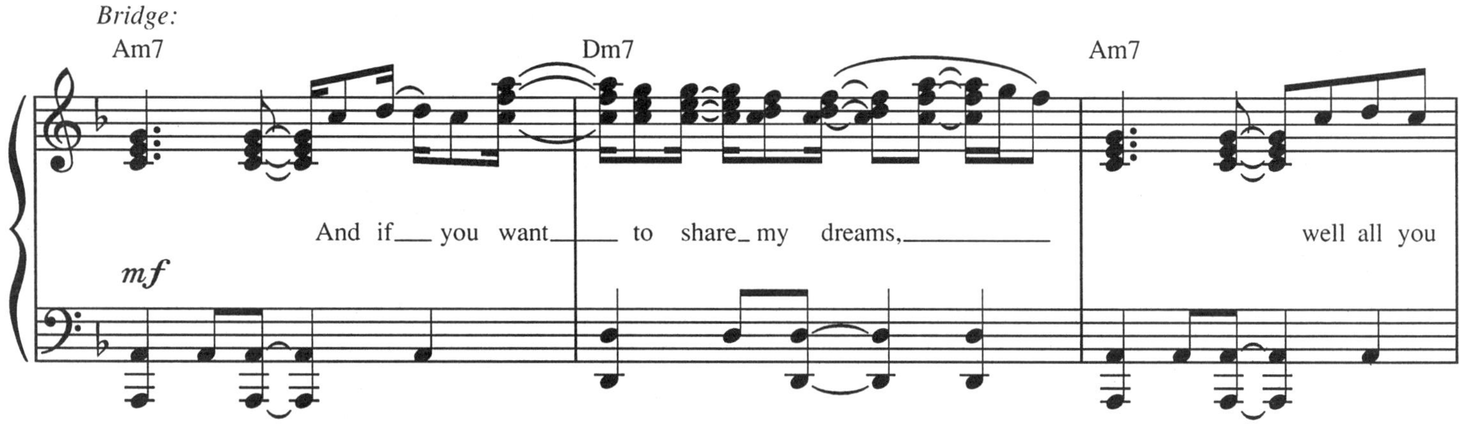
Bridge:
Am7
Dm7
Am7
mf
And if you want to share my dreams,
well all you

Dm7
C
B♭
have to do is say it, say it. Let me

F
C
hear you loud and clear, 'cause I need you if you wan - na be, if you

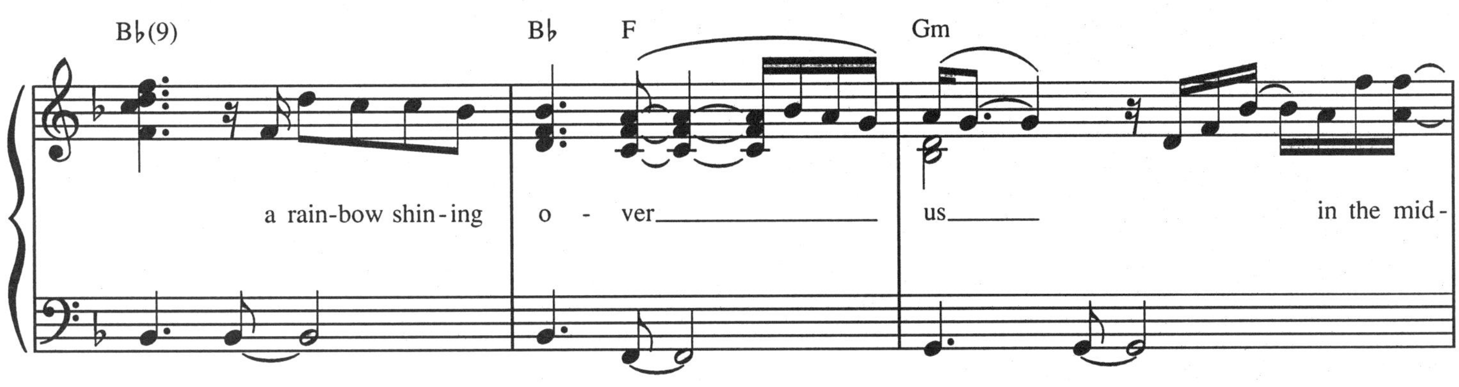

Verse 2:
Do you need a friend right now
On the road that you're going to?
If you get lost, just call me, I'll be there;
Yes, I'll be right there.
'Cause though I may not have the answers,
At least I know what I'm looking for.
Yes, I can do without the sorrow.
There's a day after tomorrow, so I'm leaving it behind.

Chorus 2:
I'm free, I'm free.
Things are only as important as I want them to be.
We'll have a breath of sunshine when the rain goes away,
I pray, I pray.

JUST ANOTHER DAY

Words and Music by
JON SECADA and
MIGUEL A. MOREJON

Moderately ♩ = 108

Em G

mp

Ped. * Ped. * Ped. * Ped. * Ped. * (sim.)

D C

G Em

D/E Cmaj7 D G

Verse:
Em
G
1. Morn-ings a - lone...
When you come home, I breathe
D
C
a lit - tle fast - er,
G
Em
ev - ery time we're to - geth - er,
oh.
D/E
C
It'd nev - er be the same
(Bkgrd.: It'd nev - er be the same
D
G
Em
D/E
if you're not here.
)
How can you stay a - way,

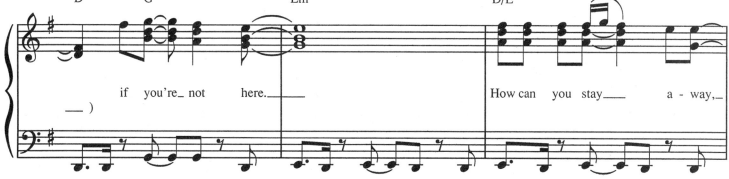

C
D
G
How can you stay a - way so long?
(How can you stay a - way so long?)
Bridge:
D
C
1. Why can't we stay to - geth - er?
D
Just
C
give me a rea - son, give me a rea - son, 'cause
Chorus:
G
D
Em
I, I don't wan - na say it,

Bm Am7

I don't wan - na find an - oth - er way,

G D

make it through the day with - out you.

D7sus G D

I, I, I can't

Em Bm Am7

re - sist trying to find ex - act - ly what I missed. It's

G D 1.

just an - oth - er day with - out you. It's

Verse 2:
Making the time,
Find the right lines to make you stay forever.
What do I have to tell you?
Just trying to hold on to something.
(Trying to hold on to something good.)
Give us a chance to make it.
(Give us a chance to make it.)

Bridge 2:
Don't wanna hold on to never . . .
I'm not that strong, I'm not that strong.
(To Chorus:)

Bridge 3:
Why can't you stay forever?
Just give me a reason, give me a reason.
(To Chorus:)

LATELY

Words and Music by
STEVIE WONDER

Slowly ♩ = 60

1. 2.

D♭ Bbm7 Gbmaj9 D7(#9 b13)

mp

(with pedal)

Ebm7 Gb/Ab Ab13(b9) Gbmaj9 Fm7 Ebm7 Gb/Ab Ab7

Verse:

D♭ Bbm7

1. Late - ly I___ have had___ the strang - est feel - ing
2. Late - ly I've___ been star - ing in___ the mir - ror,

Ebm7 Ab7 Bb7(b13)

with no viv - id rea - son here___ to find.___
ver - y slow - ly pick - ing me___ a - part;___

Ebm
Bb7(b13)
Ebm7
Gb/Ab
Ab7
Yet, the thought of los - ing you's been hang - ing 'round my
trying to tell my - self I have no rea - son with your
Db
Ebm9
Ab
Bbm7 Ab/C
3
3
mind.
heart.
Db
Bbm7
Far more fre - quent-ly you're wear - ing per - fume
Just the oth - er night while you were sleep - ing, I
Ebm7
Ab7
Bb7(b13)
with, you say, no spe - cial place to go. But
vague - ly heard you whis - per some-one's name. But

Ebm
Bb7(b13)
Ebm7
Gb/Ab
Ab7
when I ask will you be com - ing back soon, you don't
when I ask you of the thoughts you're keep - ing, you just
Db
Ebm7
Abm7
Db13
know, nev - er know.
say noth-ing's changed.
Well,
cresc.
To Coda
Gbmaj7
Gbm7
Cb13
I'm a man of man - y wish - es,
hope my pre - mo - ni - tion miss - es,
mf
Fm7
Bb9sus
Bb9
but what I real - ly feel, my eyes won't let me hide, 'cause they

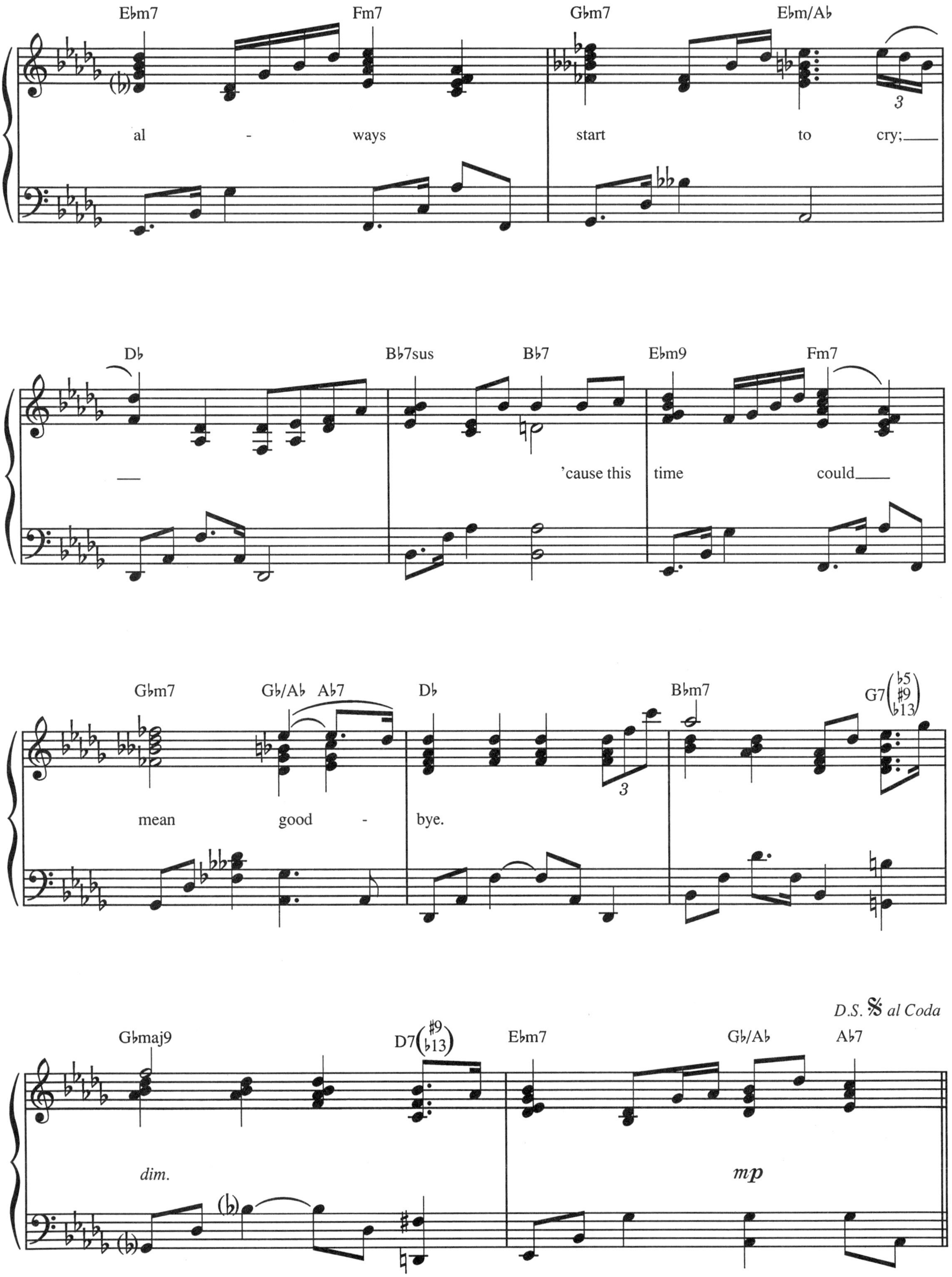

Ebm7
Fm7
Gbm7
Ebm/Ab
al - ways start to cry;
Db
Bb7sus
Bb7
Ebm9
Fm7
'cause this time could
Gbm7
Gb/Ab
Ab7
Db
Bbm7
G7(b5 #9 b13)
mean good - bye.
D.S. 𝄋 al Coda
Gbmaj9
D7(#9 b13)
Ebm7
Gb/Ab
Ab7
dim.
mp

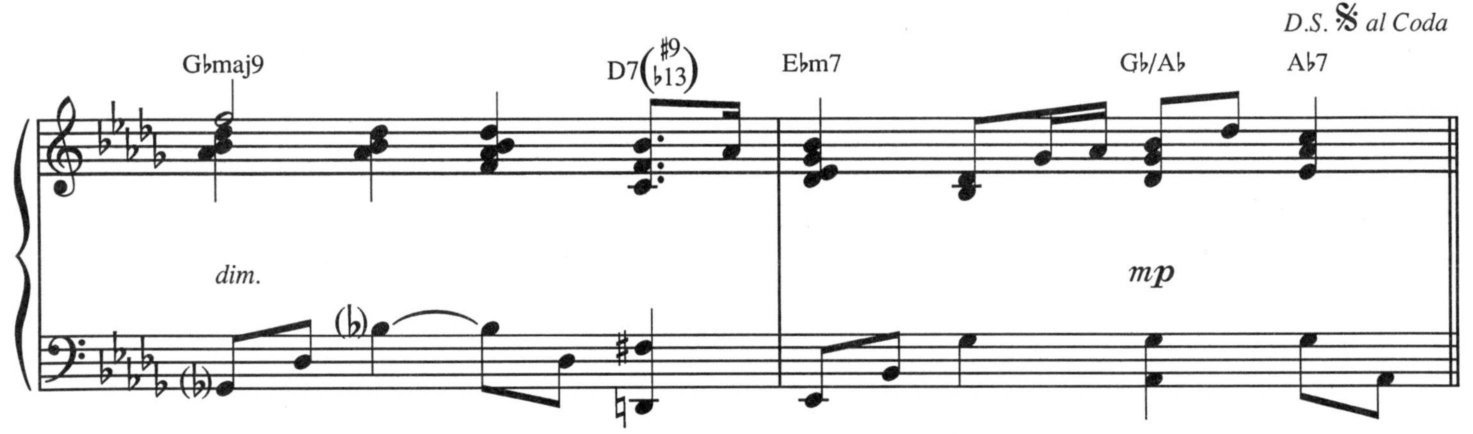

Coda
Bbm7
Db/Eb
Eb7
but what I real - ly feel, my
cresc.
eyes won't let me hide, 'cause they
Abm7
Bbm7
Bm7
Db7
al - ways
start to
f
Gb
Eb7sus
Eb7
Abm7
Bbm7
cry;
'cause this
time could
Bm7
Cb/Db
Gb
Ebm7
Gb/Db
mean good - bye.
Cbmaj7
Gb/Bb
Abm7
Abm7/Db
Bbm7
Ebmaj13
8va
rit.

LIVE AND LET DIE

Words and Music by
PAUL McCARTNEY and
LINDA McCARTNEY

Slowly
G
Bm
C
D7
D7-9
mf
When you were young and your heart was an o - pen book,
(2nd time, instrumental till *)
G
Bm
C
C (D bass)
Cm (D bass)
You used to say live and let live. (You know you did, you know you did, you know you
G
Bm
C
A
did.) But if this ev - er - chang - ing world in which we live in makes you
3

D
B♭
G7
C (G bass)
give it a cry,
Say live and let die!
Live and let
Gdim
G7
C (G bass)
die,
Live and let
die,
Live and let
die.
Gm
3fr
ff
To Coda
C9
8va lower ad lib. till *
What does it mat - ter to ya,
mf

G7
D7
when you got a job to do you got-ta do it well,
You got-ta
Em
F
Gm
3fr
give the oth-er fel-low hell!
ff
D. C. al Coda
Coda
Gm
3fr
Eb m
(Gb bass)
T

LOST IN YOUR EYES

Lyrics & Music by
TOM PETTY

Lost in Your Eyes - 3 - 1

Am7
D
G/B
Chorus:
C
G/B
you nev - er re - al - ized that
I could have stood there
cresc.
f
Am7
G
C
G/B
Am7
G
lost in your eyes.
Stood there wait-ing and
not re - al - ized
C
G/B
Am7
G
Cmaj7
love is-n't eas - y, it
is-n't al - ways kind.
I could have stood there
To Coda
1.
D.S.
N.C.
G
C/G
N.C.
G
C/G
lost in your eyes.
2.
G
Bridge:
D
C
And though, some - times
I won - der,
yes, I
won - der,
I real-ly, real-ly

Verse 2:
Guess I understand it, guess I sort of have to,
Guess I kind of see.
Just because it could have been, doesn't mean it had to ever mean a thing.
And baby, baby, I could say it all the time, that . . .
(To Chorus:)

Verse 3:
Guess I understand it, guess I sort of have to,
Guess I kind of see.
Just because it could have been, doesn't mean it had to ever mean a thing.
And baby, baby, you never realized that . . .
(To Chorus:)

LOVE OF MY LIFE

Words and Music by
CARLY SIMON

G
A
But you've got to know
But get it through your head
that
D
Bm7
A
F♯m7
Em7
you're the love of my life, you are the love of my life.
No Chord
D
Bm7
A
You are the love of my life, you are the
Em7
N.C.
F♯m7
love of my life.
From the mo - ment I first saw

Bm7
Em7
G
A
— you, the sec - ond that you were born,— I knew that
D
Bm7
A
Em7
you were the love— of my life, quite sim - ply the love
D/F♯
G
A
1. D
2. D
of— my life. life.
B♭
C
Am
Dm
Gm7
3fr.
You can drive me cra - zy. You can drive me
f

F
Gm7
3fr.
F/A
an - y - where.
Here are the keys
just
do as you please,
it may not
Bbmaj7
D
al - ways be eas - y.
But you're the love of my life,
rit.
a tempo
Bm7
A
F#m7
Em7
N.C.
D
my heart is rid - ing on a run - a - way train.
You are the love of my
Bm7
A
Em7
N.C.
life,
through all the pleas - ure and pain.
From the

F♯m7
Bm7
Em7
mo - ment I first saw you, I knew it right a - way
G
A
D
Bm7
I knew that you were the love of my life, sim - ply the
mf
Em7
D/F♯
love of my life. You are the love, the great
p
love of my life.
rit.

LOVE SHOULDA BROUGHT YOU HOME

Words and Music by
BO WATSON, BABYFACE and
DARYL SIMMONS

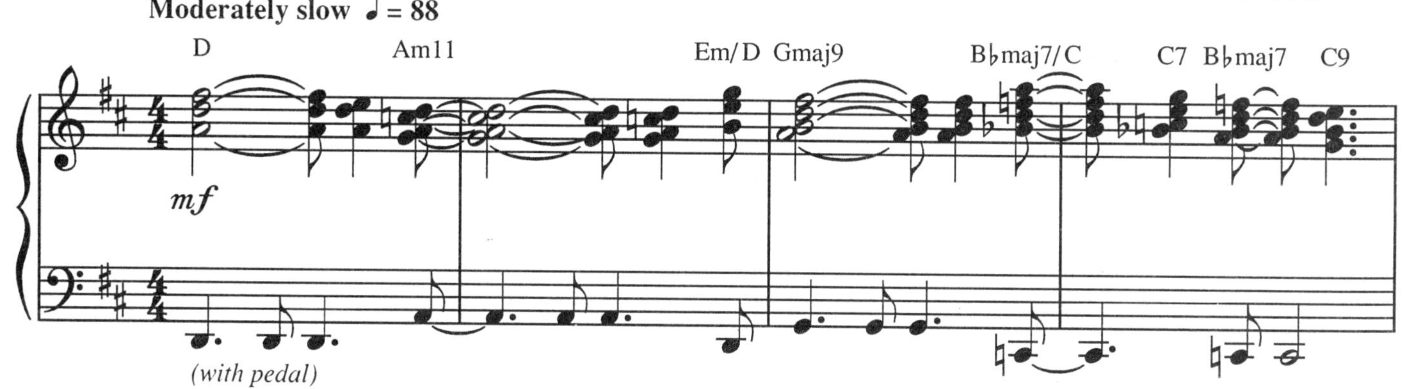

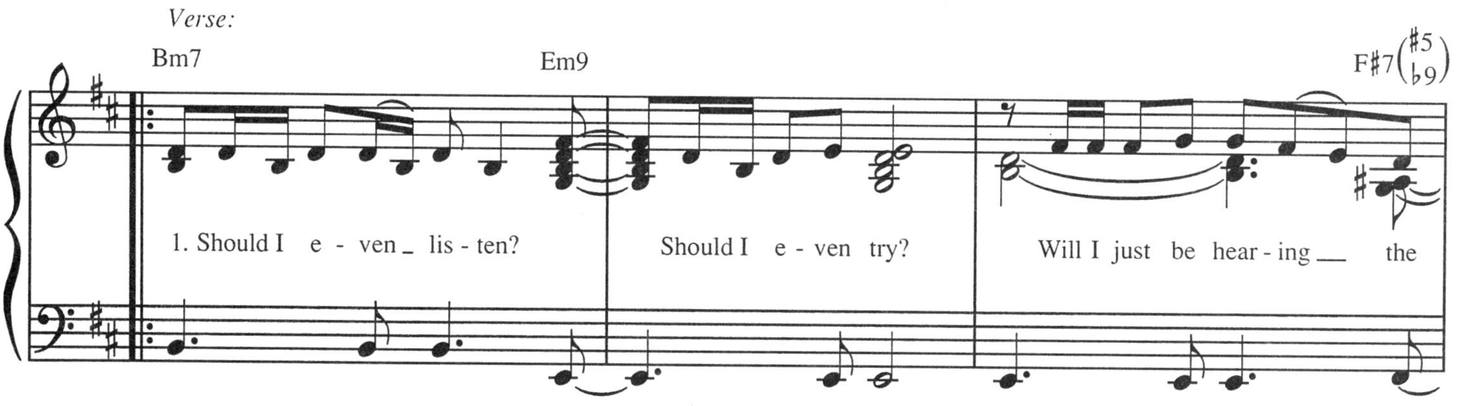

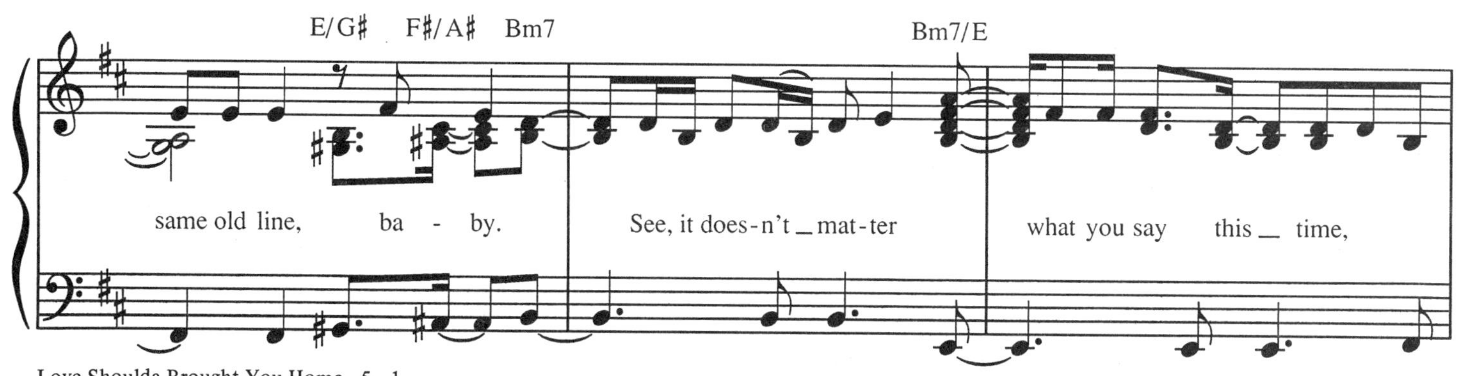

Em7 F#7(#5 b9) Gmaj9 F#m7
'cause our whole re - la - tion-ship is built on one lie. You say things aren't the way
Em7 Dmaj7 Cmaj7 Bm7 Gmaj7/A Bm7 Gmaj7
they seem, but still you can't come straight with me. How can
F#m7 Em7 F#m7 G F#m7 Gmaj7/A
you think that you're in love when you don't know the mean -
Chorus:
D/A D Am7
- ing of love.
Love should have brought you, brought you home last night. You should-a been
Gmaj7 Bbmaj7/C C9 Bbmaj7/C C9 A/B Bm7
with me, should-a been right by my side, ba - by. If you cared

1.
E13
E9
Em7
F♯m7
Gmaj9
F♯
E/G♯
F♯/A♯
_ an - y - thing for me, ___ then
love would-a brought you to me last night. ___

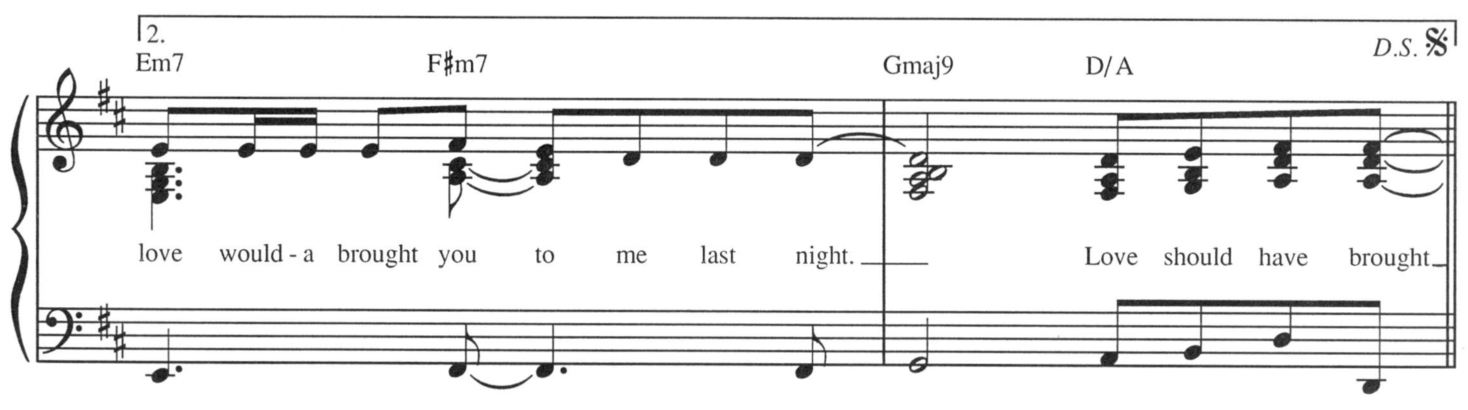
2.
Em7
F♯m7
Gmaj9
D/A
D.S. 𝄋
love would - a brought you to me last night. ___
Love should have brought _

3.
Em7
F♯m7
Em7
F♯m7
you would have been sin - cere, and
I would-n't be in tears, and

Em7
F♯m7
B♭maj7
Dmaj7
Em7
F♯m7
love would-a brought you to me last night. ___
Oh, ba - by,

Bridge:
Gmaj7
Gm7
Gm6
D/F♯
why, why do men think that love's just for the mo - ment, not

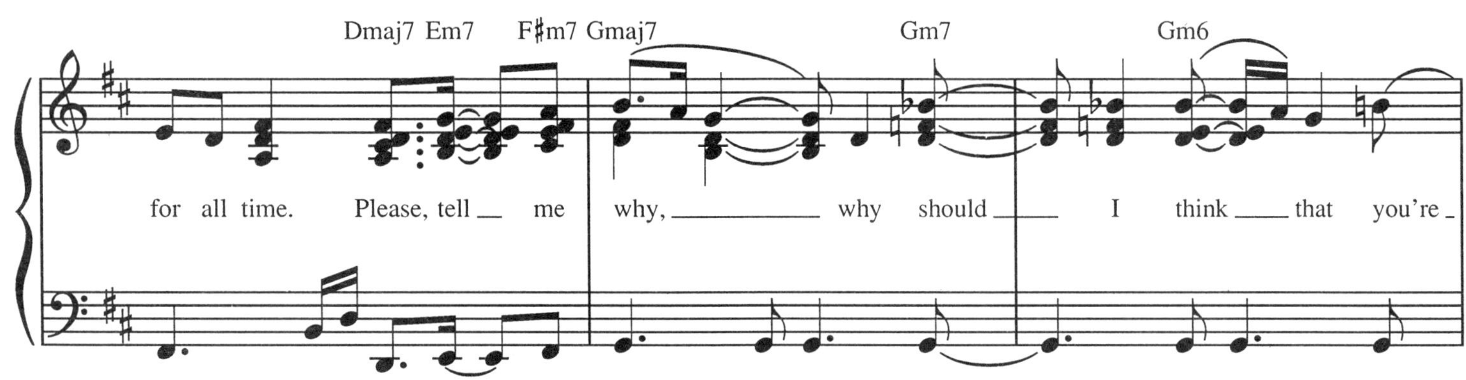
Dmaj7 Em7
F♯m7 Gmaj7
Gm7
Gm6
for all time. Please, tell me why, why should I think that you're

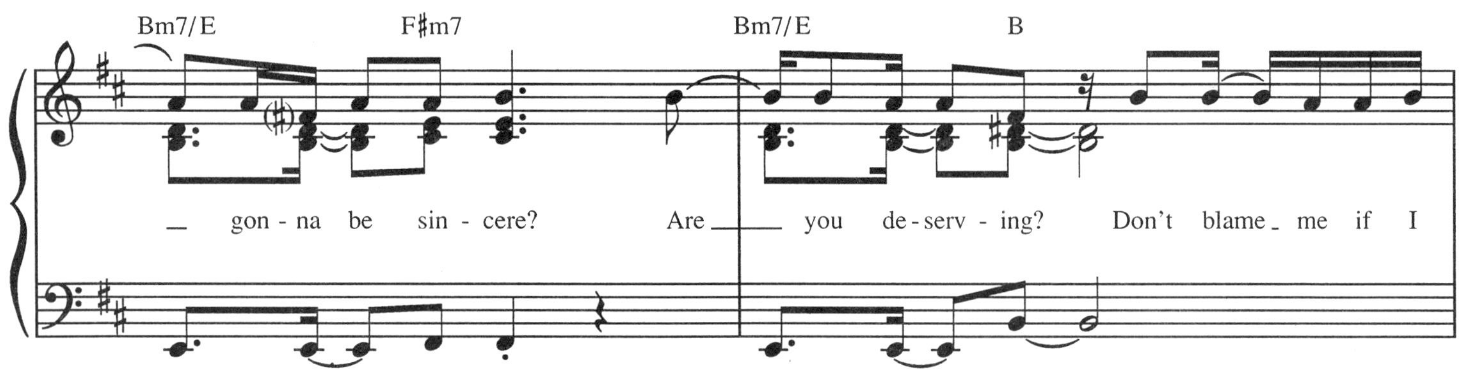
Bm7/E
F♯m7
Bm7/E
B
gon - na be sin - cere? Are you de - serv - ing? Don't blame me if I

Em7
F♯m7
F
Em7
D/A
just don't be - lieve it, just don't be - lieve that you'll al - ways be here.
Love should have brought

D
Am7
Gmaj7
B♭maj7/C
you, brought you home last night. You should-a been with me, should-a been right

C9 B♭maj7 C9
A/B
Bm7
E13
E9
by my side, ba - by. If you cared an - y - thing for me, then

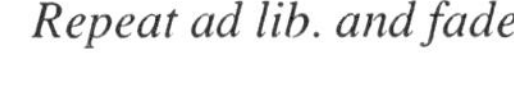
Repeat ad lib. and fade

Em7
F♯m7
Gmaj9
D/A
love would-a brought you to me last night. Love should have brought

Verse 2:
Gotta hand it to ya,
Had me there for awhile.
I was so in love with you,
I couldn't see past your smile.
Now I smell the coffee, boy.
I got a wake-up call.
And it left a message that you
Just don't care at all.
You can't expect me to believe
That she does not mean anything.
You say that you love only me.
Your kind of love, darlin', I just don't need.
(To Chorus:)

MARY JANE'S LAST DANCE

Words and Music by
TOM PETTY

Rock ♩ = 88

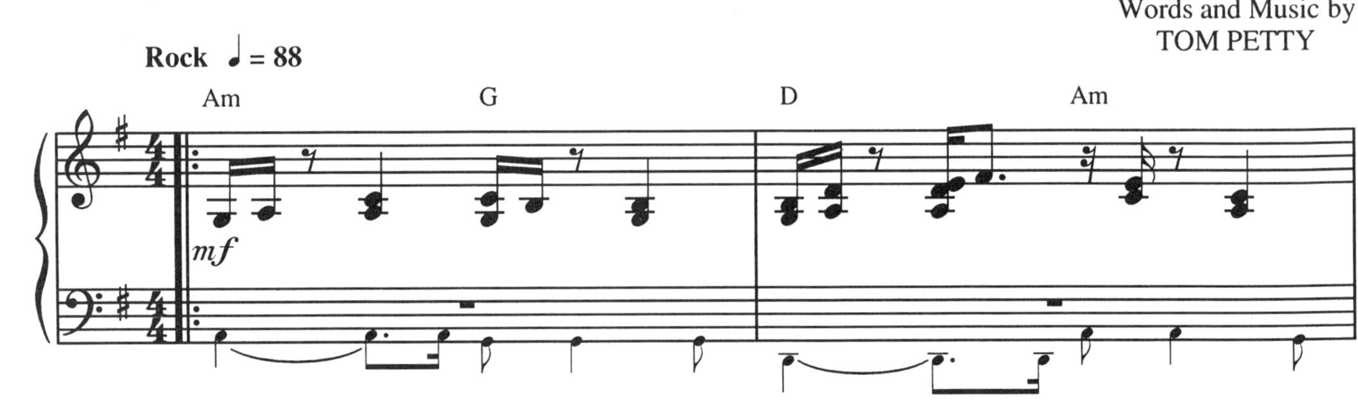
Am
G
D
Am
mf

G
1.
D
Am
2.
D
Am

Verse:
G
D
Am
1. She grew up in a In - di - an - a town, had a
good look-in' ma-ma who nev - er was a-round. But she

G
D
Am
grew up tall__ and she grew up right_ with them
In - di - an - a boys on an In - di - an - a night.

1.
G
D
Am
G
Hoo.

D
Am
2.
G
D
Am
Hoo.
2. Then she
on.
Keep mov-in' on.

To Next Strain
3.4.
G
D
Am
G
Oh my, my, oh hell yes —

D
Am
G
hon - ey, put on that par - ty dress.
Buy me a drink, sing me a song,

Chorus:
D
Am
Em7
take me as I come 'cause I can't stay long.
Last dance with Mar - y Jane,

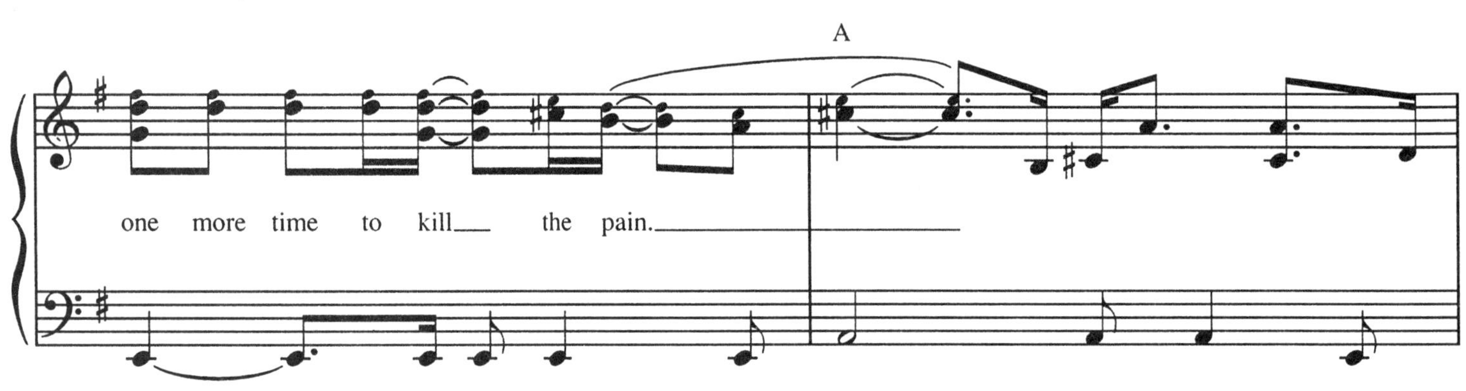
A
one more time to kill the pain.

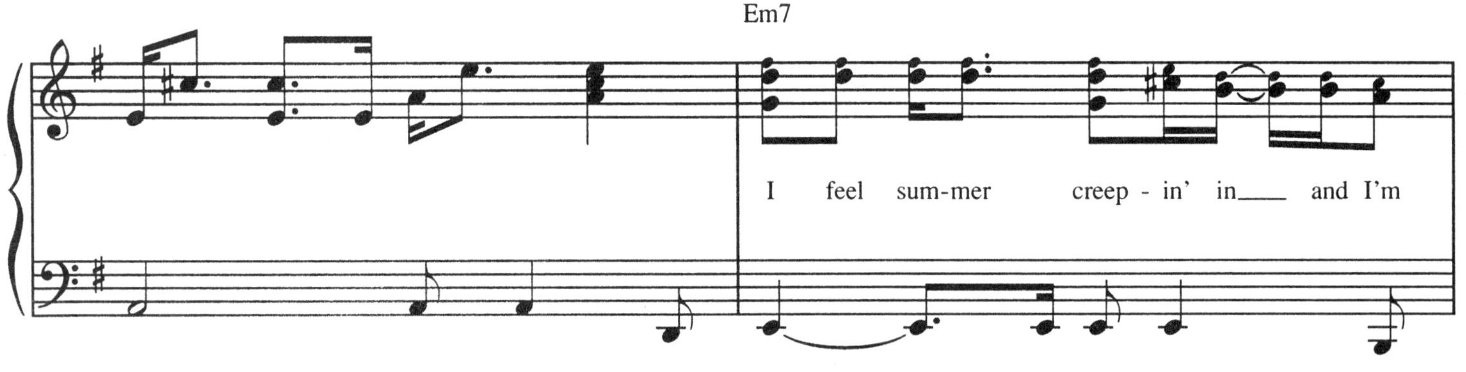
Em7
I feel sum-mer creep - in' in and I'm

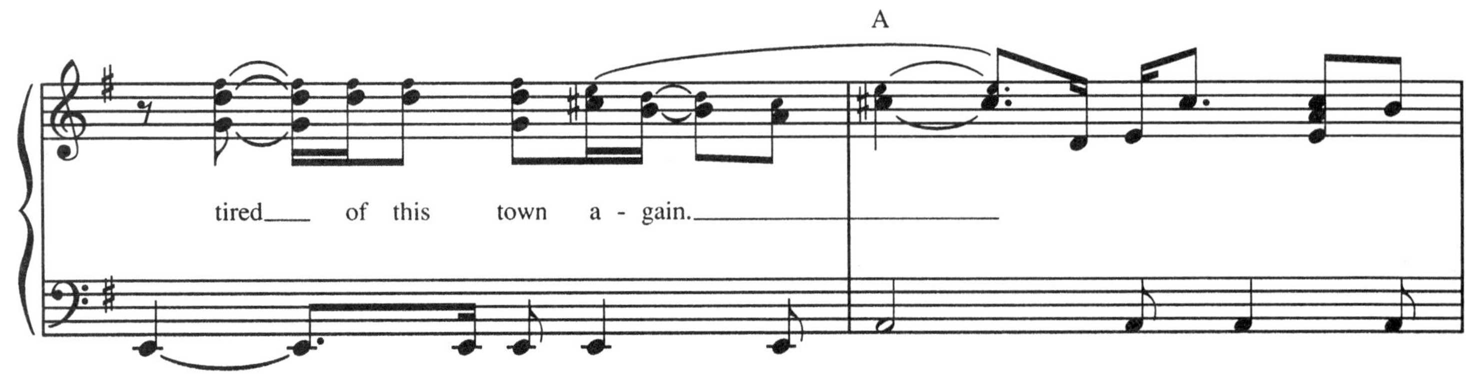
A
tired of this town a - gain.

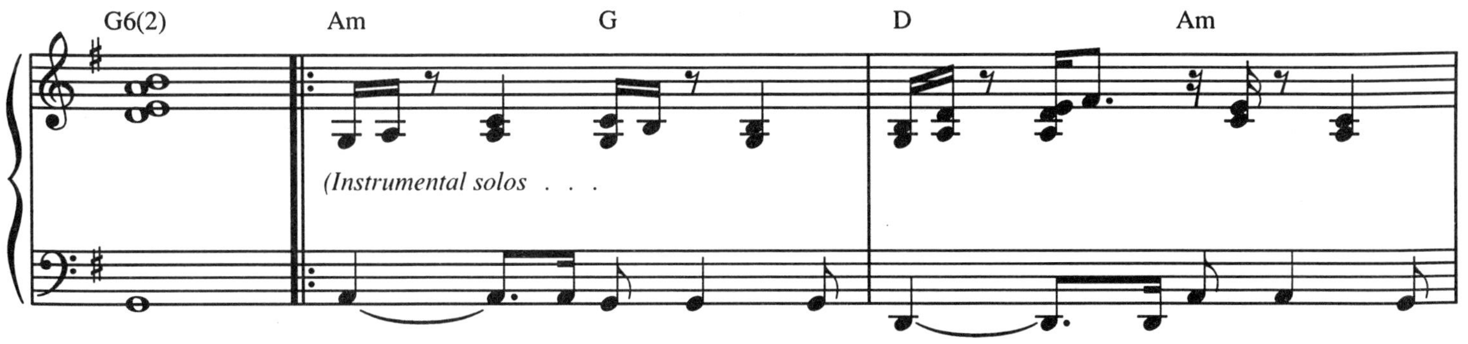

Verse 2:
Then she moved down here at the age of eighteen,
She blew the boys away; was more than they'd seen.
I was introduced and we both started groovin',
She said, "I dig you, baby, but I got to keep movin'."
(To Chorus:)

Verse 3:
Well I don't know but I been told, you never slow down, you never grow old.
I'm tired of screwin' up, tired of goin' down,
Tired of myself, tired of the town,
Oh my, my, oh hell yes - Honey put on that party dress.
Buy me a drink, sing me a song,
Take me as I come 'cause I can't stay long.
(To Chorus:)

Verse 4:
There's pigeons down on Market Square,
She's standing in her underwear.
Lookin' down from a hotel room,
Nightfall will be coming soon.
Oh my, my, oh hell yes, you got to put on that party dress.
It was too cold to cry, when I woke up alone.
I hit my last number, I walked to the road.
(To Chorus:)

MASTERPIECE

Words and Music by
KENNY NOLAN

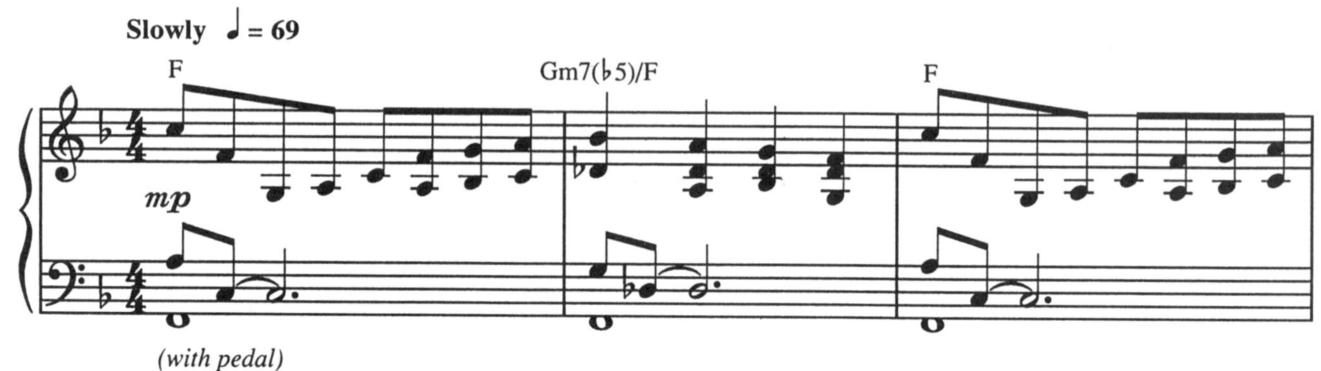
Slowly ♩ = 69
F
Gm7(♭5)/F
F
mp
(with pedal)

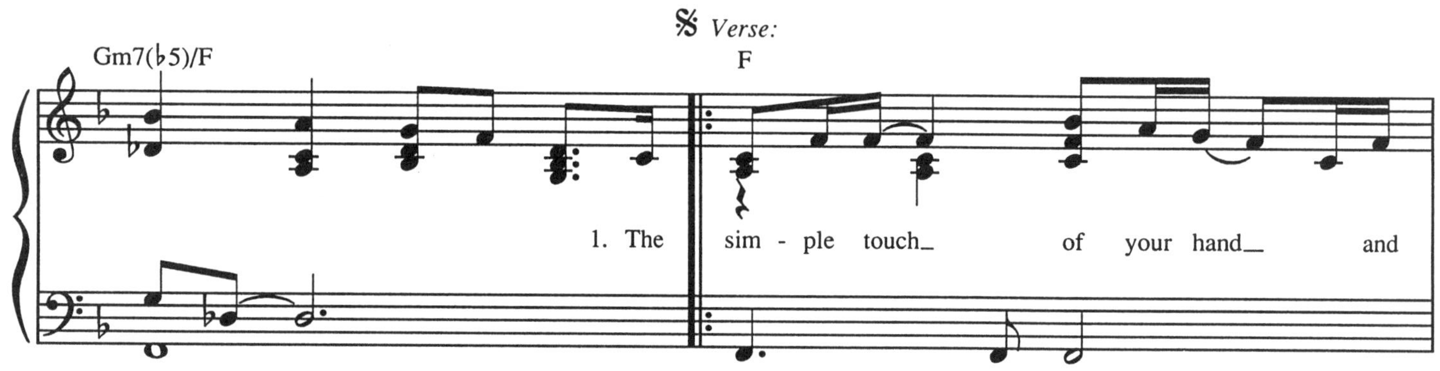
Gm7(♭5)/F
Verse:
F
1. The
sim - ple touch_ of your hand_ and

Gm7(♭5)/F
F
ev - ery - thing_ is right.__ The
gen - tle way_ you look at me__

Gm7(♭5)/F
F
Am7
when we kiss_ good-night.__ You've
giv - en me_ the free - dom no

B♭(2)
B♭m6
F
oth - er love has known and now I
thank you, girl.
(Thank you, girl.)
1.3.
B♭/C
Thank you, girl.
(Thank you, girl.) 2. The
2.4.
B♭/C
D♭/E♭
E♭/F
now I know, ooh
cresc.
Chorus:
D♭maj7
I've found a mas - ter - piece in
mf
Cm7
E♭/F
you, a work of art it's
B♭m7
D♭maj7/E♭
D♭/E♭
E♭/F
D♭maj7
true. And I trea-sure you, my love. Ooh,
I've found a mas-ter-piece in
Cm7
B♭m7
you, a work of art it's true. And I trea-sure
1.
B♭/C
D.S.
you. 3. Some -
dim.

2.
To Next Strain
3.4. etc.
Repeat ad lib. and fade
B♭/C
you.
B♭/C
you.

Bridge:
F
B♭m
When I'm lost__ and in - se-cure, you build me up__ and make_ me sure.

F
D♭/E♭
E♭/F
D.S.S. 𝄋𝄋
Ev - ery - thing will turn out right,_ my love. Oh,

Verse 2:
The countless ways you've touched my heart
Is more than I can say.
The beauty that you've shown to me takes my breath away.
A picture perfect painting, that's what our love is.
And yes I need you so, and now I know . . .
(To Chorus:)

Verse 3:
Sometimes I wonder what I'd be had I not found you.
A lost and lonely soul,
This world could show me nothing new.
But now my life's a canvas, painted with your love.
And it will always be, and now I see . . .

Verse 4:
The two of us together, thru time will never part.
This fairy tale we're sharing is real inside our hearts.
Let it be forever, never let it end.
This promise I do make,
Heaven is ours to take.
(To Chorus:)

MERCY, MERCY ME (THE ECOLOGY)/ I WANT YOU

"Mercy, Mercy Me" - Written by MARVIN GAYE
"I Want You" - Written by LEON WARE
and ARTHUR ROSS

F♯m7
F♯maj7/B
no. Where did all the blue skies go? Poi - son is the wind that blows
1.2.
3.4.
from the north, west, south and east.
near by are dy - ing.
from the north, west, south and
Verse:
Emaj7
C♯m9
4.6. Oh, mer - cy, mer - cy me. Oh, things
east.
F♯m7
ain't what they used to be. What a-bout this o - ver crowd-
F♯maj7/B
C♯m9 C♯m
- ed land? How much more a - buse from man can she stand?

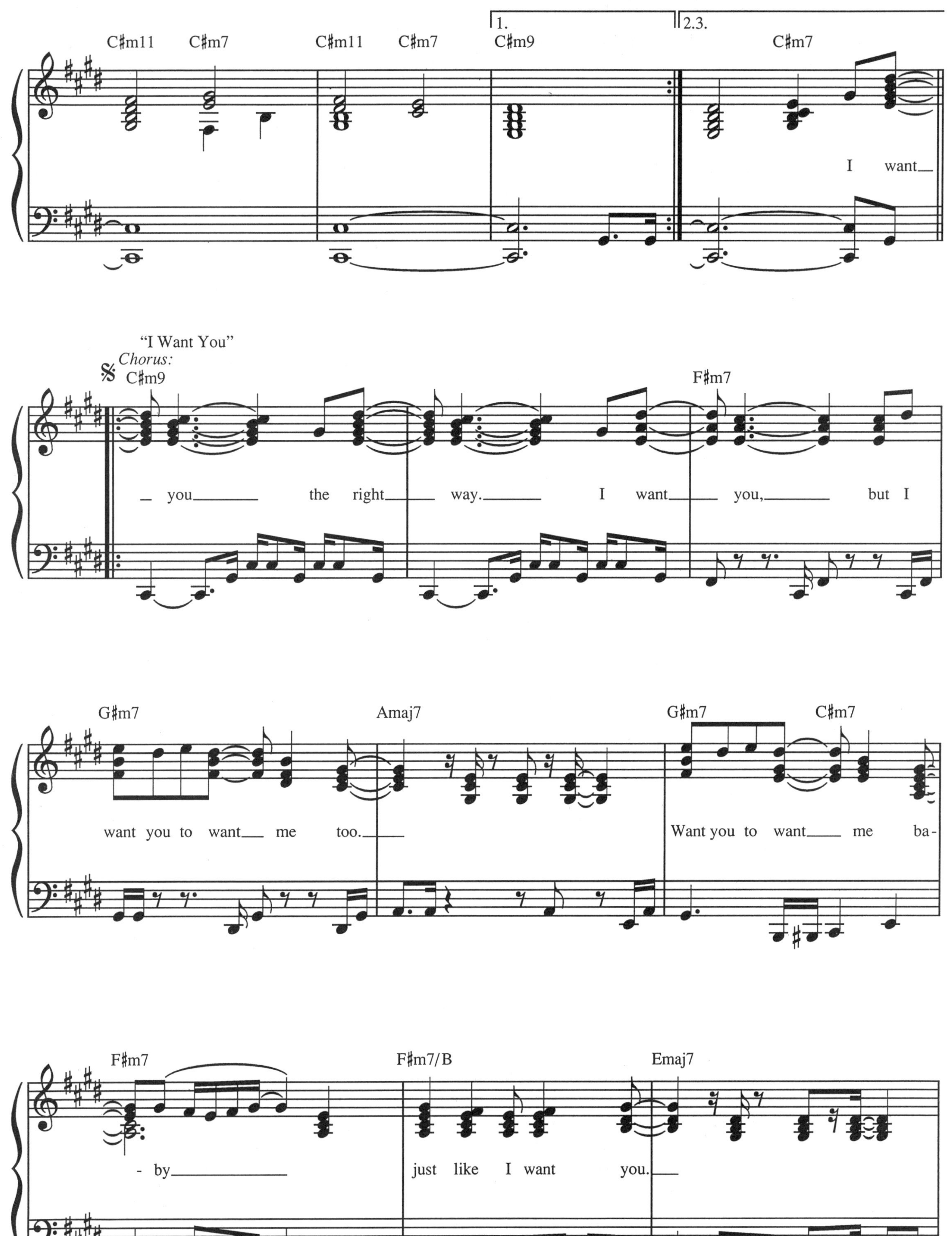

1.
2.3.
C♯m11
C♯m7
C♯m11
C♯m7
C♯m9
C♯m7
I want
"I Want You"
Chorus:
C♯m9
F♯m7
you the right way. I want you, but I
G♯m7
Amaj7
G♯m7
C♯m7
want you to want me too.
Want you to want me ba-
F♯m7
F♯m7/B
Emaj7
- by
just like I want you.

1.2.
To Next Strain
3.4.
Repeat ad lib. and fade
Verse:
G#sus
G#7(♭13)
G#sus
G#7(♭13)
C#m9
1. Oh,
I want
I'll give you all
the love you want in re-turn, sweet dar-lin'.
F#m7
A/B
G#7sus
Your hap-pi-ness is all I crave.
G#7(♭13)
C#m9
Ooh, it's too bad, it's just too sad you don't

F♯m7
A/B
want me now.
But
I'm
gon-na change your
mind

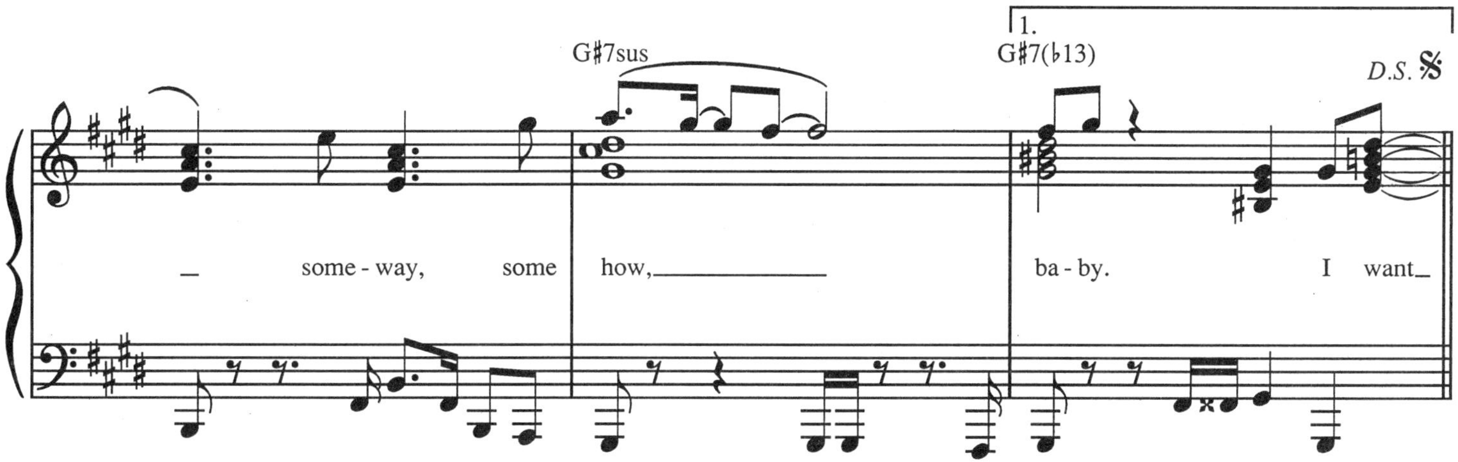
G♯7sus
1.
G♯7(♭13)
D.S. 𝄋
some - way,
some
how,
ba - by.
I
want

2.
G♯7(♭13)
C♯m7 C♯m
C♯m11 C♯m7
C♯m11
D.S.S. 𝄋𝄋
there.
I want you.
Woh.

"Mercy, Mercy Me"
Verse 2:
Oh, mercy, mercy me.
Oh, things ain't what they used to be, no, no.
Oil wasted on the oceans,
And our seas are fish full of mercury.

Verse 3:
Oh, mercy, mercy me.
Oh, things ain't what they used to be, no, no.
Radiation underground and in the sky,
Animals and birds who live nearby are dying.

"I Want You"
Verse 2:
A one way love is just a fantasy.
Ah, sugar, to share is precious, pure and fair.
Don't play with something you should cherish for life, baby.
Don't you want to care?
Lonely? I'm there.

MI TIERRA
(MY HOMELAND)

Musica y Letra:
ESTEFANO
Inspiraciones:
GLORIA ESTEFAN

Moderate salsa ♩ = 100
C♯m
mf
N.C.
Verse:
1. De mi tie-rra be - lla, de mi tie-rra san - ta,
2. Si-guen los pre - go - nes, la me-lan-co-lí - a,
C♯m
oi-go e-se gri-to de los tam-bo - res, y los tim-ba - les al cum - ban-
y ca-da no-che jun-to a la lu - na si-gue el güa-ji - ro en-to-nan-do el

G♯7
F♯m
C♯m
- char.
son.
Y‿e-se pre - gón que can-ta‿un her-ma - no, que de su
Y ca-da ca - lle que va‿a mi pue - blo, tie-ne‿un que-
G♯7
C♯m
tie - rra vi - ve le - ja - no, y que‿el re - cuer - do le‿ha-ce llo - rar.
ji - do, tie-ne‿un la - men - to, tie - ne nos - tal - gia co - mo su voz.
U - na can-
Y‿e-sa can-
F♯m
C♯m
G♯7
ción que vi-ve‿en - to - nan - do, de su do - lor de su pro-pio llan - to, y
ción que vi-ve‿en - to - nan - do, co - rre en‿la san - gre si - gue lle - gan - do, con
3
3
C♯m
N.C.
se la‿es - cu - cha pe - nar.
más fuer - za‿al co - ra - zón.
La
f

Chorus:
C♯m
G♯7
tie - rra te due - le, la tie - rra te da, en
F♯m
G♯7
C♯m
me - dio del al - ma, cuan - do tú no es - tás. La
G♯7
tie - rra te em - pu - ja de ra - íz y cal, la
To Coda I
To Coda II
F♯m
G♯7
C♯m
tie - rra sus - pi - ra si no te ve más. La

G♯7
3
3
tie - rra don - de na - cis - tes no la pue - des ol - vi - dar, por -
F♯m
G♯7
C♯m
- que tie - ne tus ra - i - ces y lo que de - jas a - trás. La
G♯7
tie - rra te due - le, la tie - rra te da, en
F♯m
G♯7
N.C.
D.S. 𝄋 al Coda I
me - dio del al - ma, cuan - do tú no es - tás.

Coda I
C♯m N.C.
no te ve más.
1.
2.
C♯m7
F♯7
D♯m7(♭5)
G♯7
1. Instrumental solo
2. Tie-ne un que-ji - do,
¡Mi tie - rra!
Tie - ne un la - men - to,
¡Mi tie - rra!
Nun-
3.4. See additional lyrics for ad libs.
ff
1.2.3.
-ca la ol-vi - do,
¡Mi tie - rra!
La lle-vo en mi sen-ti-mien - to, ¡si se - ñor!
¡Mi tie - rra!

4.
Play 6 times
D♯m7(♭5)
G♯7(♯9)
C♯m
/B
/B♭
3
Y un día re - gre - so, yo lo sé.
D♯m7(♭5)
G♯7
D13(♯11)
C♯m7
F♯7
Instrumental solo
1.2.3.
4.
D♯m7(♭5)
G♯7
Si -
Verse 3:
C♯m7
F♯7
D♯m7(♭5)
G♯7
- guen los pre - go - nes, la me - lan - co - lí - a. Y ca - da
¡Mi tie - rra! ¡Mi tie - rra!

C♯m7
F♯7
D♯m7(♭5)
G♯7
no-che jun-to a la lu - na si-gue el gua-ji - ro en-to-nan-do el son. Ca-da
¡Mi tie - rra! ¡Mi tie - rra!
ca-lle que va a mi pue - blo tie - ne un que-ji-do, tie - ne un la - men - to.
¡Mi tie - rra! ¡Mi tie - rra!
D.S.S. 𝄋𝄋 al Coda II
La nos - tal - gia de su voz le lle-ga con fuer - za al co-ra-zón. La
¡Mi tie - rra!

Additional ad libs:
Oigo ese grito ... ¡Mi tierra!
Vive el recuerdo ... ¡Mi tierra!
Corre en mi sangre ... ¡Mi tierra!
La llevo por dentro ¡como no! ... ¡Mi tierra!

Canto de mi tierra bella y santa, ... ¡Mi tierra!
Sufro ese dolor que hay en su alma, ... ¡Mi tierra!
Aunque estoy lejos yo la siento ... ¡Mi tierra!
Y un día regreso yo lo sé.
(To Instrumental Solo:)

English lyrics:
Verse 1:
From my beautiful homeland,
From my holy homeland,
I hear the cry of the drums and the timbales partying.
And a refrain is sung by a brother who lives far from his homeland,
And the memories make him cry.
The song that he sings springs from
His pain and his own tears,
And we can hear him cry...

Verses 2 & 3:
The refrain continues, as does the melancholy
And each night by the light of the moon
The country boy sings his s-o-n
And each street that leads to my village
Has a cry, a lament
It has a nostalgia, like its voice
And the song that keeps repeating,
Flows in my blood, ever stronger
On its way to my heart.
(To Chorus:)

Chorus:
Your homeland hurts you,
Your homeland strikes your soul when you're gone.
Your homeland pushes you forth from its roots,
Your homeland sighs when you're not there.
The land where you were born, you can never forget
Because it holds your roots and everything you've left behind.

Ad libs:
It has a cry ... My homeland.
It has a lament ... My homeland.
I'll never forget her ... My homeland.
I carry her in my emotions, yes sir ... My homeland.

I hear her cry ... My Homeland.
The memories live ... My homeland.
She flows through my blood ... My homeland.
I carry her inside me, yes indeed.

I sing of my homeland, beautiful and holy,
I suffer the pain that's in her soul.
Although I'm far away, I can feel her
And one day I'll return ... I know it.

MORE THAN WORDS

Lyrics and Music by
BETTENCOURT, CHERONE

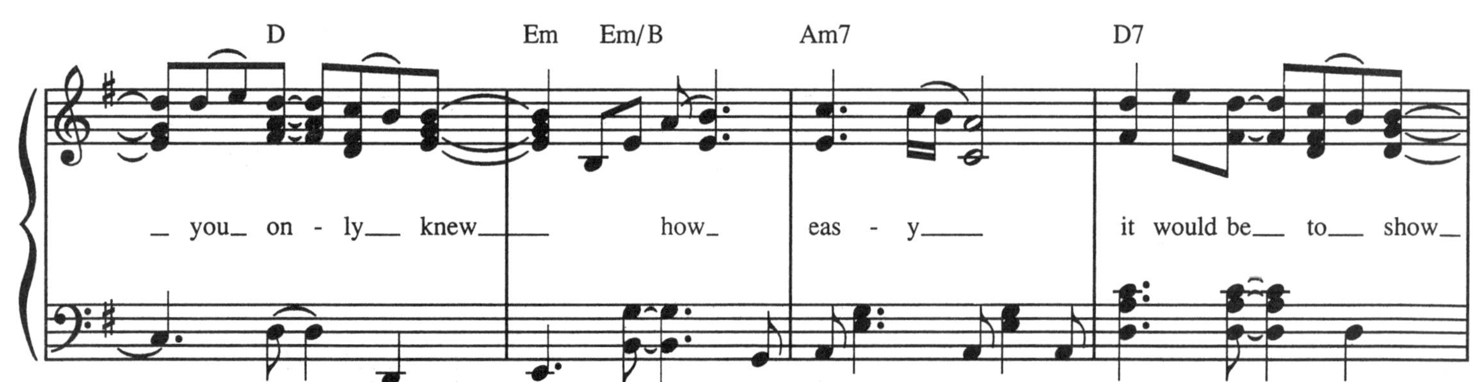

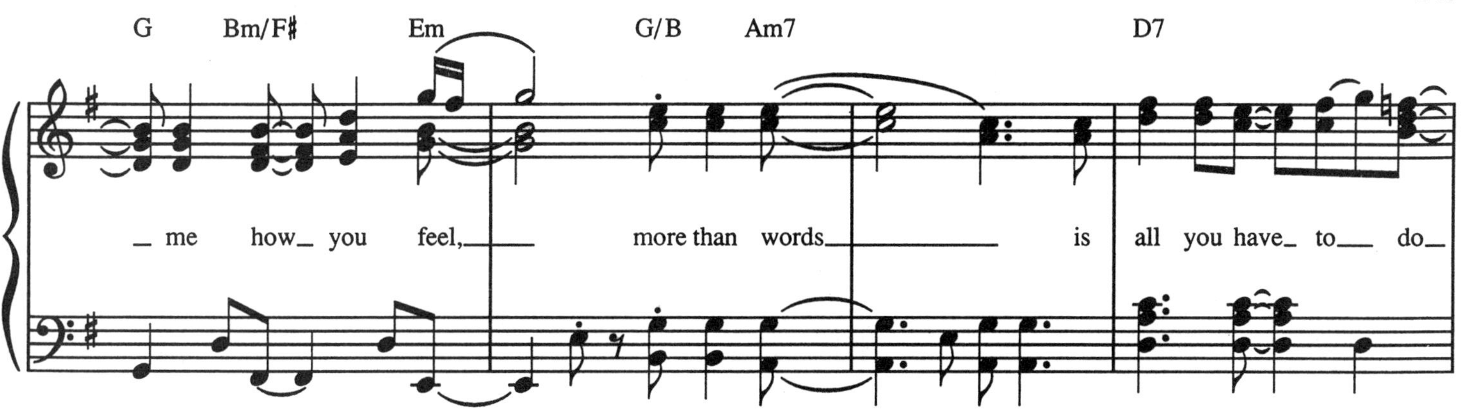
G Bm/F# Em G/B Am7 D7
_ me how_ you feel,___ more than words_______ is all you have_ to__ do_

G7 G7/B C Cm G Em7
_ to make_ it__ real.___ Then, you would - n't have_ to say_____ that you love_

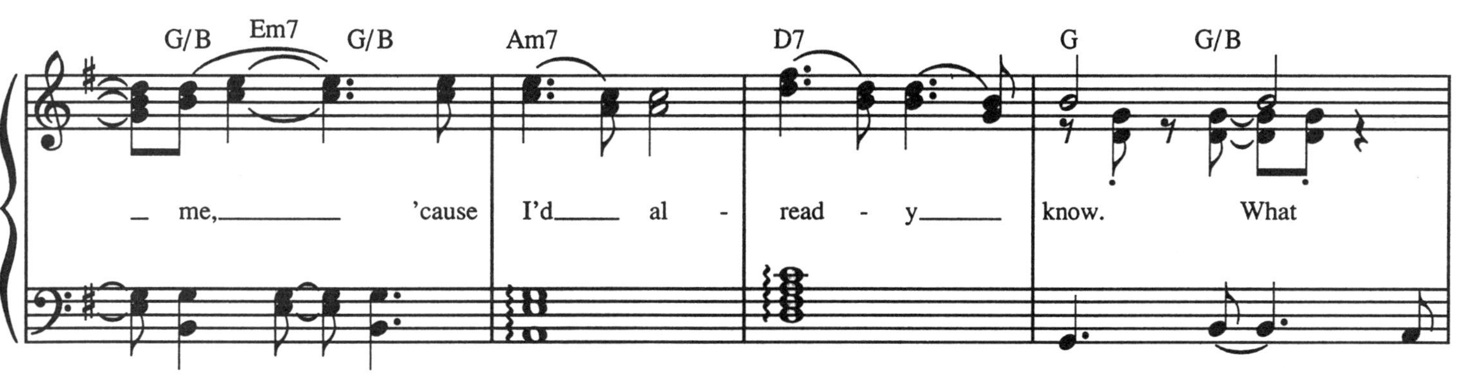
G/B Em7 G/B Am7 D7 G G/B
_ me,_____ 'cause I'd___ al - read - y____ know. What

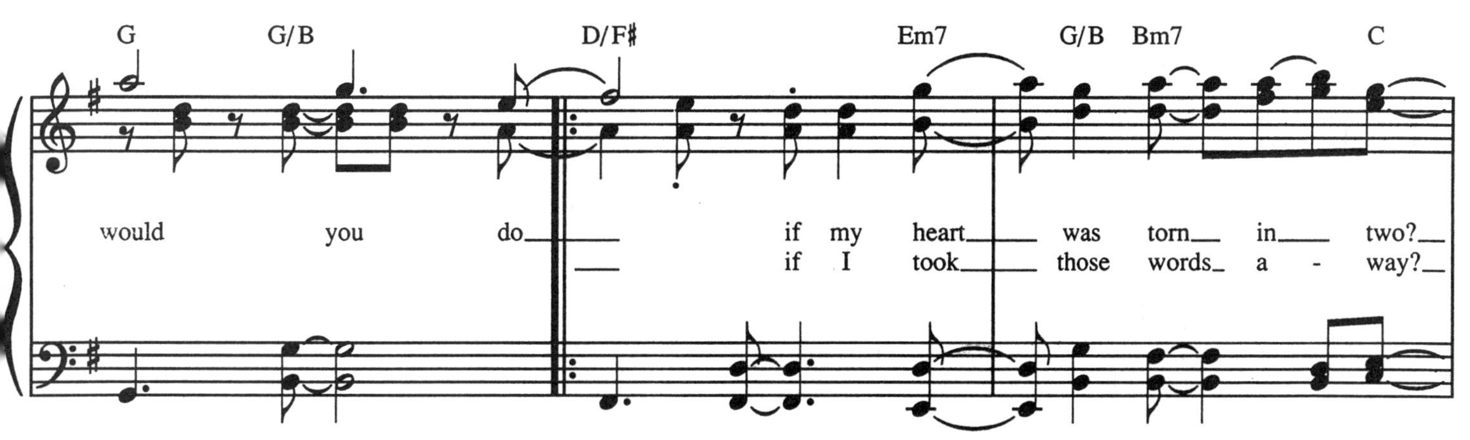
G G/B D/F# Em7 G/B Bm7 C
would you do___ if my heart___ was torn__ in___ two?__
___ if I took___ those words_ a - way?__

1. 3.
G/B Am7
D7
G
More than words to show you feel that your love for me is real.
Then, you could - n't make things new just by say -

2.
To Next Strain
4.
G/B
G
G/B
D7
D7
What would you say
- in' "I love you."
- in' "I love you."

G
G/B
C(9)
G/B
Am7
G/B
C
(La di da da di da di dai dai da.

1.
D.S. 𝄋
D
D7
G
G/B
C(9)
Am7
D7
) More than words.
La di da da di da.)

Verse 2:
Now that I have tried to talk to you
And make you understand.
All you have to do is close your eyes
And just reach out your hands.
And touch me, hold me close, don't ever let me go.
More than words is all I ever needed you to show.
Then you wouldn't have to say
That you love me 'cause I'd already know.
(To Chorus:)

MUSTANG SALLY

Words and Music by
BONNY RICE

Moderate rock ♩ = 120
C7
mf
Mus-tang Sal -

Verse:
ly,
guess you bet-ter
slow that Mus-tang down.

Mus-tang

F7
Sal-ly, now ba - by,
guess you bet-ter
slow that Mus-tang down.

C7
You been

G7
F N.C.
run-nin' all o - ver town,
ooh, I guess you got-ta put your flat feet

C7
on the ground.

Chorus:
All you wan-na do is ride a-round, Sal-ly. (Ride, Sal-ly, ride.)

All you wan-na do is ride a-round, Sal-ly.
(Ride, Sal-ly ride.)

F7
All you wan - na do is ride a - round, Sal - ly.
(Ride, Sal - ly ride.

)
C7
All you wan - na do is ride a - round, Sal - ly.

(Ride, Sal - ly, ride.)
G7
One of these ear - ly morn -

Verse 2:
I bought you a brand new Mustang,
It was a nineteen sixty five.
Now you come around, signifying a woman.
Girl, you won't, you won't let me ride.
Mustang Sally, now baby,
Guess you better slow that Mustang down.
You been runnin' all over town.
Oh, guess you gotta put your flat feet on the ground.
(To Chorus:)

MY LOVIN' (YOU'RE NEVER GONNA GET IT)

Lyrics and Music by
THOMAS McELROY
& DENZIL FOSTER

1.2.4.
To Next Strain
3.5.6.etc.
Repeat ad lib. and fade
lovin'. nev-er ev-er gon-na get it.
lovin'. nev-er ev-er gon-na get it.
Verse:
Ooh, bop. I re - mem - ber how it used to be.
You never was this nice, you can't fool me.
Ooh, bop. Now, you're talk - in' like you made a change.
The more you talk the more you sound the

Bridge:
E♭m9 Cm7(♭5) B♭m/F B♭m
same. Oh, what makes you think you can just walk back in - to her
E♭m9 Cm7(♭5) B♭m/F B♭m E♭m9 Cm7(♭5) B♭m/F
life with-out a good fight? Oh, oh, I just sit back
B♭m E♭m9 Cm7(♭5) B♭m/F
and watch you make a fool of your - self, 'cause you're just
1.2. D.S. 𝄋 3. B♭m13 N.C.
wast-ing your time. Oh! hear-ing her say, "No way!"
And now, it's time for a breakdown.
Nev-er gon-na get it, nev-er gon-na get it! Nev - er gon-na get it, nev-er gon-na get it! Nev-

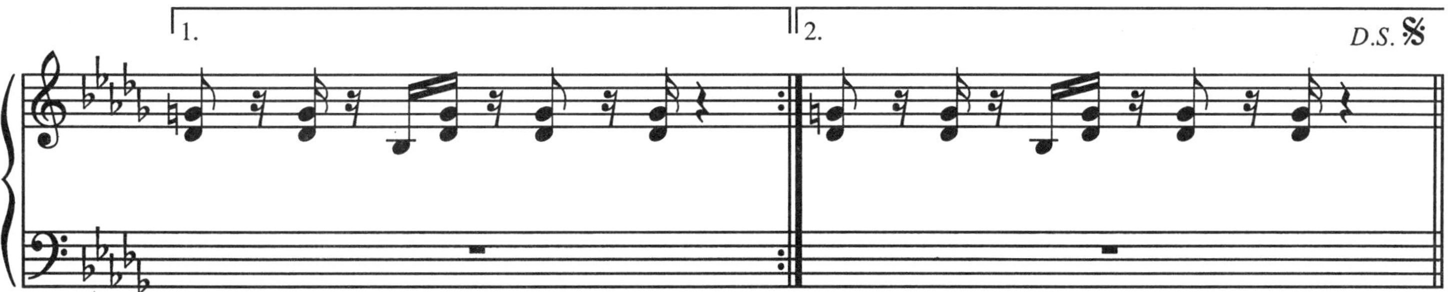

Verse 2:
Ooh, bop.
Now, you promise me the moon and stars.
Save your breath, you won't get very far.
Ooh, bop.
Gave you many chances to make change.
The only thing you changed was love to hate.

Bridges 2 & 3:
It doesn't matter what you do or what you say.
She don't love you, no way.
Maybe the next time,
You'll give your woman a little respect,
So you won't be hearing her say, "No way!"

Chorus 2:
No, you're never gonna get it, (Not this time)
Never ever gonna get it. (My lovin'.)
No, you're never gonna get it, (Had your chance
To make a change.)
Never ever gonna get it.
No, you're never gonna get it, (No not this time)
Never ever gonna get it. (My lovin'.)
No you're never gonna get it (Had your chance
To make a change.)
Never ever gonna get it. (My lovin'.)
(Repeat Chorus 2:)

Verse 3:
Ooh, bop.
Spoken: *Ooh, yes sir.*
I give to the needy, and not the greedy.
Uh huh, that's right!
Ooh, bop.
Spoken: *'Cause you see, baby,*
When you like him, you lose him, and I'm out the door!
(To Bridge 3:)

NOW AND FOREVER

Music and Lyrics by
RICHARD MARX

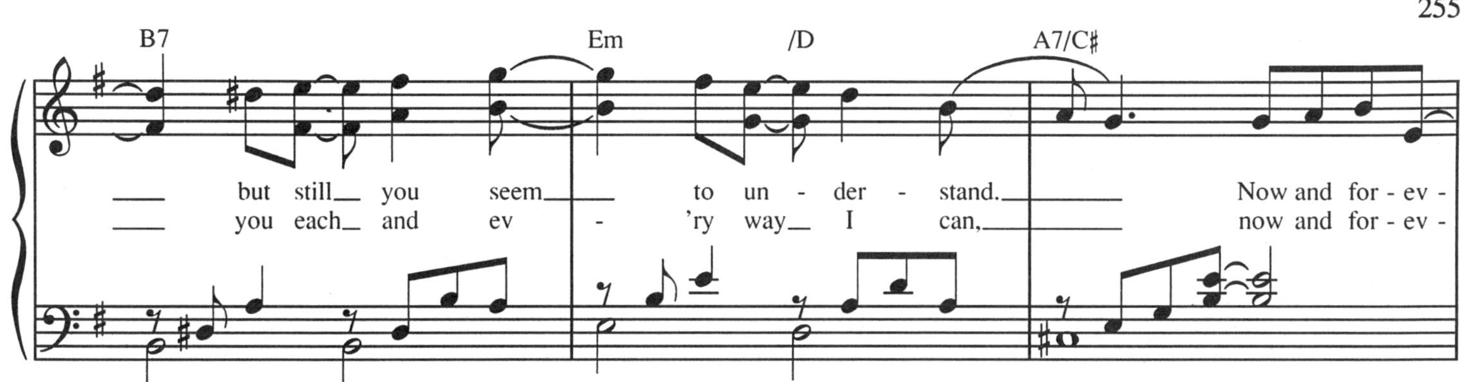
B7
Em
/D
A7/C♯
but still you seem to un - der - stand.
you each and ev - 'ry way I can,
Now and for - ev -
now and for - ev -

1.
Am7
C/D
D
G
C/G
- er,
- er,
I will be your man.
I will be your man.

2.
G
C/G
B7
Bridge:
Em
C
Now I can rest my wor - ries and
mf

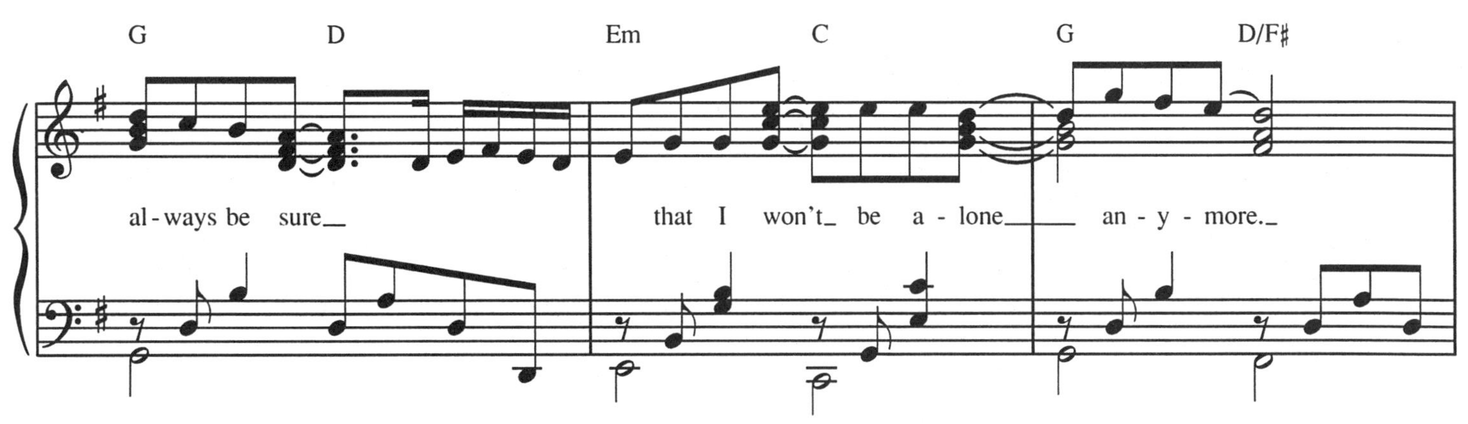
G
D
Em
C
G
D/F♯
al - ways be sure
that I won't be a - lone an - y - more.

Em C G D Am7
If I'd on - ly known you were there all the time, all this time.
Cm(♯7) Cm6 G D/F♯ Em
Am Em/G D/F♯ G D/F♯
Em Am Em/G D/F♯
C B7 Em /D
Un - til the day the o - cean does - n't touch the sand,

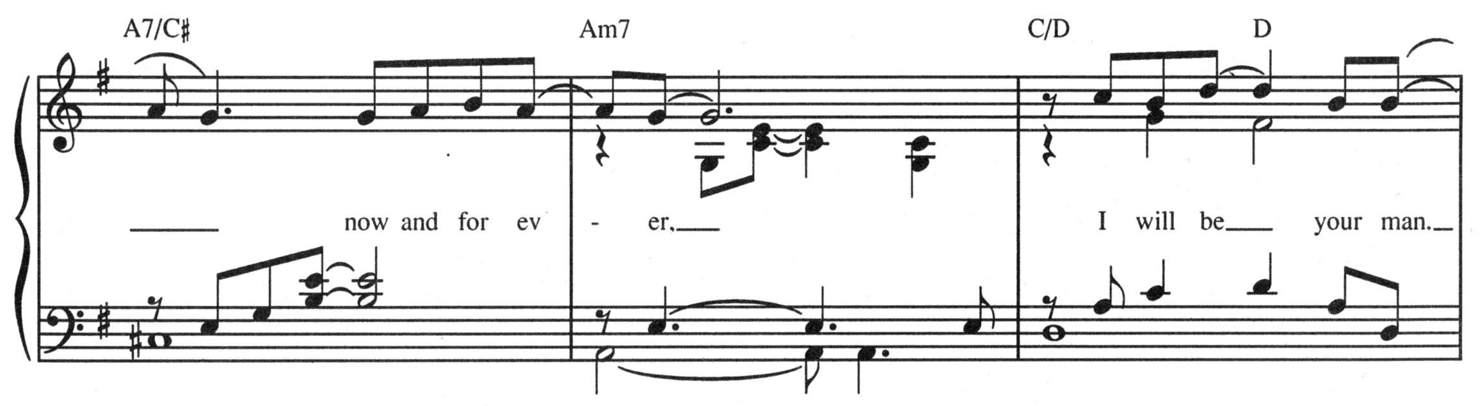
A7/C♯
Am7
C/D
D
now and for ev - er,
I will be your man.

G
C/G
Am7
Now and for - ev - er,

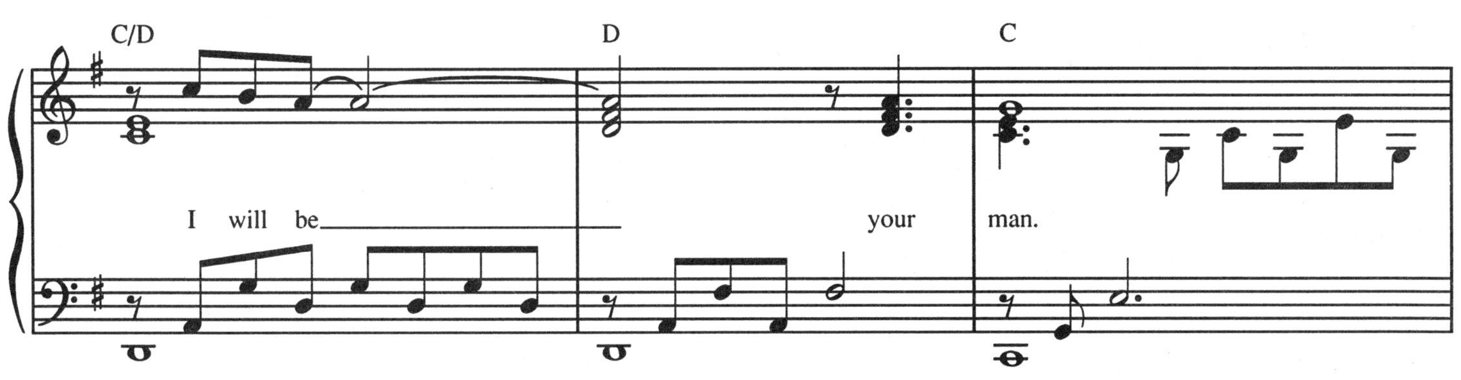
C/D
D
C
I will be your man.

Cm6
G
C/G
D/G
G
poco rit. e dim.
mp

OOH CHILD

Words and Music by
STAN VINCENT

Moderately, in a groove ♩ = 96

B♭
F/A
Gm7
B♭/C
B♭
F/A
mf

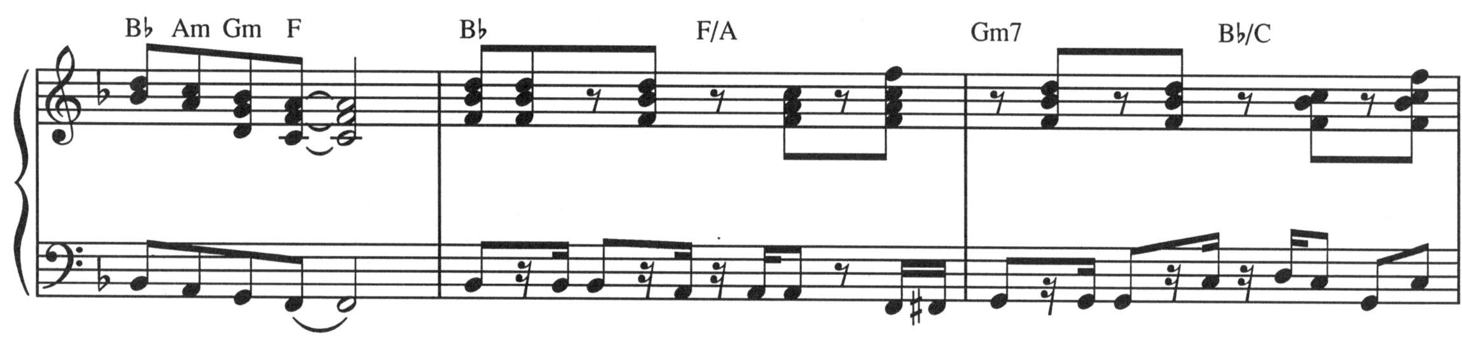
B♭ Am Gm F
B♭
F/A
Gm7
B♭/C

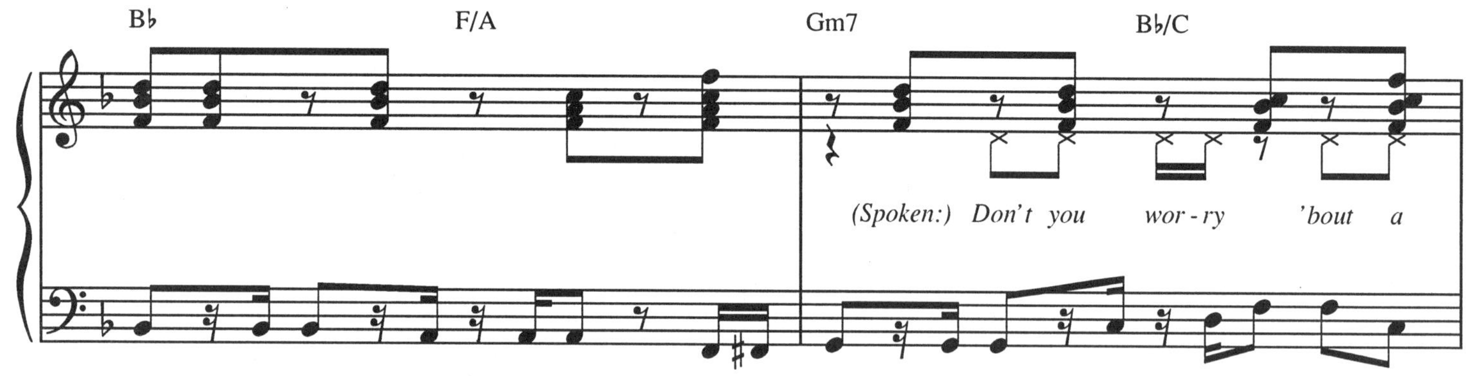
B♭
F/A
Gm7
B♭/C
(Spoken:) Don't you wor - ry 'bout a

B♭
F/A
Gm7
B♭/C
thing.
Oh, no,

Bb
F/A
Gm7
Bb/C
no.
Ooh, child, things are gon - na {get be} eas - i - er.
Ooh, child, things-'ll {get be} bright - er.
To Coda
Ooh, child, things are gon - na {get be} eas - i - er.
Ooh, child, things-'ll {get be} bright - er.

D♭maj7
A♭/C
B♭m7
D♭/E♭
Some - day, yeah, we'll put it to-geth-er and we'll get un - done,
D♭maj7
A♭/C
B♭m7
D♭/E♭
some - day, when your head is much light - er.
D♭maj7
A♭/C
B♭m7
D♭/E♭
Some - day, yeah, we'll walk in the rays of a beau-ti - ful sun,
D♭maj7
A♭/C
B♭m7
D♭/E♭
some - day when the world is much bright - er.
B♭
F/A
Gm7
B♭/C
La, la, la, la, la, la, la, la.

B♭
F/A
Gm7
B♭/C
La, la,__ la, la,________ la.__
B♭
F/A
Gm7
B♭/C
La, la, la,__ la, la,__ la, la, la.____
B♭
F/A
Gm7
B♭/C
La, la,__ la, la,________ la.__
D♭maj7
A♭/C
B♭m7
D♭/E♭
Some - day, some-day, we'll put it to-geth-er and we'll get it un - done,__
D♭maj7
A♭/C
B♭m7
D♭/E♭
some - day, when your head is much light - er.__

Dbmaj7
Ab/C
Bbm7
Db/Eb
Some - day, some-day, we'll walk in the rays of a beau-ti-ful sun,
Dbmaj7
Ab/C
Bbm7
Db/Eb
some - day when the world is much bright - er.
Bb
(Spoken:) Don't you wor-ry a - bout a
thing. Life is up and down. You got-ta keep mov - in' on.
D.S. 𝄋 al Coda

Coda
B♭
F/A
Gm7
B♭/C
Ooh, child, things-'ll get bright - er on - ly right
F
C/F
B♭/F
now,
right
now.
(Bkgrd.) Right
Fmaj9
(Lead vocal ad lib.)
now.
B♭maj7/F
Right
now.
1.2.
3.
Right
Right
now.

Inspired by the Columbia Pictures' Feature Film "THE PRINCE OF TIDES"

PLACES THAT BELONG TO YOU

Lyrics by
ALAN and MARILYN BERGMAN

Music by
JAMES NEWTON HOWARD

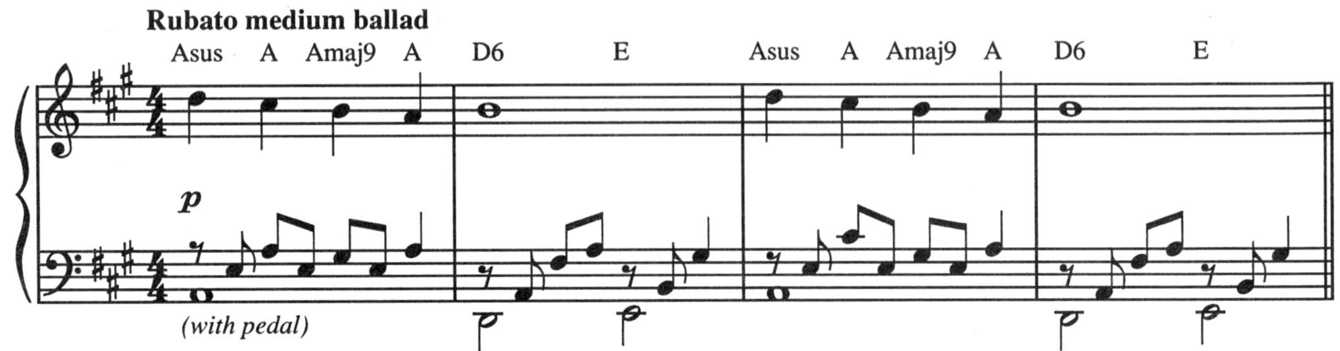

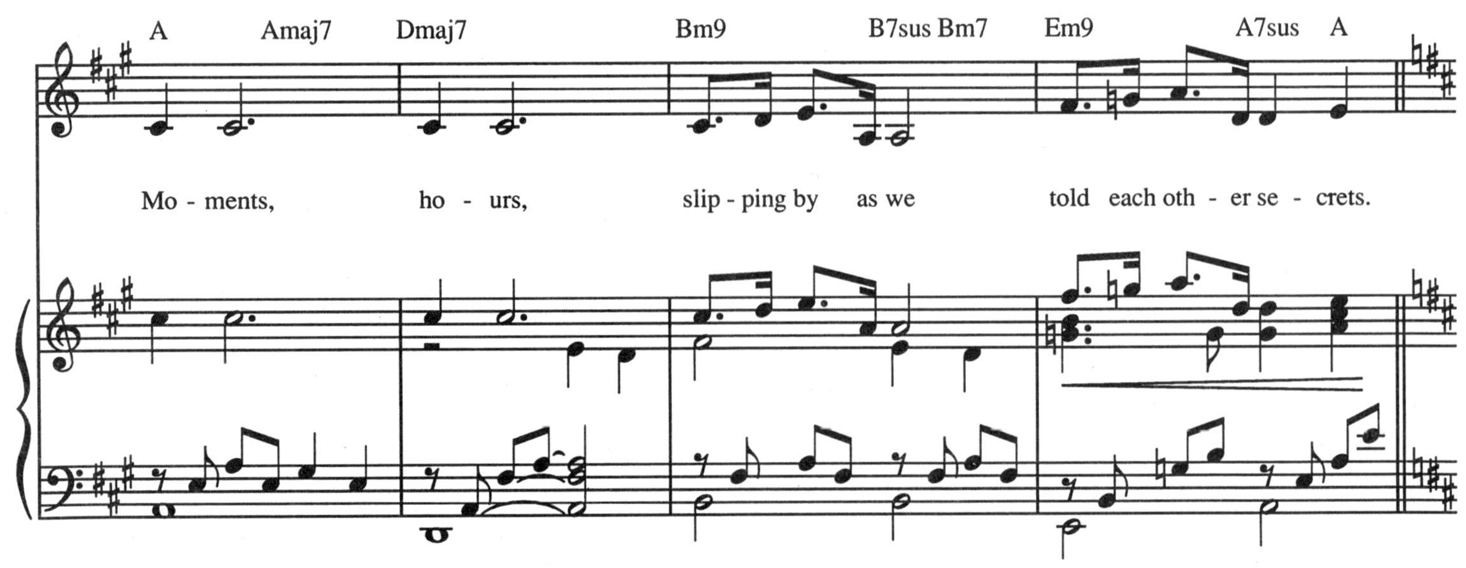

Dmaj7
F♯maj7
Em7(add4)
A
A/G
F♯m7
Bm7
Some - how I'll nev - er let go of the mem - 'ries.
mp
Em7
Asus
Bm7(add2)
A(add2)
G
D(add9)/F♯
Some-thing al - ways seems to re - mind me of how it was, of
Em7
G/A
F♯/A♯
Bm(add2)
Esus4 2
E
A
Amaj7
what it was, when it was all there was. Laugh - ter,
p

Dmaj7
Bm9
Bm9/E
Esus
E
A
Amaj7
love songs, foot-steps that I hear make me think you're near me. Po - ems,
cresc. poco a poco
Dmaj7
Bm9
Em9
A7sus
A
Dmaj7
F♯m7
pic - tures, let - ters nev - er mailed, boats that nev - er sailed. Re - mem - ber that
mf
Cmaj9
Am9
F♯m7
Bm
Em7
Asus
ev - en though we can't be to - geth - er, we're more for hav-ing loved one an -

Bm(add2) A(add2) G D(add9)/F♯ Cmaj9 Dsus4/2 D♯dim
-oth - er. We shared the sky, we learned to fly.
Emaj7 G♯m7 Dmaj9 Bm9 G♯m7 C♯m7 F♯m7 B5 B7sus
Some-day when some-one else-'s arms are a-round us, when time has put some dis-tance be-
f
C♯m(add2) B(add2) A E(sus2)/G♯ F♯m7 E(sus2)/G♯
-tween us, the years will kind-ly show how mem-'ries come and go. They

Amaj7 A/B G♯5/B♯ C♯(add2) E/F♯ F♯
ebb and flow like the tides.
dim.
B Bmaj7 Emaj7 C♯m9 C♯m9/F♯ E/F♯ F♯
There are qui - et plac - es in my heart ev - er since we part - ed.
mp
B Bmaj7 Emaj7 C♯m9 C♯m9/F♯ E/F♯ F♯
Gen - tle, ten - der, trac - es of a song, plac-es that be-long to
B(add2) B Bmaj7 Emaj7 C♯m9 E/F♯ F♯7sus F♯ B(add2)
you.
dim.
p

REACH OUT, I'LL BE THERE

Words and Music by
BRIAN HOLLAND, LAMONT DOZIER
and EDDIE HOLLAND

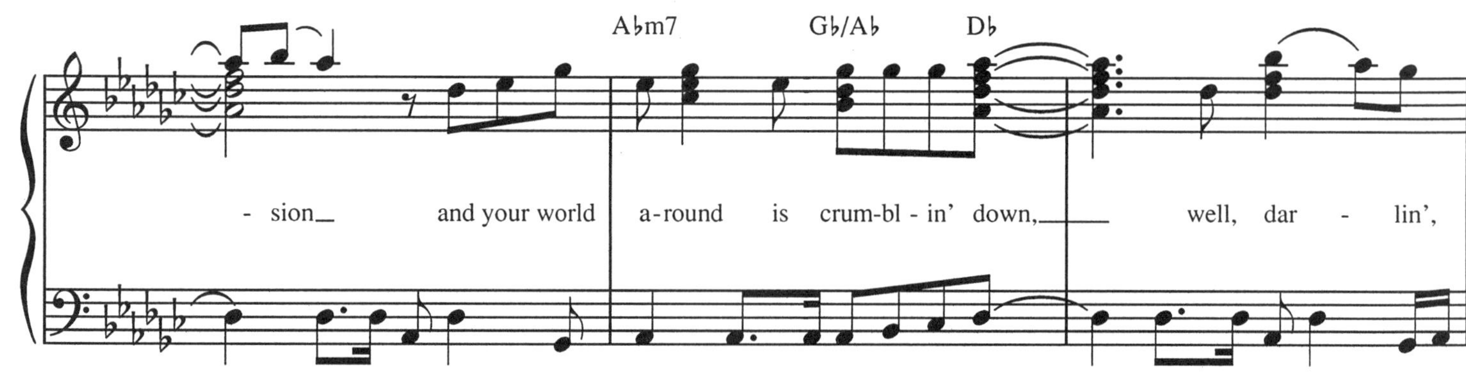
A♭m7
G♭/A♭
D♭
- sion__ and your world a-round is crum-bl - in' down,____ well, dar - lin',

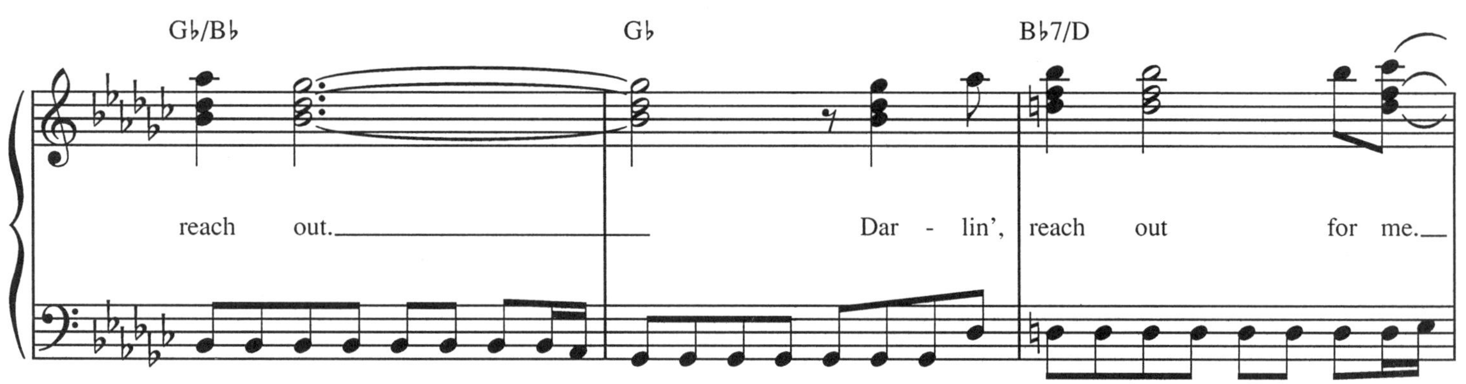
G♭/B♭
G♭
B♭7/D
reach out.________ Dar - lin', reach out for me.__

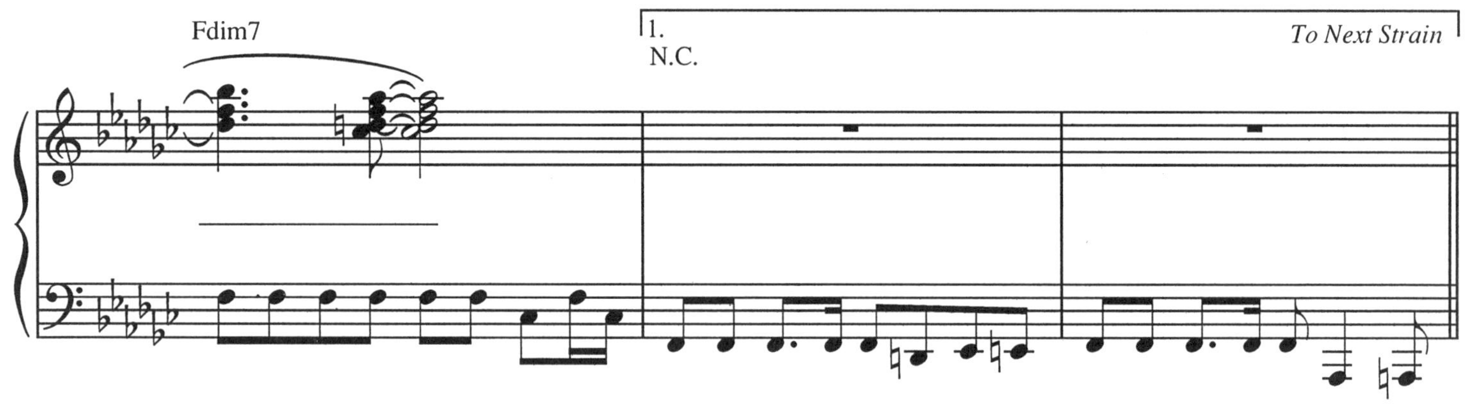
Fdim7
1.
N.C.
To Next Strain

2.3.
N.C.
Chorus:
B♭
E♭/B♭
I'll be there____ to

Verse 2:
When you feel lost and about to give up
'cause your best just ain't good enough,
And you feel the world has grown cold
and you're driftin' out all on your own,
And you need a hand to hold darlin', reach out.
Darlin', reach out for me.

Chorus 2:
I'll be there with a love that will shelter you.
And I'll be there with a love that will see you through.
I'll be there to give you all the love you need.
And I'll be there, you can always count on me.

Verse 3:
I can tell the way you hang your head,
you're without love and now you're afraid,
And through your tears you look around,
but there's no peace of mind to be found,
I know what you're thinkin', you're alone now,
no love of your own, but darlin', reach out.
Darlin', reach out for me.

Chorus 3:
I'll be there to give you all the love you need.
And I'll be there, you can always count on me.
I'll be there with a love that will shelter you.
And I'll be there with a love that will see you through.
(Ad lib. vocals)

PLEASE FORGIVE ME

Words and Music by
BRYAN ADAMS
and ROBERT JOHN "MUTT" LANGE

Slowly ♩ = 69
A(2)
D6
E7sus
pp
mp

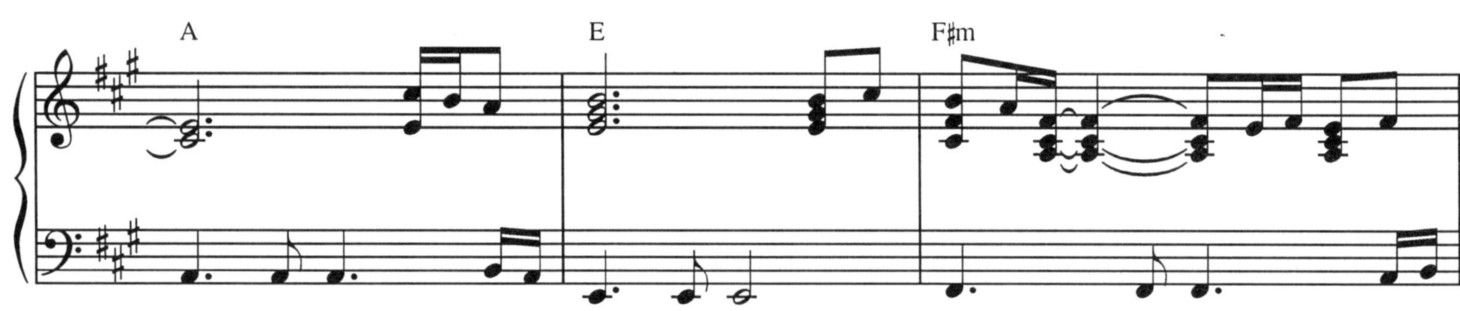
A
E
F♯m

C♯m
D(2)
A/E
Verse:
A
1. It still feels like our first night to - geth - er.

E
F♯m
Feels like the first kiss and it's get - tin' bet - ter, ba - by.

C♯m
D(2)
A
No one can bet - ter this.
We're still hold - in' on, you're still the
E
A
one.
The first time our eyes met
C♯7
F♯m
the same feel - in' I get
on - ly feels much strong - er,
C♯7(♭9)
A
and I wan - na love you long - er.
You still turn the fire on.
E
Esus
E
A
F♯m
A
D
So, if you're
mf
feel - in' lone - ly, don't.

E
A
Asus
A
You're the on - ly one I'll ev - er want. I on - ly
F♯m
A
D
wan - na make it good.
E
F♯m
D
So, if I love you a lit - tle more than I should, please for -
mp
Chorus:
A
E/A
A
F♯m
E/F♯
F♯m
give me, I know not what I do. Please for - give me, I can't stop lov-in' you. Don't de -
D
E/D
D
A
E/A
A
A/C♯
ny me this pain I'm go-in' through. Please for - give me, if I need you like I do. Please Oh, be -
mf

1.

E F♯m/E E D6 A E

lieve me, ev-'ry word I say is true. Please for - give me, I can't stop lov-in' you.

mp

A E F♯m A/E

2. It still

D.S. 𝄋 2.

A E F♯m

feels like our best times are to - geth - give me, I can't stop lov-in' you.

mf

D F♯m E F♯m D F♯m A D

(Instrumental solo . . . *cresc.* *. . . end solo)*

Bridge:

E D A D

The one thing I'm sure of is the way we make love.

f

E D A D
The one thing I de - pend_ on is for us to stay_____ strong.
F♯m D
With ev - 'ry word and ev - 'ry breath_ I'm pray - in',_____ that's why I'm
F♯m/E E
say - in',_____ please for
mp
Chorus:
B F♯/B B
- give me,_ I know not what I do._ Please for -
G♯m F♯/G♯ G♯m E F♯/E E
give me,_ I can't stop lov-in' you._ Don't de - ny me_ this pain I'm go-in' through._Please for -
B F♯/B B B/D♯
give me,_ if I need you like I do._ Babe, be -
mf
F♯ G♯m/E F♯ E6
lieve me,_ ev-'ry word I say is true._ Please for -
mp

B
F♯/B
B
B/D♯
F♯
G♯m/F♯
F♯
E6
give me,__ if I can't stop lov-in' you._ Now,__ be - lieve_ me,__ I don't know what I'd do.__ Please for-

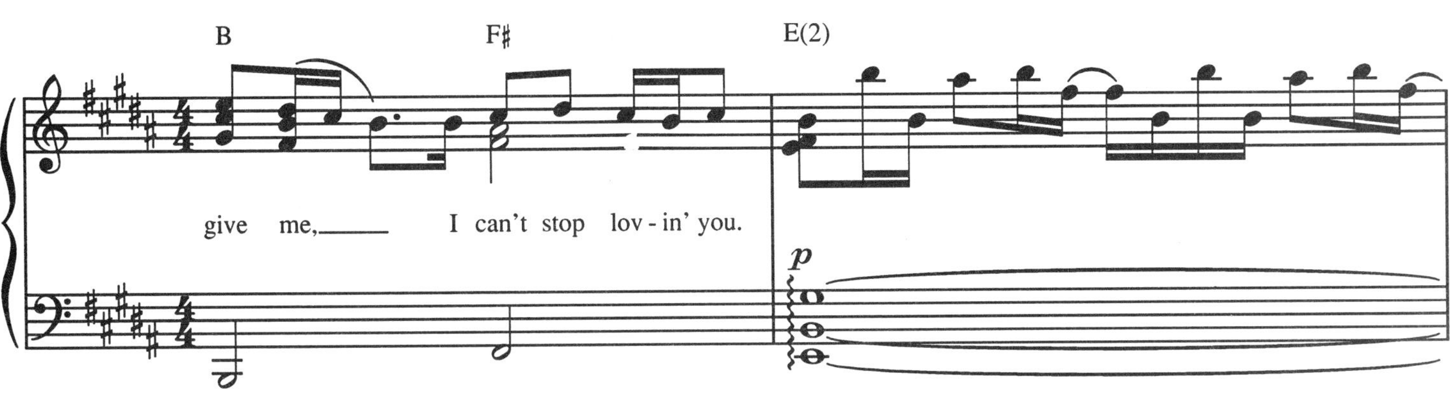
B
F♯
E(2)
give me,_____ I can't stop lov - in' you.
p

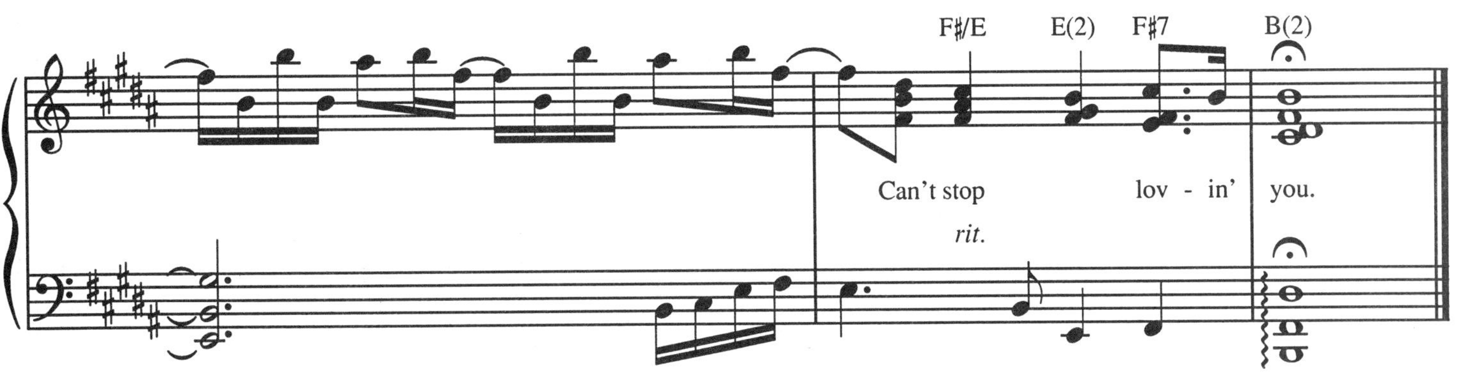
F♯/E
E(2)
F♯7
B(2)
Can't stop lov - in' you.
rit.

Verse 2:
It still feels like our best times are together.
Feels like the first touch, we're still gettin' closer, baby.
Can't get close enough.
We're still holdin' on, you're still number one.
I remember the smell of your skin, I remember everything.
I remember all your moves, I remember you, yeah.
I remember the nights, you know I still do.
So, if you're feelin' lonely, don't.
You're the only one I'll ever want.
I only wanna make it good.
So, if I love you a little more than I should, . . .
(To Chorus:)

REACH OUT TO ME

Words and Music by
LARRY WEIR, MICHAEL DAMIAN,
TOM WEIR and MICHAEL PARNELL

Moderate disco ♩ = 126
E♭
B♭
mf

F
E♭(9)

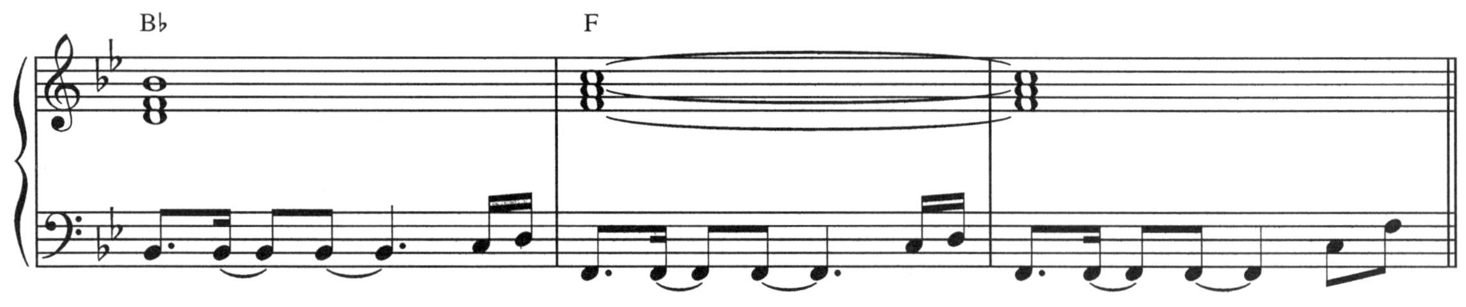
B♭
F

Verse:
B♭
3
F
Gm
1. I know you'll soon be off on your own,
2. You've be - come much more than a friend.
(mf)

B♭
F
Gm
and you'll be
This kind of
man-y
feel-ing,
miles_ from your
it___ will nev-er
home.
end.

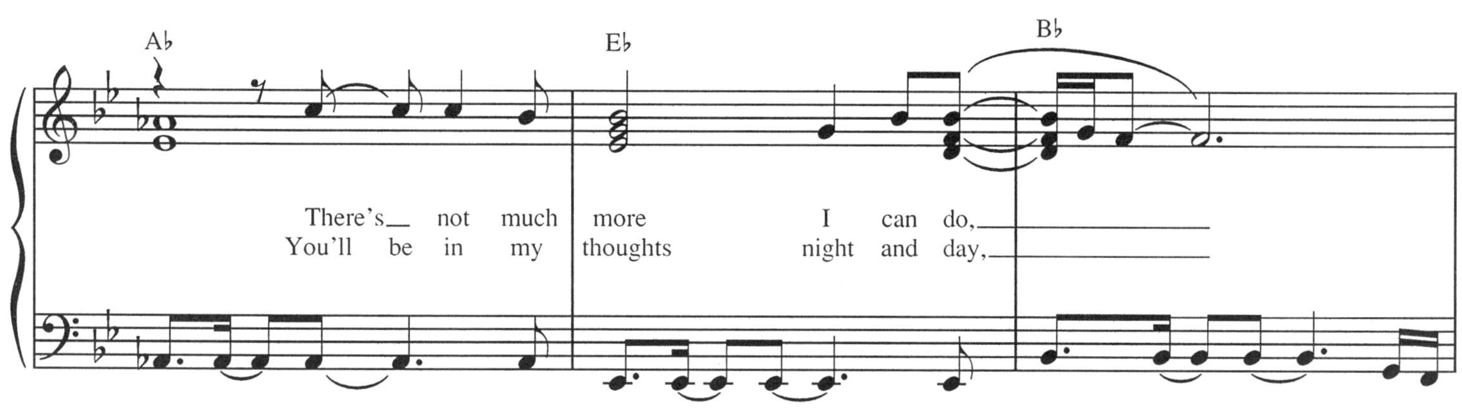
A♭
E♭
B♭
There's__ not much
You'll be in my
more
thoughts
I can do,
night and day,

A♭
E♭
ex-cept to say___ how much_ I'll miss
I'll wrap my arms a - round_ you__ and

F
Chorus:
E♭(9)
you.
pray.
If you
cresc.
reach out to me, you know_
f

B♭
F
E♭(9)
I'll be right there.
If you
reach out to me, you'll have
B♭
F
some - one who cares.
If you
E♭(9)
B♭
Gm
reach out to me, no mat - ter what or from an - y - where,
C7
E♭
F
To Coda
just
reach out to me and I will see you
1.
2.
Gm
F
B♭
there.
there.
dim.

A♭
E♭
B♭
Reach out to
me.
A♭
E♭
Cm7
F
D.S. 𝄋 al Coda
If you
𝄌 Coda
Gm
there
F
Just
E♭
reach out to me and I will see you
F
B♭
there.

E♭(9)
B♭
If you reach out to me, you'll have some - one who cares.
F
E♭(9)
If you reach out to me, no mat - ter what or from an - y - where,
B♭
Gm
C7
just
E♭
F
B♭
reach out to me and I will see you there.
Reach out to me.

RESTLESS HEART

Words and Music by
ANDY HILL and PETER CETERA

Moderate Soft Rock

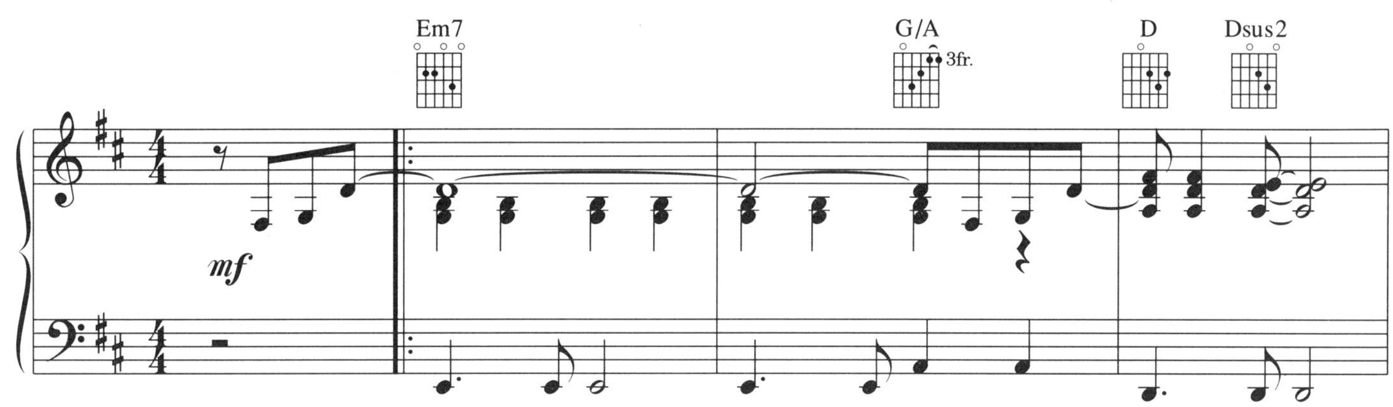

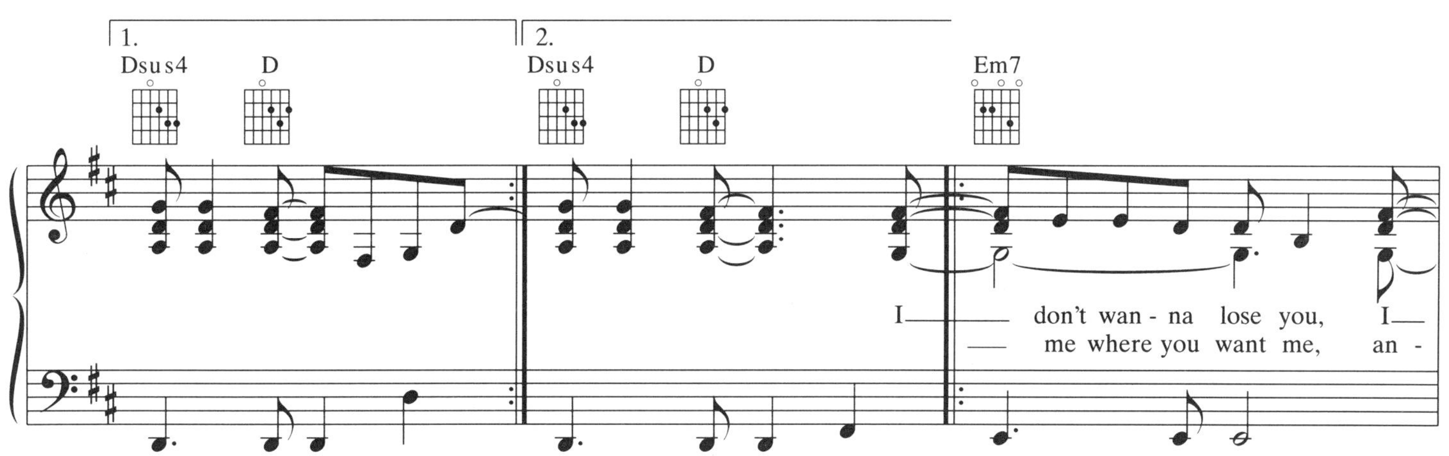

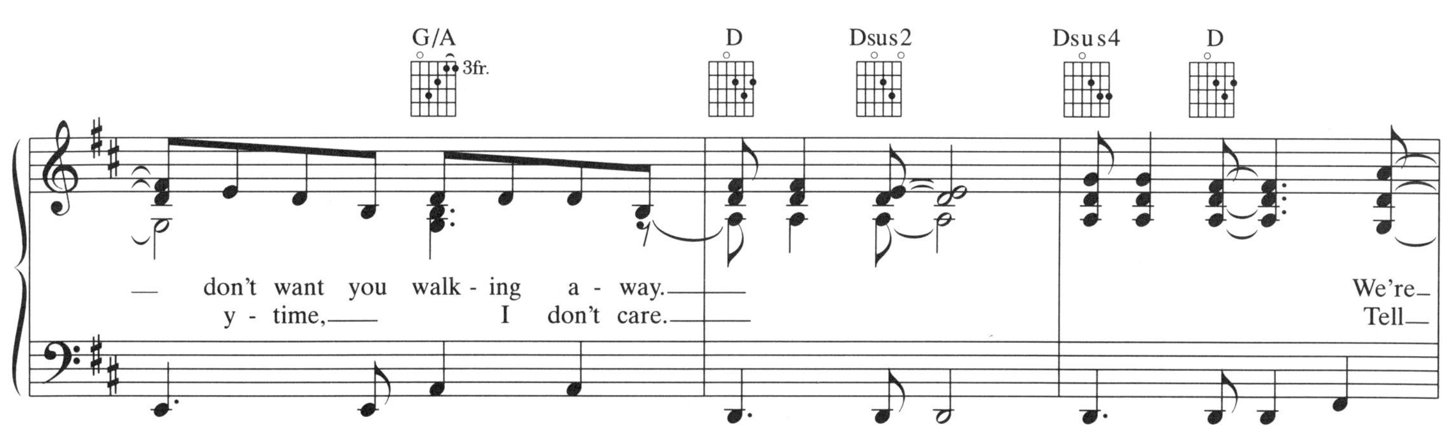

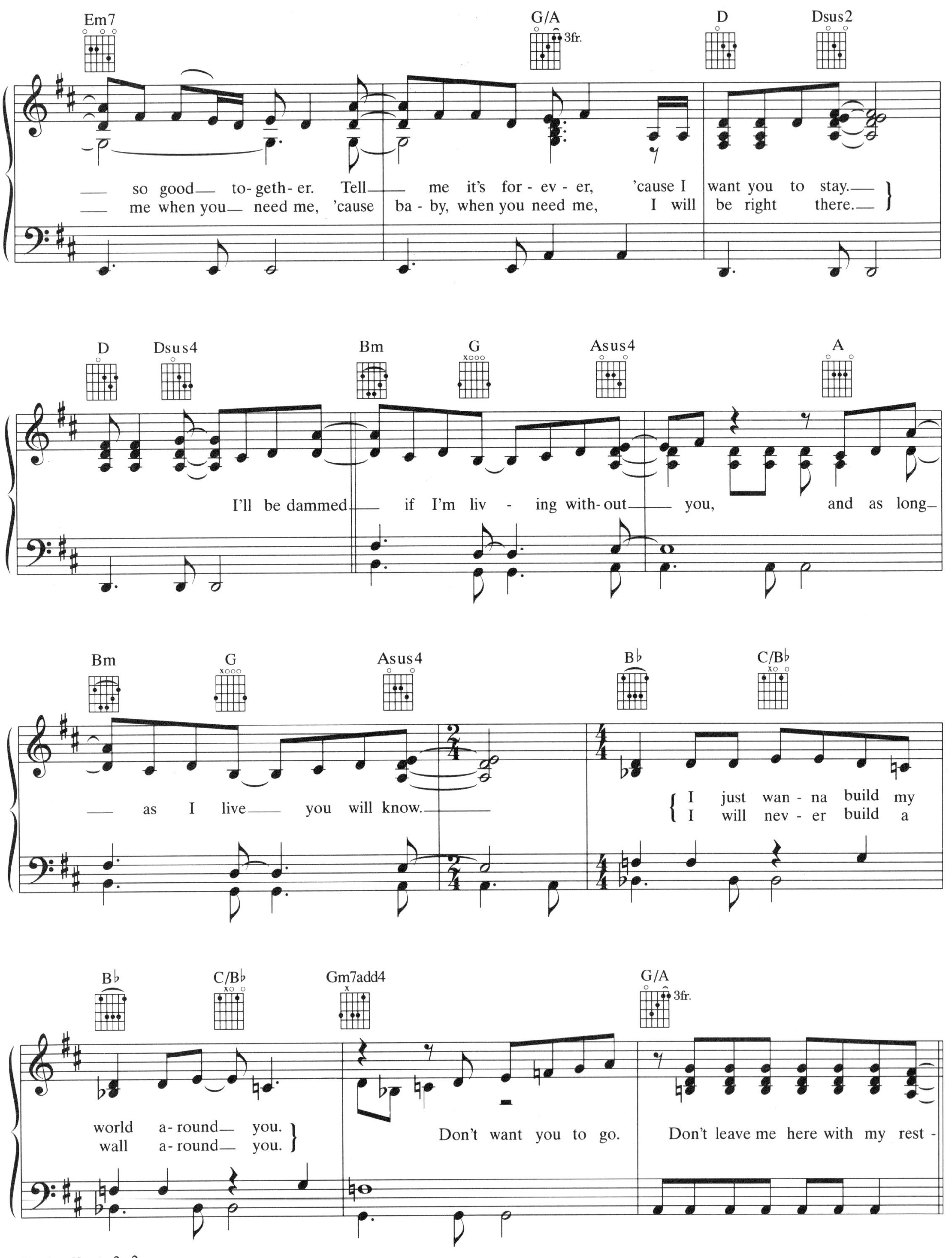
Em7
G/A
3fr.
D
Dsus2
so good— to-geth-er. Tell— me it's for-ev-er, 'cause I want you to stay.—
me when you— need me, 'cause ba-by, when you need me, I will be right there.—
D
Dsus4
Bm
G
Asus4
A
I'll be dammed— if I'm liv-ing with-out— you, and as long—
Bm
G
Asus4
B♭
C/B♭
— as I live— you will know.—
I just wan-na build my
I will nev-er build a
B♭
C/B♭
Gm7add4
G/A
3fr.
world a-round— you.
wall a-round— you.
Don't want you to go.
Don't leave me here with my rest-

D
Em7
G/A
3fr.
D
G
less heart,
the one you filled with e - mo - tion, ba - by, right from the start.
Em7
G/A
Bm7
Em7
G/A
'Cause the hard - est part is be - ing a - lone with my rest -
1.
G
G/A
D
Dsus2
less heart, mm, with my rest - less heart.
Dsus4
D
2.
G
G/A
D.S. and fade
Tell less heart.
Don't leave me here with my rest -

RUN TO YOU

Words and Music by
JUD FRIEDMAN and ALLAN RICH

Dbm6/Ab
Ab/Eb
Bb/D
that you just don't see._ But if___ you would on - ly take the__ time,_ I
al-ways in con-trol._ But at night,_ I come home and turn the__ key,_ there's
Dbm6/Fb
Eb7sus
C7/E
Fm7
know in my heart you'd find,___ oh,_____ a girl who's scared some-times, who
no - bod - y there, no one cares for me. Oh,_____ what's the sense of try - ing
Dbm6/Fb
Ab/Eb
is - n't al-ways strong.___ Can't_ you see the hurt in me? I
hard to find your dreams?___ With - out__ some-one to share them with, tell,

Chorus:
B♭m7/E♭
E♭
D♭2
B♭m7
B♭m7/E♭ E♭
feel so all a - lone.
me, what does it mean?
I wan-na run to you,
oo,
I wan-na
cresc.
rit.
a tempo
mf
A♭(2)
F7(♭9/♯5)
F7(♭9)
B♭m7
run to you,
oo.
Won't you
hold me in your arms
and
B♭m7/E♭
E♭
D♭(2)
B♭m7
B♭m7/E♭ E♭
keep me safe from harm?
I wan-na run to you,
oo
But if I
A♭(2)
F7(♭9/♯5)
F7(♭9)
D♭maj7
come to you,
oo,
tell me
will you stay,
or

1.
2.
Db♭m6/F♭ E♭7sus E♭7 A♭ D♭/A♭ A♭ D♭m(4)/A♭ D♭m/A♭
will_ you_ run a - way?_ Each
dim.
Fm D♭m6/F♭ A♭/E♭
way?_ Run_ a - way._
B♭/D
Bridge:
B♭m7 A♭/C
I need you here, I need you here to wipe a-way my tears,_ to kiss a -
B♭/D B♭m7/E♭ Fsus F
way my fears._ If you on - ly knew how much I wan - na
poco rit.

Chorus:
E♭(2)
Cm7
Cm7/F
F
B♭(2)
run to you, oo.
I wan-na run to you, oo,
a tempo
G7(♭9 ♯5)
G7(♭9)
Cm7
Cm7/F
F
won't you hold me in your arms and keep me safe from harm? I wan-na
E♭(2)
E♭m6/G♭
B♭(2)
G7(♭9 ♯5)
G7
run to you, oo.
But if I come to you, you, tell me,
dim.
E♭maj7
E♭m6/G♭
F7sus
F7
B♭
E♭m6/B♭
B♭
will you stay, or will you run a - way?
mf
rit.
dim.
mp

SAID I LOVED YOU . . . BUT I LIED

Composed by MICHAEL BOLTON
and ROBERT JOHN "MUTT" LANGE

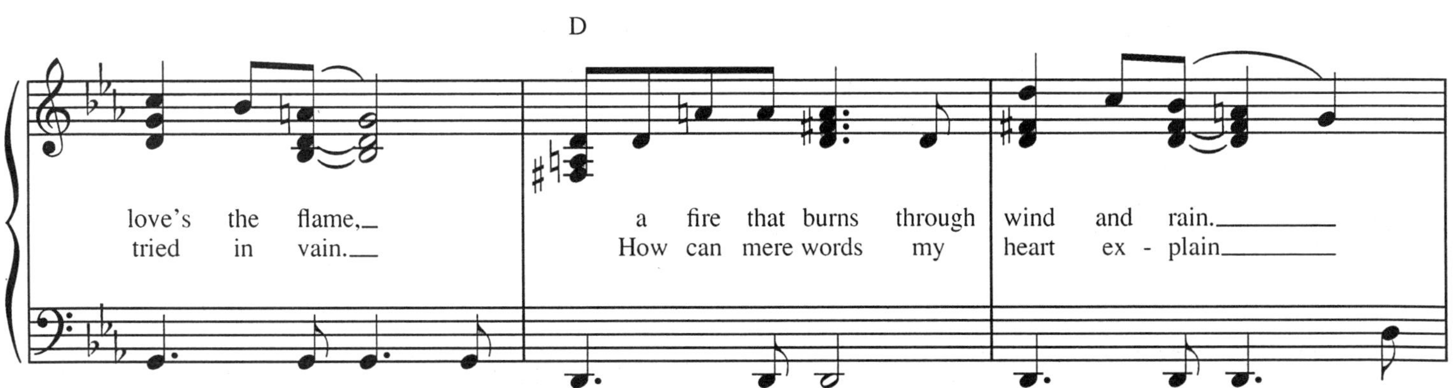

Cm
A♭
E♭
Shine your light on this heart of mine
this taste of heav - en so deep, so true,
till the end of
I've found in

𝄋𝄋 Bridge:
B♭
Cm
A♭
time.
you?
(1.3.) You came to me like the dawn through the night, just shin -
So man - y rea-sons in so man - y ways, my life

B♭
B♭sus
B♭
Cm
- in' like the sun.
has just be - gun.
Out of my dreams and
Need you for - ev - er, I

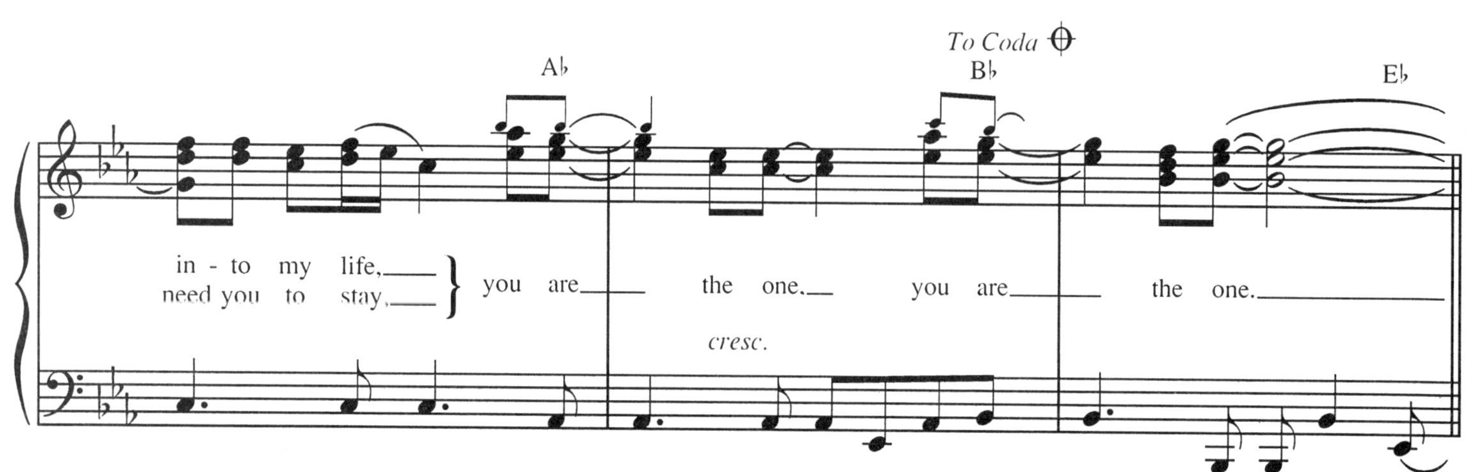
A♭
To Coda
B♭
E♭
in - to my life,
need you to stay,
you are the one, you are the one.
cresc.

Chorus:
B♭
Cm
A♭
E♭
B♭
Said I loved you, but I
lied,
mf

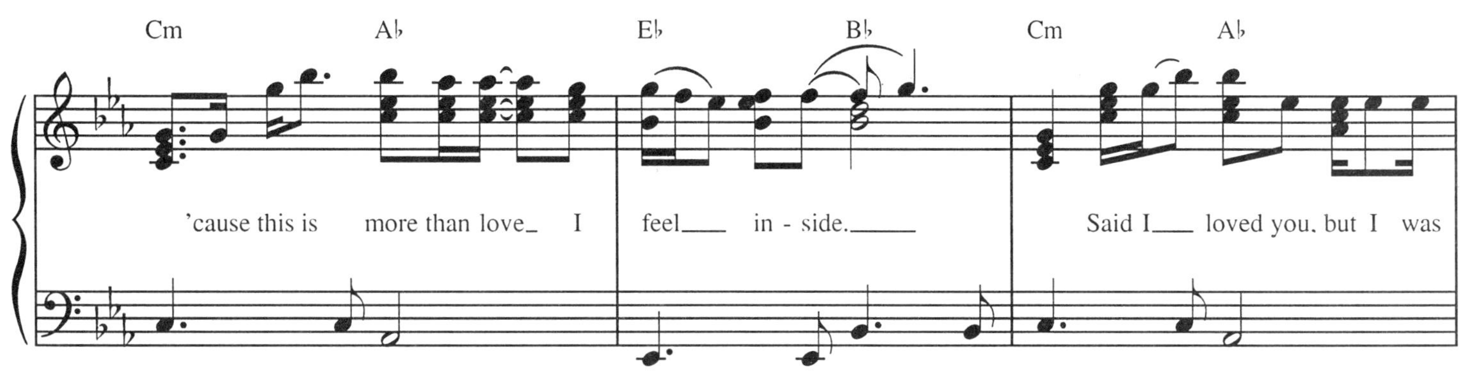
Cm
A♭
E♭
B♭
Cm
A♭
'cause this is more than love I
feel in - side.
Said I loved you, but I was

E♭
B♭
Cm
A♭
E♭
B♭
wrong,
'cause love could nev - er, ev - er
feel so strong.

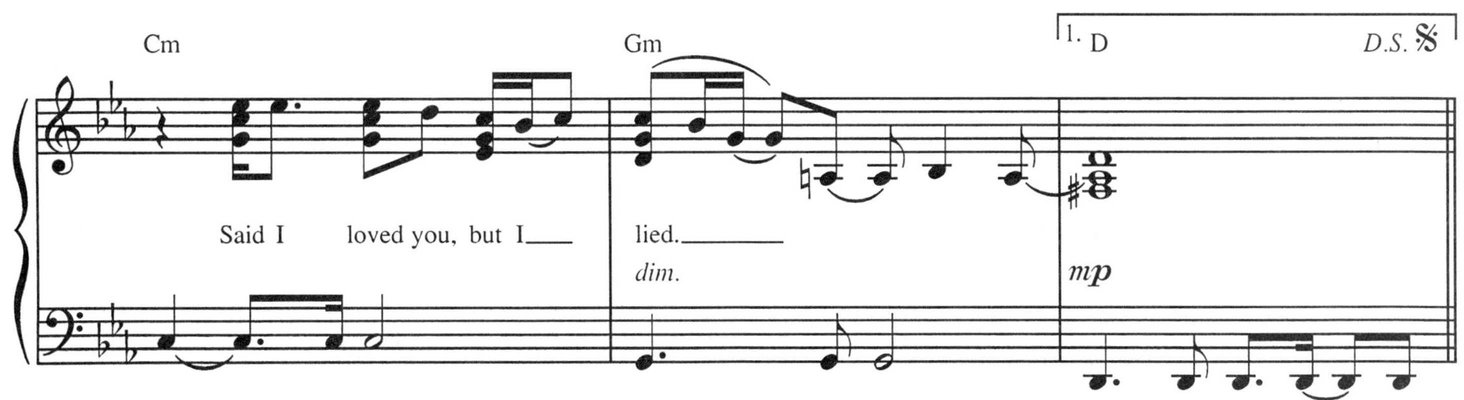
Cm
Gm
1. D
D.S. 𝄋
Said I loved you, but I
lied.
dim.
mp

2.
D
E♭m
A♭m7/C♭
D♭
mp
G♭
C♭
B♭
E♭m
A♭m7/C♭
D♭
D.S.S. 𝄋𝄋 al Coda
G♭
C♭
⊕ Coda
B♭sus
N.C.
3
the one.
F
C
Dm
B♭
F
C
Said I loved you, but I
lied,
'cause this is
more than love I
mf

Dm
B♭
F
C
Dm
B♭
feel__ in - side.___
Said I__ loved you, but I was
wrong,________

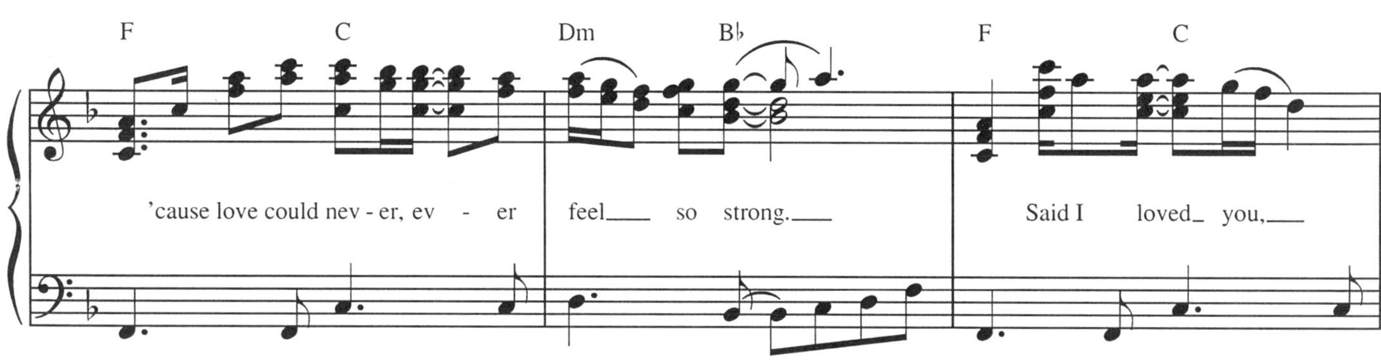
F
C
Dm
B♭
F
C
'cause love could nev - er, ev - er
feel__ so strong.__
Said I loved_ you,__

Dm
Am
'cause this is more than love_ I
feel____ in - side.__________

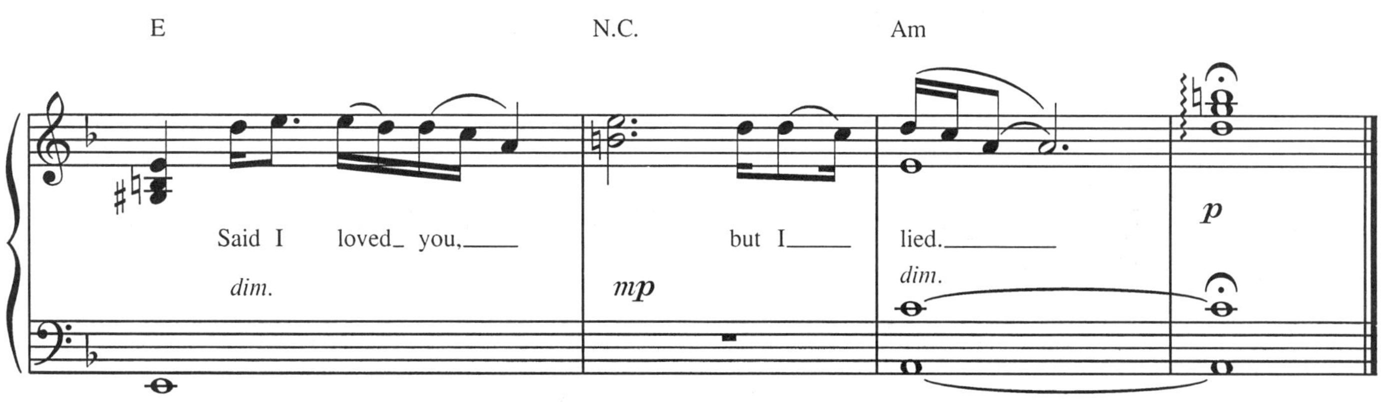
E
N.C.
Am
Said I loved_ you,___
but I___
lied.______
dim.
mp
dim.
p

SHOW ME THE WAY

Lyrics and Music by
DENNIS DE YOUNG

G♭ A♭m7 D♭/F E♭m C♭ D♭sus D♭
feel this emp - ty place in - side; so a - fraid that I've lost my faith. Show me the
mf
Chorus:
G♭ D♭ C♭ G♭ D♭ C♭
way, show me the way. Take me to - / Bring me to -
f
To Coda
G♭ D♭/F E♭m7 G♭/D♭ A♭m7 D♭sus D♭
night to the riv - er and wash my il - lu - sions a - way.
night to the moun-tain and take my con - fu - sion a - way.
Please show me the
G♭ C♭/G♭ D♭/G♭ C♭/G♭
way.
1. D.S. 2.
2. And
Bridge:
B♭ E♭m
and if I see a light, should I be - lieve? Tell me, how will I

A♭7 A♭m7 D♭sus D♭ D♭sus D♭ A B/A Amaj7 B/A
know?
D.S.S. 𝄋𝄋 al Coda
A B/A A B/A Amaj7 B/A D♭ C♭/D♭ D♭ C♭/D♭
Show me the
Coda G♭ D♭ C♭ G♭ D♭ C♭
way, show me the way. Take me to -
G♭ D♭/F E♭m7 G♭/D♭ A♭m7 D♭sus D♭
night to the riv - er and wash my il - lu - sions a - way. Show me the
G♭ D♭ C♭ G♭ D♭ C♭
way, show me the way. Give me the

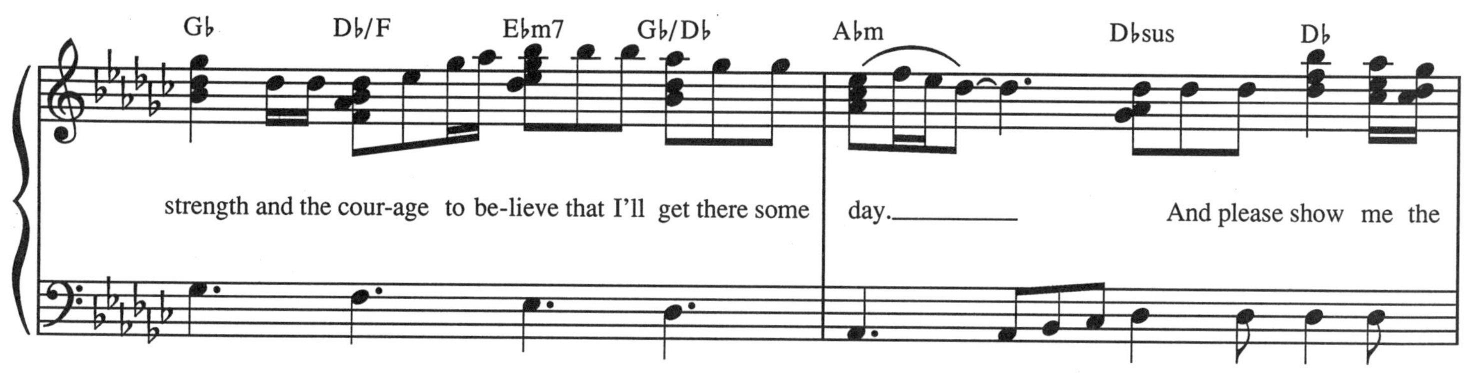
Gb Db/F Ebm7 Gb/Db Abm Dbsus Db
strength and the cour-age to be-lieve that I'll get there some day. And please show me the

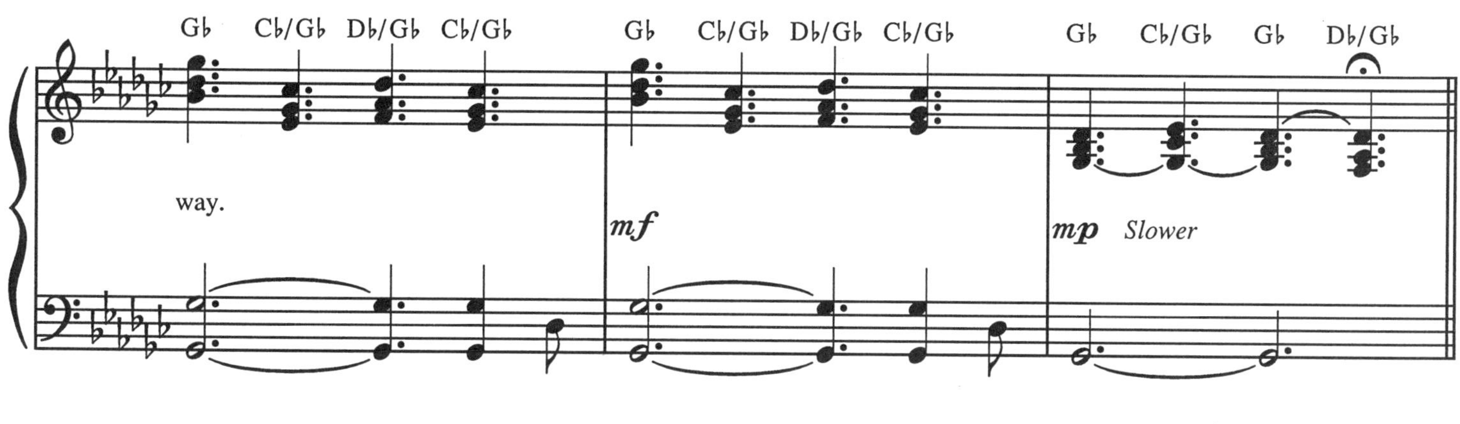
Gb Cb/Gb Db/Gb Cb/Gb Gb Cb/Gb Db/Gb Cb/Gb Gb Cb/Gb Gb Db/Gb
way.
mf
mp Slower

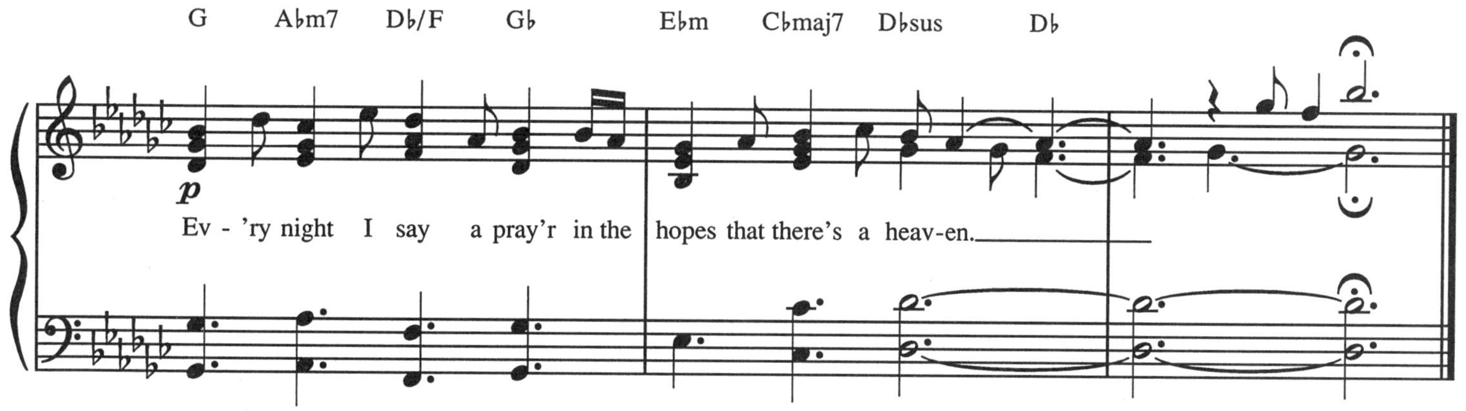
G Abm7 Db/F Gb Ebm Cbmaj7 Dbsus Db
p
Ev - 'ry night I say a pray'r in the hopes that there's a heav-en.

Verse 2:
And as I slowly drift to sleep
For a moment dreams are sacred.
I close my eyes and know there's peace
In a world so filled with hatred.
Then I wake up each morning and turn on the news
To find we've so far to go.
And I keep on hoping for a sign
So afraid I just won't know.
(To Chorus:)

SINCE I DON'T HAVE YOU

Words and Music by
JOSEPH ROCK, JAMES BEAUMONT
and THE SKYLINERS

Slowly ♩. = 72

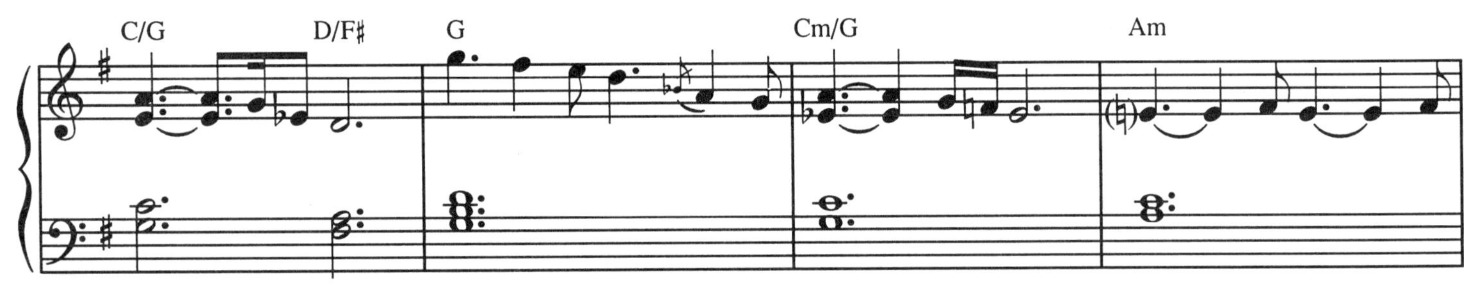

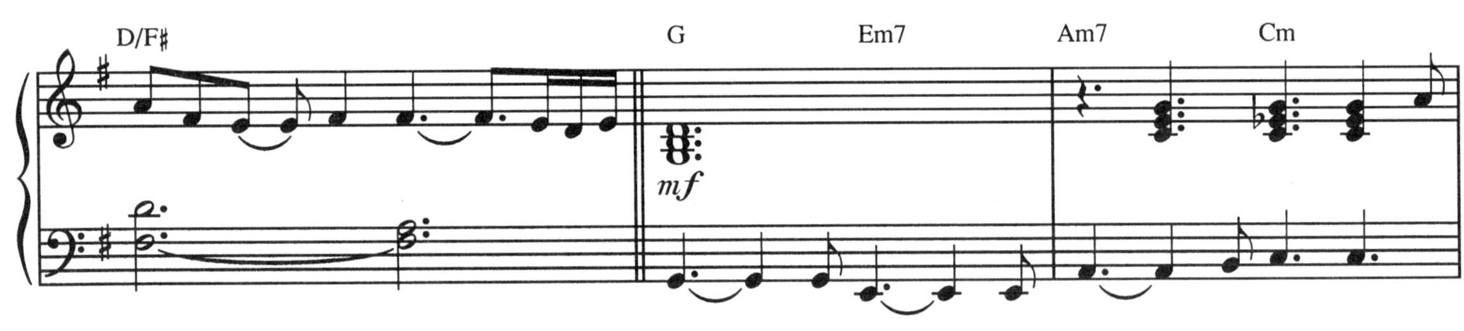

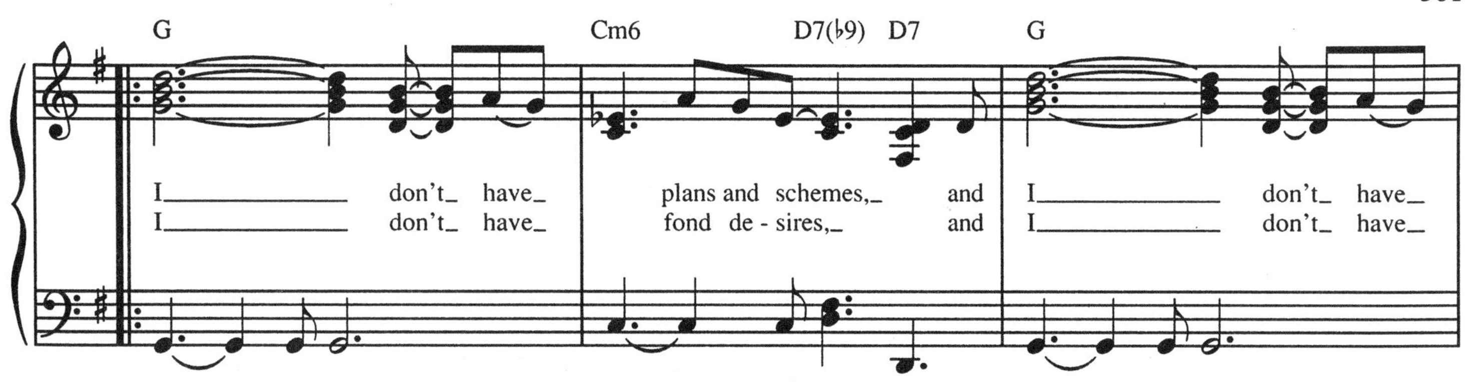
G
Cm6
D7(♭9)
D7
G
I_____ don't_ have_
plans and schemes,_ and
I_____ don't_ have_
I_____ don't_ have_
fond de - sires,_ and
I_____ don't_ have_

Cm6
D7(♭9)
D7
G
Cm6
hopes and dreams._
hap - py hours._
I_____ don't have_____ an - y - thing

1.
2.
Am
D
Am
since_ I don't_ have
you._____ And
since_ I don't_____ have
I don't have

G
Am
G
you._____
hap-pi-ness and I guess
I___ nev-er will_____ a - gain._____

Am
G
When you walked out on me,
in walked old mis - er - y,
Am
D
and he's been here since
then.
G
Cm6
D
D7
G
Cm6
D
D7
G
Cm6
Am
D

G Cm6 D7(♭9) D7 G

I ______ don't_ have_ love to share,_ and I ______ don't_ have_

Cm6 D7(♭9) D7 G Cm6

one who cares._ I ______ don't have ______ an - y - thing

Am D G Em7

since_ I don't_ have you. ______ You,_ you,_

Am7 D G Em7 1. Am7 D

you, ______ oh, ______ oh. ______ You,_ you,_ you, ______ oh, ______ oh. ______

2. Am7 D G Em7 G

You, ______ oh, ______ oh. ______ You,_ you,_ oh. ______

SOME PEOPLE'S LIVES

Words and Music by
JANIS IAN and
RHONDA FLEMING

C
Gm7
Am
Some lives wear out like old ten-nis shoes no one can
Gsus G Am/G G
F
Gsus G
use. Well, it's sad but it's true. Did-n't an - y - bod - y tell them?
F
G
F
Am/G G
Dm7
Did-n't an - y - bod - y see? Did-n't an - y - bod - y love them like you love

G
C
Gm7
me?
Some
peo-ple's
eyes
fade
like
their
dreams,
too
Am
Gsus G Am/G
G C/G G7
C
tired
to
rise,
too
tired
to
sleep.
Some
peo-ple
Gm7
Am
Gsus
laugh
when
they
need
to
cry,
and they
nev - er
know
G
F
G
F
why.
Did - n't
an - y - bod - y
tell
them
that's not
how
it
has
to

G
F
Am/G
G
Dm7
G
Dm6/F
be?
Did-n't an - y - bod - y
love_ them
like
you
love
me?
E
E7/G♯
Asus4 2
Am
E/A
Am
Asus4 2
Am7
D
Em7
Some peo - ple ask___
if the
tears have
to
fall.___
Then why take
your chanc-
D7/F♯
Gsus4 2
G
Am/G
G
C/G
G7
C
- es?
Why
both - er
at___
all?
And
some
peo-ple's
lives
are as
rit.
a tempo
rit.
a tempo
Gm7
Am
Gsus4 2
cold
as
their___
lips,
they just
need
to
be___
rit.
rit.

G F Am/G G F

kissed. Does-n't an - y - bod - y tell___ them? Does-n't an - y - bod - y

a tempo

a tempo

G F Am/G G Dm/F E E7(#9) G#dim7

see? Does-n't an - y - bod - y love___ them like you love

Am Em/G F C/E Dm7 F/G G7 C Dm/C C Dm/C F/C

me? 'Cuz that's all they need.___

rit. *a tempo*

rit. *a tempo*

C N.C.

rit.

8vb

TEARDROPS

Words and Music by
ZEKKARIYAS/ZERIIYA ZEKKARIYAS

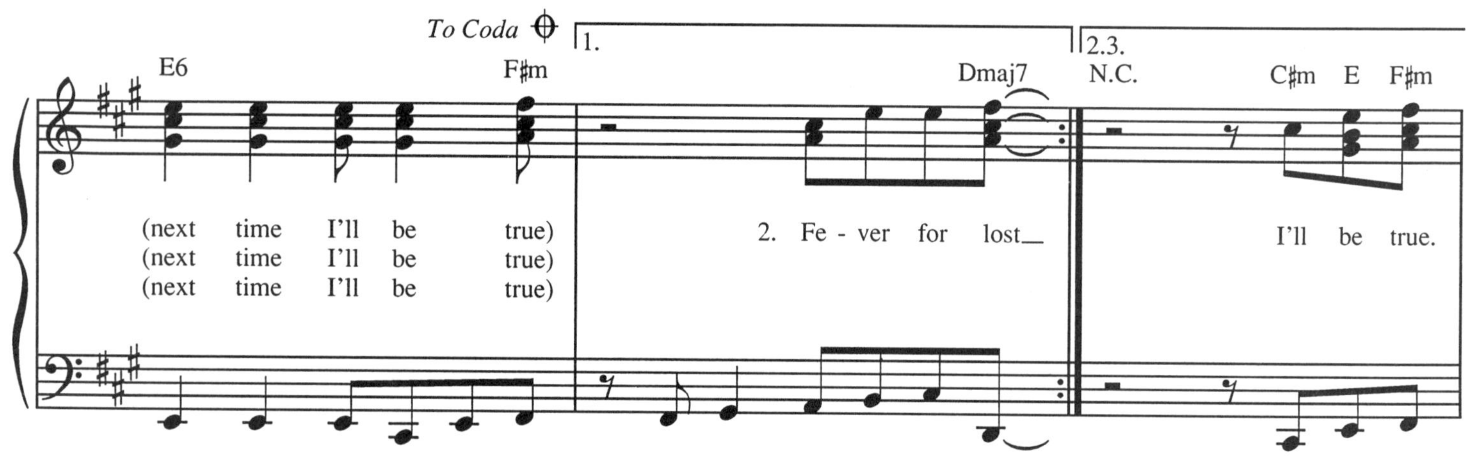
To Coda
1.
2.3.
E6
F♯m
Dmaj7
N.C.
C♯m E F♯m
(next time I'll be true)
(next time I'll be true)
(next time I'll be true)
2. Fe - ver for lost
I'll be true.

Bridge:
N.C.
Dmaj7
Bm7
Foot - steps on the dance floor (re -

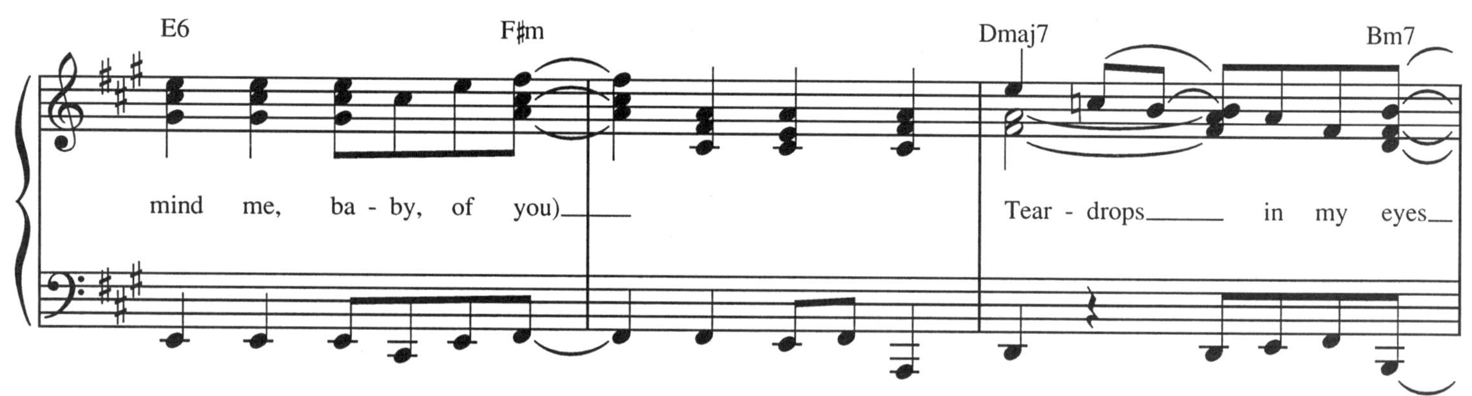
E6
F♯m
Dmaj7
Bm7
mind me, ba - by, of you)
Tear - drops in my eyes

E6
F♯m
(next time I'll be true, yeah)

Dmaj7
Bm7
E6
F♯m
Whis - pers in the pow - der room, she cries on ev - er - y tune,
N.C.
C♯m E F♯m
N.C.
C♯m E F♯m
Chorus:
C♯m7
ev - ery tune. And the mu - sic don't feel
F♯m7
F♯m7/B
Bm7
E7
F♯m
like it did when I felt it with you. Noth-ing that
C♯m7
F♯m7
F♯m7/B
Bm7
E
I do or feel ev - er feels like I felt it with you.
1.
Esus
E
D.C.
2.
F♯m
3.
And the mu- Wo wo

D.C. al Coda
wo wo
wo wo
wo wo.
Coda
N.C.
C♯m E F♯m
I'll be true.
N.C.
C♯m E F♯m
And the mu -
Chorus:
C♯m7 F♯m7 F♯m7/B Bm7 E7
- sic don't feel like it did when I felt it with you.
F♯m C♯m7 F♯m7
Noth-ing that I do or feel ev - er feels like I
F♯m7/B Bm7 E
1. F♯m
2.
felt it with you. And the mu -
Wo wo

wo___ wo___
wo___ wo___
wo___ yeah.___
Dmaj7
Bm7
E6
1.3.etc.
F♯m
f
2.4.etc.
F♯m
Dmaj7
Bm7
E6
Wo___ wo___
wo___ wo___
wo___ wo___
1.3.etc.
F♯m
yeah,___ yeah.___
2.4.etc.
F♯m
D.S. 𝄋
yeah,___ yeah.___

STAND

Words and Music by
BRET MICHAELS, BOBBY DALL, RIKKI ROCKETT
and RICHIE KOTZEN

Stand - 4 - 1

D♭5
A♭
E♭
Stand_ for what you be - lieve!___ You know you got to
To Coda
B♭m7
D♭5
A♭
E♭
stand!_________ Stand!_____________ Stand_ for what you be - lieve!__
1.
D♭
A♭2
N.C.
_______ Ohh,_ you've got to stand_ for what you be - lieve!__
E♭
D♭(2)
A♭
E♭
mf
Al - right, al-right.
D♭(2)
A♭
2.
D♭
You got to lis-ten now! 2. Ex -
____ Hmm_ stand,__

To next strain

D♭2 A♭2 N.C. E♭ D♭(2) A♭

Stand_ for what you be-lieve.____ Some-bod-y

3. *D.S. 𝄋 al Coda*

E♭sus E♭ B♭m Cm D♭ D♭sus D♭

____ You know you've got to res - cue me.__ Come down and res - cue me.__ I know the

A♭5 D♭(2) A♭5 D♭2 A♭2

soul of this good__ man has got to be free__ when you Stand,______

N.C. B♭m7(4) D♭(2) A♭ E♭/G Fm7 E♭

stand_ for what you be - lieve.______ *(1st time only)*

(Instrumental solo . . .

1. 2.

E♭sus E♭ E♭sus E♭ B♭m7(4) E♭sus E♭ B♭m7(4)

Verse 2:
Express yourself in the face of change.
Repress yourself, you surely seal your fate.
You got to look inside, the answer lies in wait.
Resurrect, before it's too late.
(To Chorus:)

THIS OLD HEART OF MINE

(Is Weak For You)

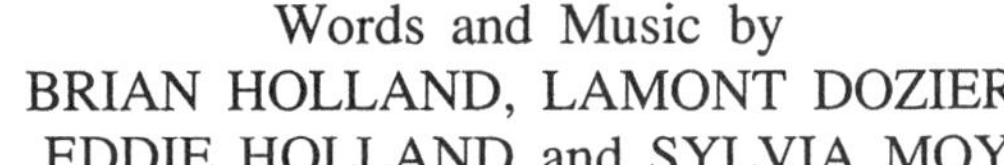

Words and Music by
BRIAN HOLLAND, LAMONT DOZIER,
EDDIE HOLLAND and SYLVIA MOY

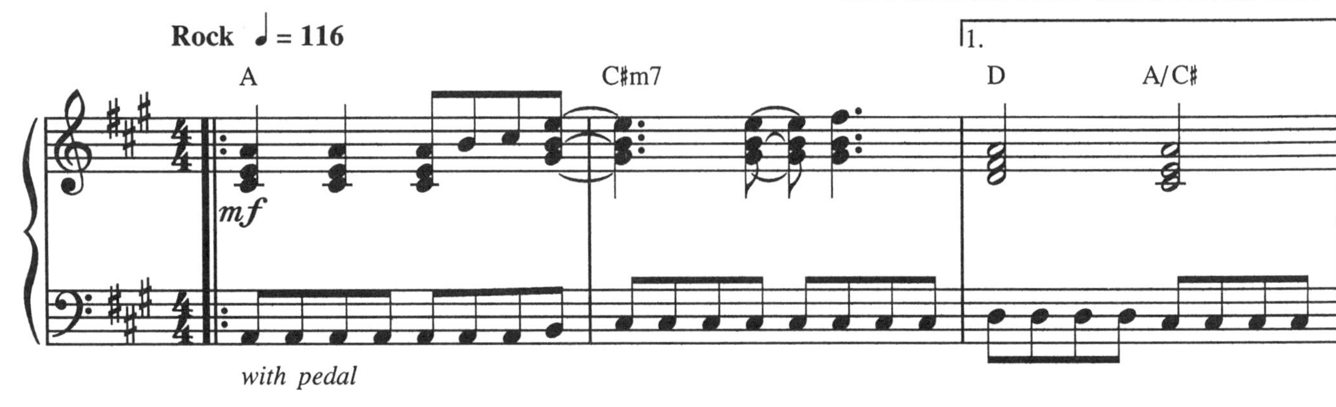

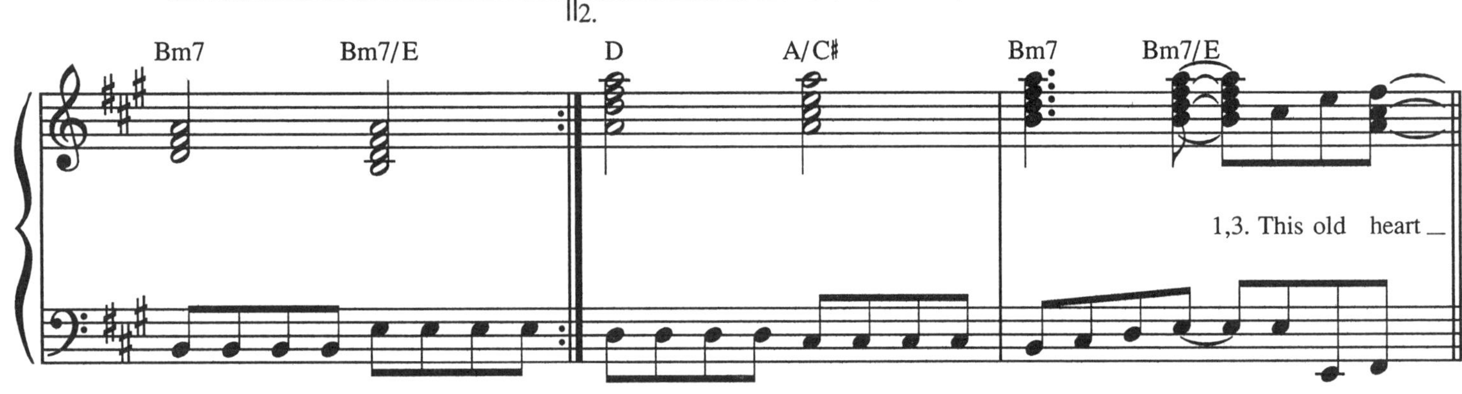

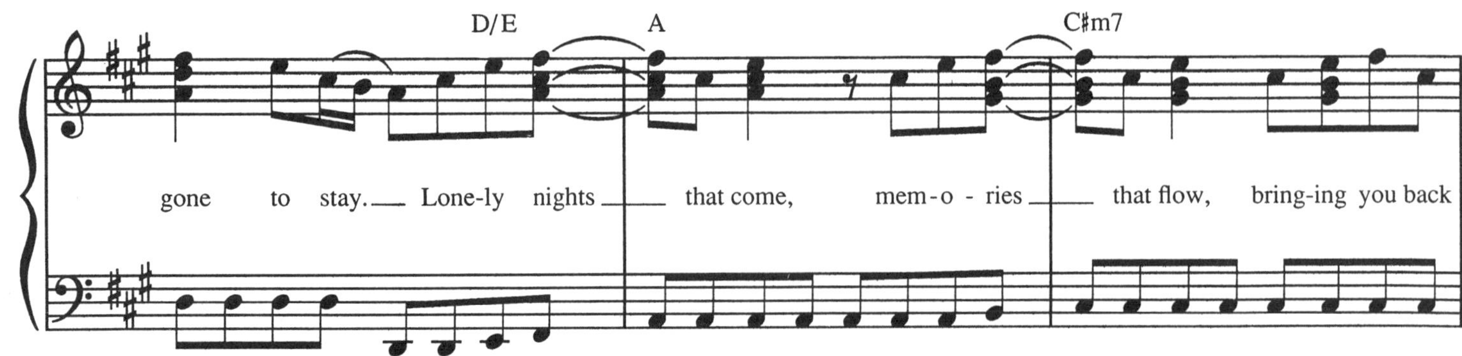

D
C♯m
Bm7
a - gain, hurt-ing me more and more.
May - be it's

E
C♯m7
F♯m
E/F♯
my mis - take to show this love that I feel in - side;

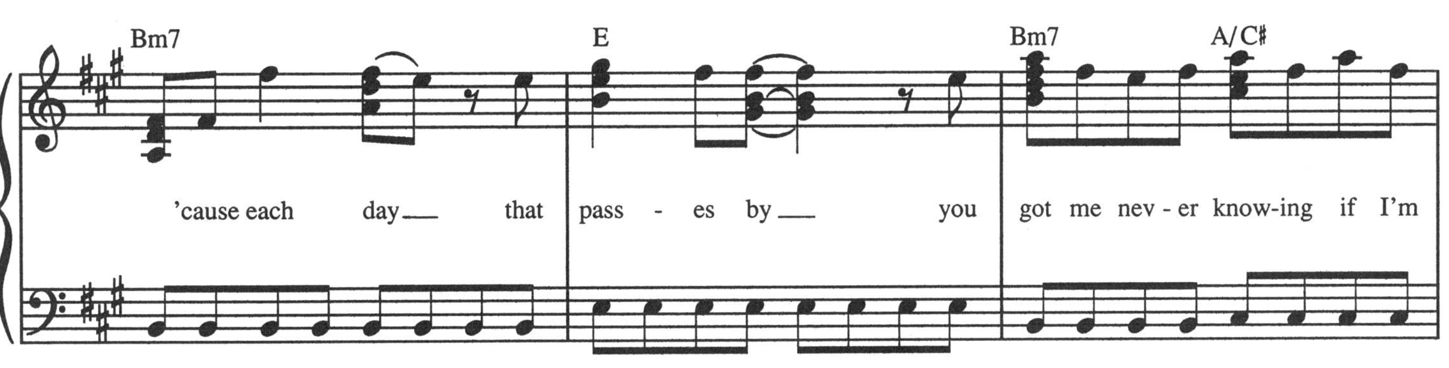
Bm7
E
Bm7
A/C♯
'cause each day that pass - es by you got me nev - er know-ing if I'm

Chorus:
To Coda
D
D/E
E
A
C♯m7
com-ing or go - ing, 'cause
1,3. I love you.
2,4. I love you.
Yes, I
This old

D
A/C#
Bm7
D/E
E
A
do, this old heart. I love you.
heart is weak for you.

1.
C#m7
D
C#m7
Bm7
D/E
E
Yes, I do, yes, I do.
This old heart, weak for

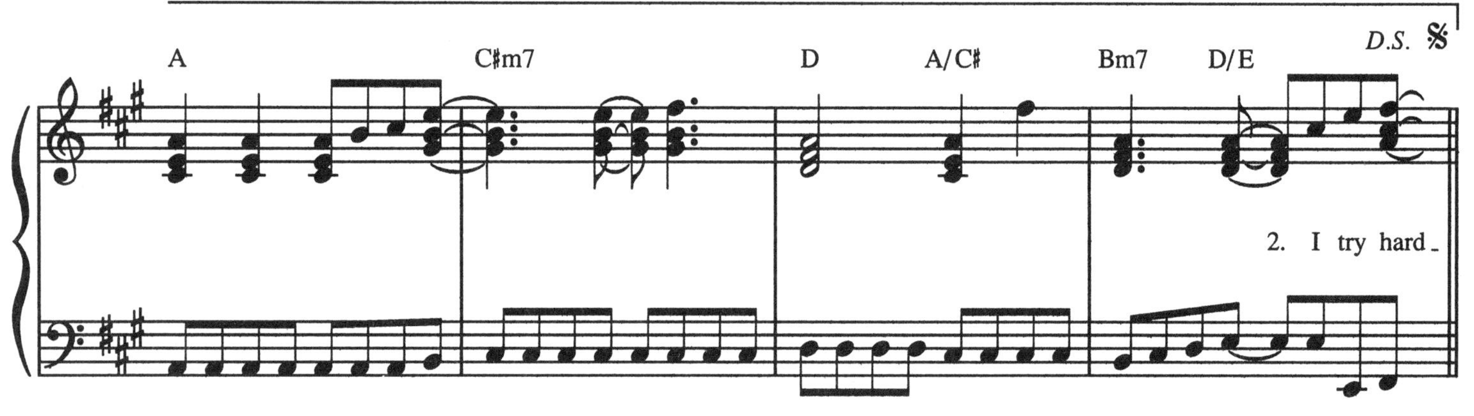
A
C#m7
D
A/C#
Bm7
D/E
D.S. 𝄋
2. I try hard

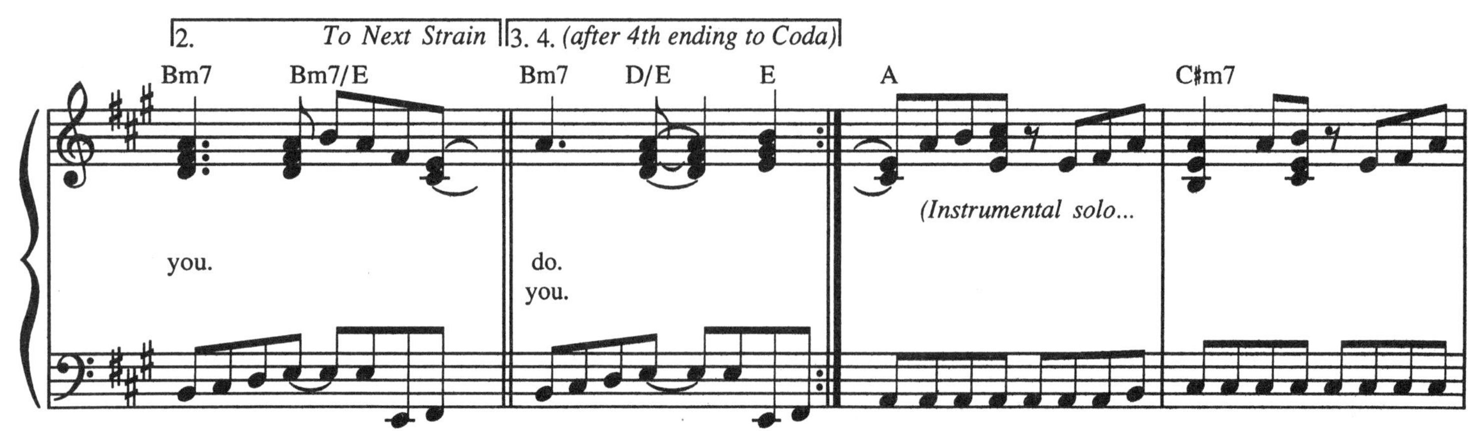
2.
To Next Strain
3. 4. (after 4th ending to Coda)
Bm7
Bm7/E
Bm7
D/E
E
A
C#m7
you.
do.
you.
(Instrumental solo...

Verse 2:

I try hard to hide my hurt inside.
This old heart of mine always keeps me cryin'.
The way you treat me leaves me incomplete,
You're here for the day, gone for the week.

But, if you leave me a hundred times, a hundred times I'll take you back.
I'm yours whenever you want me.
I'm not too proud to shout it, tell the world about it, 'cause I love you.

(To Chorus 2:)

TRUE COMPANION

Words and Music by
MARC COHN

D A E A
when it comes to love, I'm just an - oth - er fool. Yes, I'll
E A D A E A
climb a moun - tain, I'm gon-na swim the sea.
D A E A D A
There ain't no act of God, girl, could keep you
E A D A Bm/F♯ F♯m
safe from me, My arms are reach-ing out,

Bm/F♯
F♯m
A
E9sus/A
A
E9sus/A
out a - cross__ this can - yon.
D
A
E
A
D
A
I'm ask - ing you_ to be my true com - pan - ion, true__
E
A
D
A
E
A
__ com - pan - ion, true com - pan - ion.
To Coda
1.
D
A
E
A
D
A

D.S. 𝄋
2.
E D E A D A
true com - pan - ion.
cresc.
ff
E A D A E D
D A E A D A
dim.
E D
D.S. 𝄋 al Coda

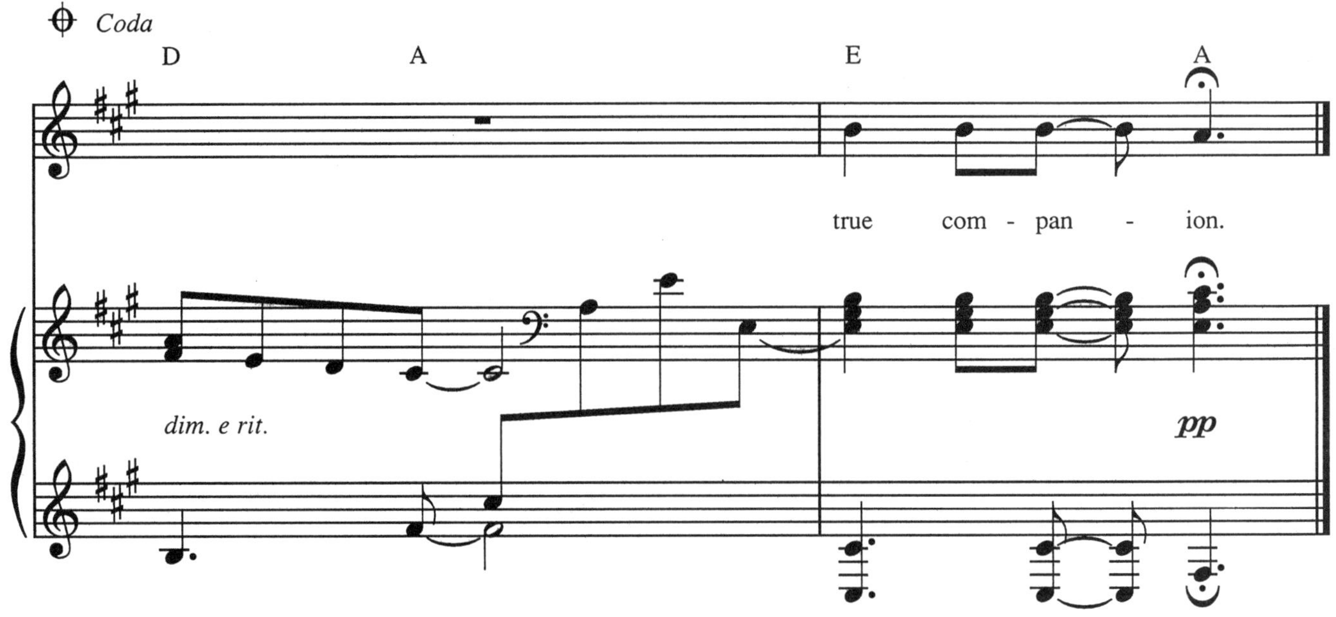

Verse 2:
So don't you dare and try to walk away;
I've got my heart set on our wedding day.
I've got this vision of a girl in white,
Made my decision that it's you all right.
And when I take your hand,
I'll watch my heart set sail.
I'll take my trembling fingers
And I'll lift up your veil.
Then I'll take you home,
And with wild abandon
Make love to you just like a true companion.
You are my true companion.
I got a true companion,
Woah, a true companion.

Verse 3:
When the years have done irreparable harm,
I can see us walking slowly arm in arm,
Just like that couple on the corner do,
'Cause girl I will always be in love with you.
And when I look in your eyes,
I'll still see that spark,
Until the shadows fall,
Until the room grows dark.
Then when I leave this earth,
I'll be with the angels standin';
I'll be out there waiting for my true companion,
Just for my true companion.
True companion,
True companion.

U CAN'T TOUCH THIS

Words and Music by
RICK JAMES, ALONZO MILLER
and M.C. HAMMER

G Am D Am G Am
su-per-dope home boy from the "Oak" town. And I'm known as such, and this is a beat, uh, U can't touch.
D Am G Am D Am
I told U home boy, U can't touch this. Yeah, that's how we're livin'
G Am D Am G Am
and U know, U can't touch this. Look in my eyes, man, U can't touch this.
1. 2. 3. 4. 5. 6.
D Am G Am G Am
Here, let me bust the funky lyrics, U can't touch this. Break it down.
Bridge:
D7
Oh, oh.

Verse 2:

Fresh new kicks and pants.
U got it like that now U know U wanna dance.
So, move out of your seat and get a fly girl and
catch this beat - while it's rollin'.
Hold on, pump a little bit
and let them know it's going on like that.
Like that cold on a mission, so fall on back.
Let 'em know that you're too much
and this is a beat U can't touch.

Chorus 2:

Yo! I told U,
U can't touch this.
Why U standin' there man?
U can't touch this.
Yo, sound the bells, school is in sucker,
U can't touch this.

Verse 3:

Give me a song, or rhythm
making 'em sweat. That's what I'm giving 'em.
Now they know U talk about the Hammer,
you're talking about a show that's hyped.
And tight singers are sweating so pass them a wipe,
or a tape to learn; what it is going to take
in the "90's" to burn the charts.
Legit. Either work hard or U might as well quit.
(To Chorus)

Verse 4:

Go with the flow. It is said
that if U can't groove to this, then U probably are dead.
So wave, your hands in the air.
Bust a few moves. Run your fingers through your hair.
This is it for a winner,
dance to this an you're gonna get thinner.
Move. Slide your rump. Just for a minute, let's all do the bump.
Bump, bump.
(To Chorus)

Verse 5:

Everytime U see me, the Hammer's just so hyped.
I'm dope on the floor. And I'm magic on the mic.
Now why would I ever stop doing this?
When others making records that just don't hit.
I've toured around the world from London to the Bay.
It's Hammer, go Hammer, M.C. Hammer, yo Hammer,
and the rest can go and play.
(To Chorus)

TWO STEPS BEHIND

Words and Music by
JOE ELLIOTT

Moderately slow ♩ = 92

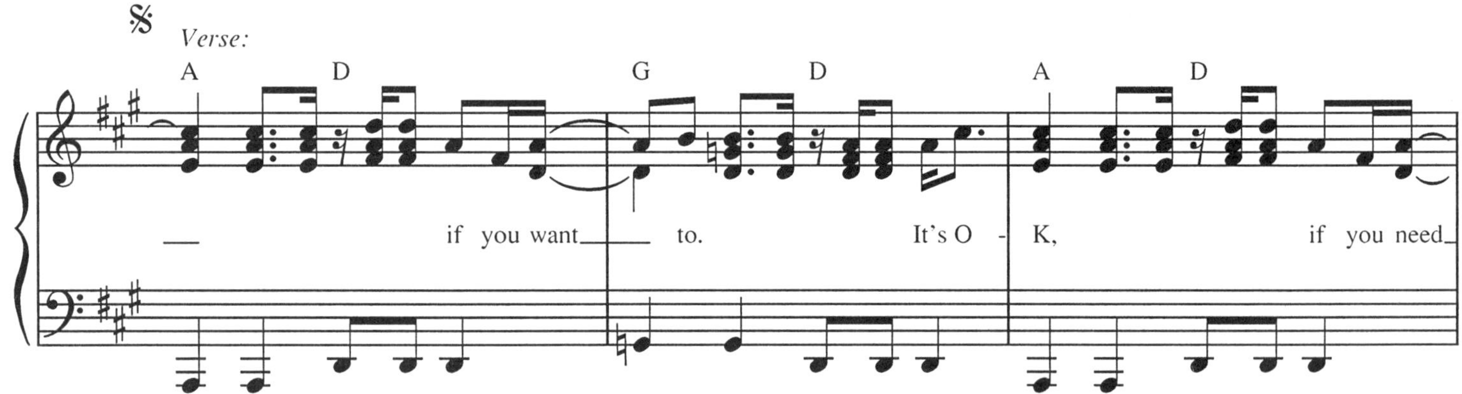

A D E D

shad - ow that's creep - ing up___ be - side___ you.

Bridge:

F♯m D

There's a mag - ic run - ning___ through your___ soul,___ but

G E N.C.

you can't___ have___ it all.___ (What - ev - er you do___

Chorus:

A D E D

___) I'll be two steps___ be - hind___ you, (Wher - ev - er you go___

A D E D

___) and I'll be there to___ re - mind___ you___ that it___

A
D
1.
E
G2
on - ly takes a
min - ute of your
pre - cious
time
to turn a - round;
D
A
D(2)
G6
D
I'll be two steps be - hind,
yeah, yeah.
A
D(2)
G6
D
D.S.
2.
E
2. Take the time
pre - cious
time
G2
D
A
Dmaj9
to turn a - round;
I'll be two steps be - hind.
G2
D6/9
A
Dmaj9
G2
D6/9
D.S.
yeah, yeah.
Oh, ho.

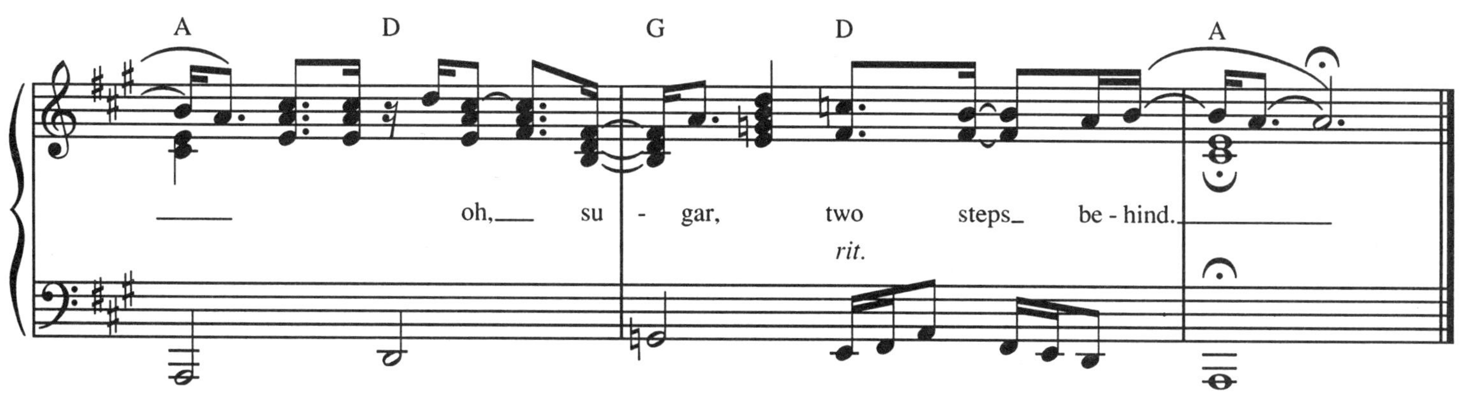

Verse 2:
Take your time to think about it.
Just walk the line; you know you just can't fight it.
Take a look around; you'll see what you can't find,
Like the fire that's burning up inside me.

Bridge 2:
Now there's a magic running through your soul,
But you can't have it all, no.
(To Chorus:)

Verse 3:
(Instrumental solo ad lib.)

Bridge 3:
There's a magic running through your soul,
But you can't have it all.
(To Chorus:)

UNTIL YOU COME BACK TO ME
(That's What I'm Gonna Do)

Words and Music by
STEVIE WONDER, MORRIS BROADNAX
and CLARENCE PAUL

Em7
A7
I want to tell you ba - by, the chang - es I've been go - ing through
F♯m7(♭5)
B7(♭9)
miss - ing you. Lis - ten you.
Chorus:
Em7
A11
Dmaj7
To Coda
Til you come back to me, that's what I'm gon - na do.
1.
D.S.
2.
To Next Strain
3. 4.
(4th time To Coda)
Dm7/G
G13
2. Why did you
Bridge:
Dm7
G7
Liv - ing for you my dear is like liv - ing in a world

Verse 2:
Why did you have to decide
You had to set me free?
I'm going to swallow my pride, (my pride)
And beg you to please see me.
(Baby won't you see me?)
I'm going to walk by myself
Just to prove that my love is true;
All for you baby.
(To Chorus:)

Verse 3:
Although your phone you ignore,
Somehow I must, somehow I must,
How I must explain.
I'm gonna rap on your door,
Tap on your window pane.
(Tap on your window pane.)
I'm gonnna camp on your steps
Until I get through to you;
I've got to change your view, baby.
(To Chorus:)

WHAT BECOMES OF THE BROKEN-HEARTED

Words and Music by
JAMES DEAN, PAUL RISER
and WILLIAM WEATHERSPOON

Chorus:
F♯m
C♯7/G♯
G7(♯11)
B
filled with sad - ness
and con - fu - sion.
What be-comes of the
D♯m/A♯
G♯m
E
bro - ken-heart - ed
who had love that's
now de - part - ed?
B
D♯m/A♯
G♯m
B/F♯
D♯7
E/B
F♯m7/C♯
B
I know I've got to find
some kind of peace of mind.
Help me, please.
A
C♯m
F♯m
2. The roots of love grow
all a - round,
but for me they come
D
A
D♯dim7
tum - bl - in' down.
Ev - ery day, heart - aches
grow a lit - tle stron - ger,

Verse 3:
I walk in shadows, searching for light,
Cold and alone, no comfort in sight.
Hoping and praying for someone who cares,
Always movin', but goin' nowhere.
(To Chorus:)

Verse 4:
Instrumental solo
(To Verse 5:)

Verse 5:
I'm searching though I don't succeed, no.
For someone's love, there's a growing need.
All is lost, there's no place for beginnning,
And all that's left is an unhappy ending.
(To Chorus:)

WALKING IN MEMPHIS

Words and Music by
MARC COHN

*chord symbols in parentheses indicate implied harmony

(Am) (F) (G) (C) (Am) (F)
Del - ta Blues_ in the mid-dle of the pour - ing rain.___
(G) (C) (Am) (F) (G) (C)
W.__________ C. Han - dy, won't you look down o - ver me?_
(dou-ble u____)
(Am) (F) (G) (C) (Am) (F)
_ Yeah,__ I got a first class___ tick - et, but I'm as
Chorus:
(G) C Am F G C
blue as a boy__ can be.______ Then I'm walk-ing in Mem - phis,

**implied harmony with no bass

(G7sus)
(C/G)
(G7sus)
to the gates of Grace - land, then I watched him walk_ right through._
(C/G)
F2
G7sus
C
Am
_ Now, se - cu-ri-ty, they did not_ see him. They just
F2
G7sus
C
Am
F2
G7sus
hov - ered 'round his_ tomb._ But there's a pret - ty lit - tle thing_ wait -
C
Am
F
N.C.
3
3
C
ing for the King,_ down in the Jun - gle_Room. When I was walk-ing in Mem -

Chorus:
F G C Am F G C
- phis, I was walk-ing with my feet ten feet off of Beale.
Am F G C Am
Walk-ing in Mem - phis, but do I real - ly
F G C7sus C7 C7sus C7
feel the way I feel? They've got
mp
dim.
mp
Bridge:
C7sus C7 C7sus C7
cat-fish on the ta - ble. They've got

C7sus
C7
C7sus
C7
gos - pel in the air.
And Rev - er - end Green
Rubato - vocal ad lib.
E7
F7
F♯dim7
be glad to see you
when you have - n't got a
Rubato
G7 C/G G7 N.C.
(F)
(G)
(C)
prayer.
But boy you got a prayer in Mem - phis...
a tempo
a tempo
(Am)
(F)
(G)
(C)
(Am)
(F)
Now,

Verse:
(G) (C) (Am) (F) (G) (C)
Mu - ri - el plays pi - a - no ev - ery Fri - day at the Hol - ly - wood.
(Am) (F) (G) (C) (Am) (F)
3
And they brought me down to see her, and they
(G) (C) (Am) F2 G7sus C
asked me if I would do a lit - tle num -
mf
cresc.
Am7 F2 G7sus C Am7
- ber. And I sang with all my might. She said,

F2 G7sus C Am7 F2 N.C.
"Tell_ me, are you a Christ - ian, child?"_ And I____ said, "Ma'am, I am________
cresc.
f
Chorus:
C F G C Am
to-night." Walk-ing in Mem - phis, I was walk-ing with my
F G C Am F G C
feet ten feet__ off of Beale.___ Walk-ing in Mem - phis,
1.
Am F C/E Dm C Am
but do I real - ly feel the way__ I feel?___ Walk - ing in Mem -

2.
F G Csus (G) (C) (Am) (F)
feel the way I feel?
(G) (C) (Am) (F) (G) (C)
Put on my blue
(Am) (F) (G) (C) (Am) (F)
suede shoes and I board-ed the plane. Touched down
(G) (C) (Am) (F) (G) (C)
in the land of the Del - ta Blues in the mid-dle of the pour - ing rain.
dim.

(Am) (F) (G) (C) Am
_ Touched down___ in the land of the Del - ta Blues___ in the
mp
rit.
mp
rit.
F G (F) (G) (C) (Am) (F)
mid-dle of the pour - ing_______ rain.
a tempo
a tempo
(G) (C) (Am) (F) (G) (C)
(Am) F G C
dim. e rit.
p

COME TO MY WINDOW

Lyrics and Music by
MELISSA ETHERIDGE

D
C(9)
G
the hand of death.
You don't know how far I'd go to
use this precious ache. And
you don't know how much I'd give or
how much I can take. Just to reach
Em
you. Just to reach
you. Oh, to reach you,
oh.
Chorus:
Am
Come to my win - dow.
Crawl in - side, wait

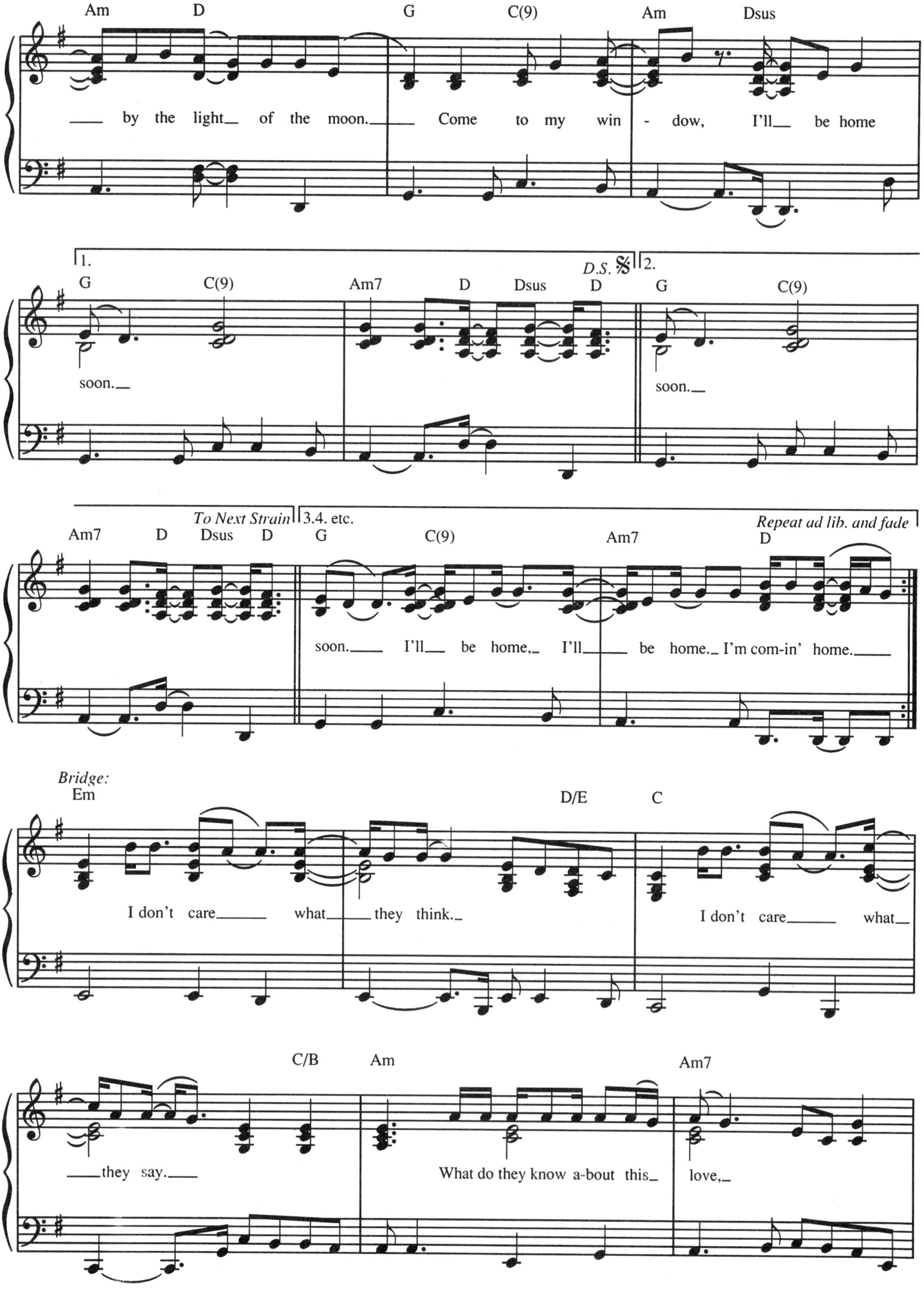

Am D G C(9) Am Dsus
___ by the light___ of the moon.___ Come to my win - dow, I'll___ be home
1.
G C(9) Am7 D Dsus D
D.S. 𝄋
soon.___
2.
G C(9)
soon.___
Am7 D Dsus D
To Next Strain
3.4. etc.
G C(9) Am7 D
Repeat ad lib. and fade
soon.___ I'll___ be home,___ I'll___ be home.___ I'm com-in' home.___
Bridge:
Em D/E C
I don't care___ what___ they think.___ I don't care___ what___
C/B Am Am7
___they say.___ What do they know a-bout this___ love,___

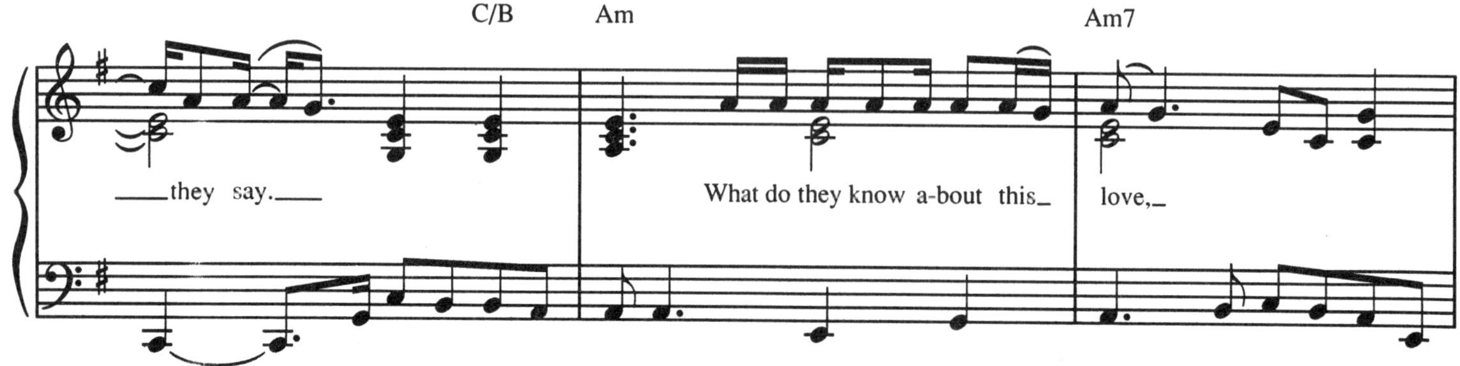

Verse 2:
Keeping my eyes open, I cannot afford to sleep.
Giving away promises I know that I can't keep.
Nothing fills the blackness that has seeped into my chest.
I need you in my blood, I am forsaking all the rest.
Just to reach you,
Just to reach you.
Oh, to reach you.
(To Chorus:)

WHEN SOMETHING IS WRONG WITH MY BABY

Words and Music by
ISAAC HAYES and DAVID PORTER

Verse 2:
He: Just what she means to me now,
Oh, you just wouldn't understand.
People can say that she's no good,
But ah, she's my woman and I know I'm her man.
She: And if he's got a problem,
Oh, I know I got to help him solve 'em.
Both: When something is wrong with my baby,
Something is wrong with me.

WHO'S LOVIN' YOU

Words and Music by
WILLIAM ROBINSON

MONOLOGUE, WITH BLUES ACCOMPANIMENT:
I'd like to talk to y'all tonight . . . about the blues.
Yeah, the blues.
Don't nobody have the blues like I have.
I may be young but I know what it's all about.
And this is how it bring down . . .

I met a girl at school one day during sandbox.
We toasted our love during milk break.
I gave her my cookies.
We fell out during fingerpainting.
So one day, I stepped up to her and I said . . .

G
D7
G
Em
C
Cm
I sit a-round with my head hang - ing down. And I won-der who's lov-in'

1.
2.
G
D
N.C.
G
Bm
you. I, I, I, you. Life with-out love

Em
Bm
is oh, so lone-ly. I don't think, I don't think I'm gon - na

Em
C
D
make it. All my life, all my love, ba - by, be -
(all my life,)

G D/F♯ Em A7 D7

longs to you on-ly. Come on, come on and take it, girl. Come on and take it. Be-cause

G Em G

all, all I can do, all I can do since

Em E♭ D

you been gone is cry. Ooh,

C7 D

don't ev-er won-der or wor-ry your pret-ty head

C7 G D7

'bout what I do. Don't you know I sit a-round with my

G D/F♯ Em D C Cm
head, yeah, hang-ing down. And I won - der who's

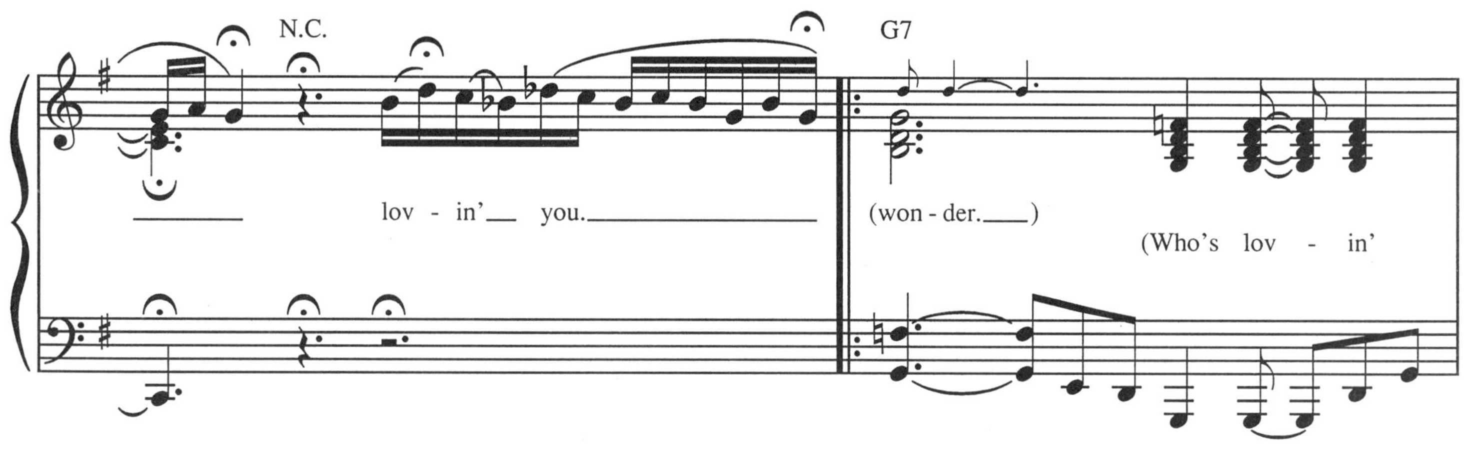
N.C. G7
lov - in' you. (won - der.)
(Who's lov - in'

C7 1.2. G7
I, I got - ta know.
you?) (Who's lov - in'

C7 3. G7 C7 C♯dim7 G/D A♭13 G7
I, I, I, I, I, know. Oh! Oh! Oh! Oh yeah!
you?)

WHY MUST WE WAIT UNTIL TONIGHT?

Lyrics & Music by
BRYAN ADAMS &
R.J. LANGE

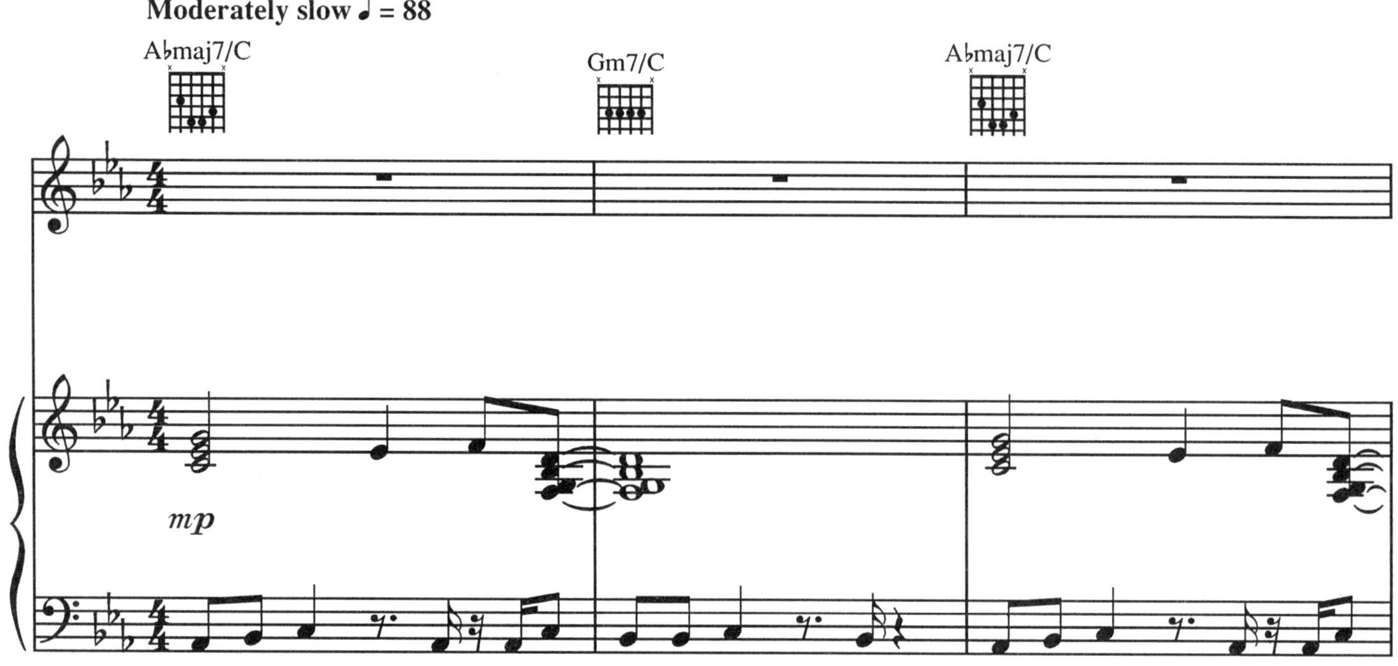

A♭maj7/C
Gm7/C
A♭maj7/C
- night?
Tell me why,
Gm7/C
A♭maj7/C
Gm7/C
why must we wait un - til to - night?
You wan - na take a lit - tle
Verse:
A♭maj7/C
Gm7/C
A♭maj7/C
time,
you wan - na drink me like a fine wine.
slow,
show me ev - 'ry lit - tle move you know.

Gm7/C
A♭maj7/C
Gm7/C
Like the book of love, line by line. But I wan-na play
Take a lit-tle love and watch it grow. But I wan-na lay
Cm
Fm
with you, you,
with you, you, my dar - ling,
B♭/C
Gm/C
Cm
right now. Go all the way with you, ba-
right now. Make love all day with you, ba-

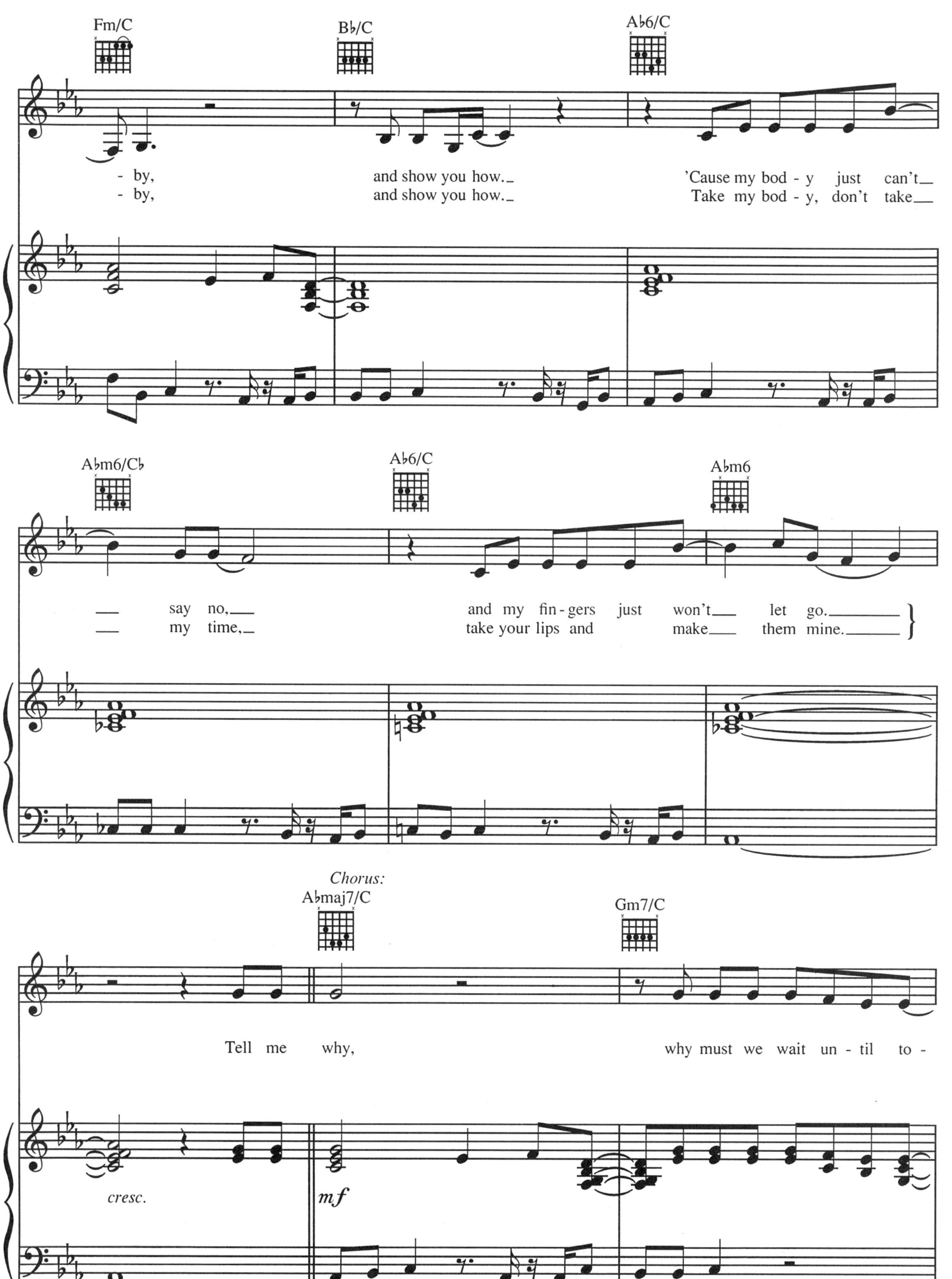
Fm/C
Bb/C
Ab6/C
- by,
- by,
and show you how.
and show you how.
'Cause my bod - y just can't
Take my bod - y, don't take
Abm6/Cb
Ab6/C
Abm6
say no,
my time,
and my fin-gers just won't let go.
take your lips and make them mine.
Chorus:
Abmaj7/C
Gm7/C
Tell me why,
why must we wait un - til to -
cresc.
mf

A♭maj7/C
Gm7/C
A♭maj7/C
- night?
Tell me why,
Gm7/C
A♭maj7/C
Gm7/C
why when I've wait-ed all my___ life?
You're touch-ing me,
A♭maj7/C
Gm7/C
A♭maj7/C
I'm touch-ing you,
ooh,___ what should I do?_ Now tell me why,

1.
Gm7/C
Cm
why must we wait un - til to-night?
2. You like to take it real
2.
Gm7/C
Cm
why must we wait un - til to - night?
Fm/C
B♭/C
Gm/C

Cm
Fm/C
B♭/C
A♭6/C
A♭m6/C♭
A♭6/C
'Cause my bod - y just can't say no,
and my fin - gers just won't
A♭m6/C♭
N.C.
let go.
Ba - by,
oh, tell me

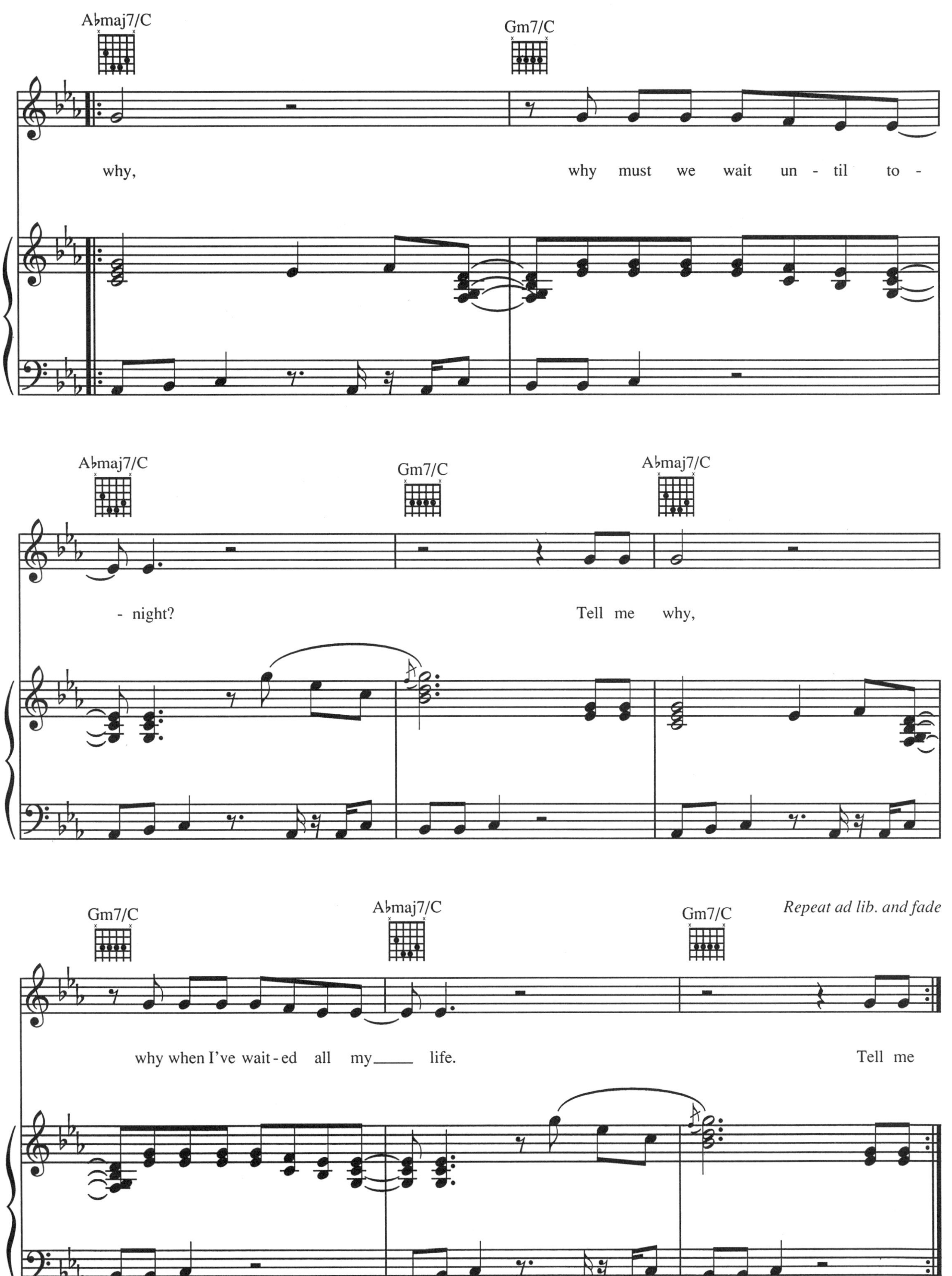
A♭maj7/C
Gm7/C
why,
why must we wait un - til to -
- night?
Tell me why,
why when I've wait - ed all my ___ life.
Tell me
Repeat ad lib. and fade

WITH YOU

Words and Music by
RAYMOND REEDER

Chorus:
Db/Eb Eb/G C C7(b13) Fm Bb9 Eb/Db Ab(2)/C
_ con - trol ___ of ___ me. ___ When I'm with you, ___ it's for real _
To Coda
Ab/C Eb/F Fm7 Bbm7 Db/Eb Eb Dbmaj7 Ab(2)/C Bbm7
___ what I feel ___ when I'm _ with you. ___
1. D.S. 2.3. Bridge:
Ab Db/Eb Ab Eb/G
_ 2. When I'm with you, ___ ___ Oh, ___ a spe-cial touch, _ a warm _ em -
Emaj9 Bbm7 Ab(2)/C Fm7
brace, ___ a sweet and ten - der kiss, ___ your

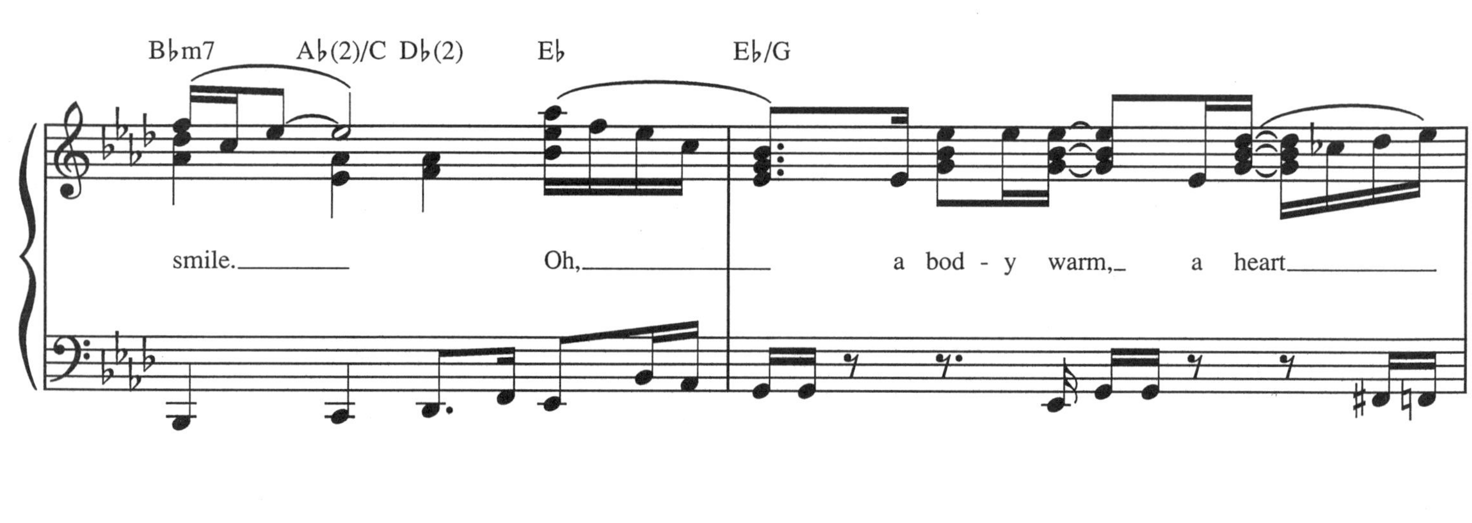
B♭m7
A♭(2)/C
D♭(2)
E♭
E♭/G
smile.
Oh,
a bod - y warm, a heart

Emaj9
B♭m7
A♭(2)/C
Fm7
so pure
that I
chill when I look,

1.
D.S. 𝄋
2.
D.S.S. 𝄋𝄋 al Coda
B♭m7
A♭/E♭
D♭/E♭
B♭m7
D♭/E♭
C7/E
look in your eyes.
3. With you,
oh, yeah,

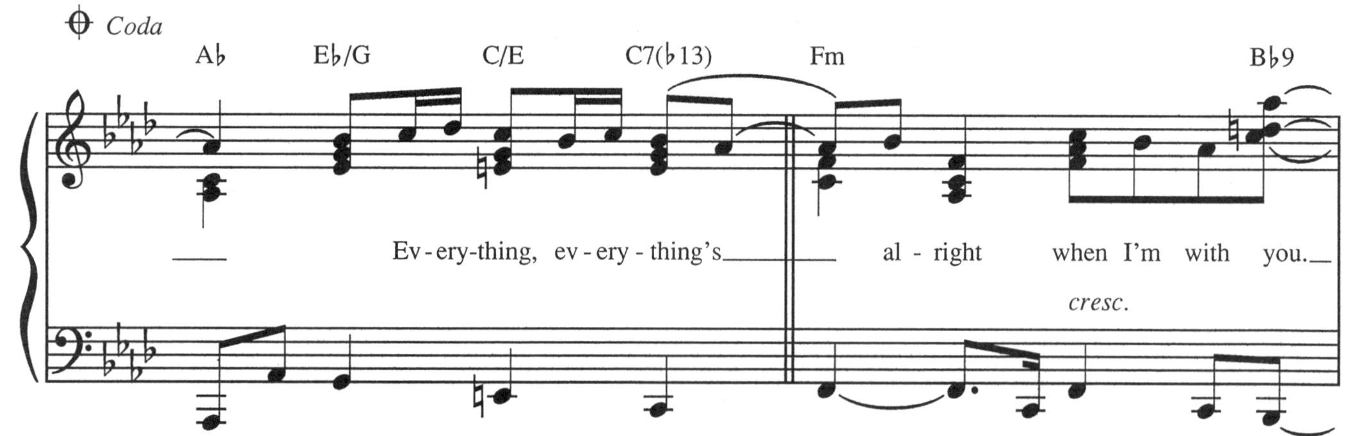
Coda
A♭
E♭/G
C/E
C7(♭13)
Fm
B♭9
Ev-ery-thing, ev-ery-thing's
al - right when I'm with you.
cresc.

A♭6(9)/C A♭/C A♭6(9)/C A♭/C
D♭6 D♭(2) D♭6 D♭
It's for
real what I feel.
It's o -
(It's for real what I feel when - ev - er you're a - round.)
f

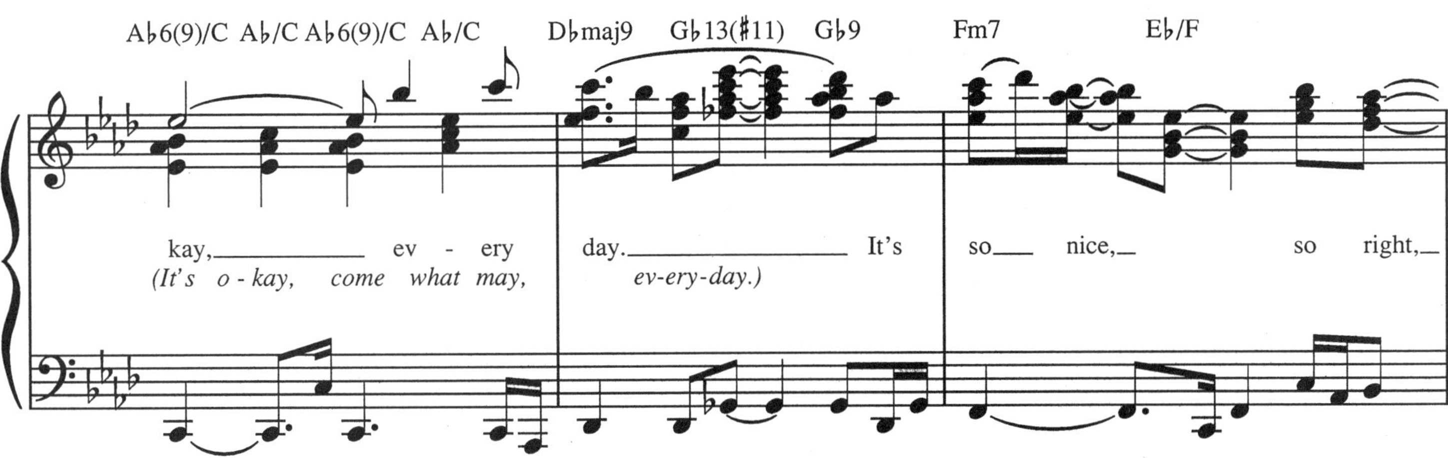
A♭6(9)/C A♭/C A♭6(9)/C A♭/C
D♭maj9 G♭13(♯11) G♭9
Fm7 E♭/F
kay, ev - ery
(It's o - kay, come what may,
day. It's
ev-ery-day.)
so nice, so right,

B♭m7 D♭/E♭
D♭maj7 A♭(2)/C B♭m7 A♭
now, when I'm with you.
dim.
mf
dim.
mp

Verses 2 & 3:
When I'm with you, I wonder why people do stop and stare and smile at us.
When I'm with you, the sun shines my way.
Maybe our love reflects its rays of light on everyone in the world.
(To Chorus:)

Bridge 2:
Oh, girl, I love you, baby.
Yeah, yeah, yeah, yes, I do.
Yeah, yeah, yeah, yes, I do.
Oh, I'd give the world to you, baby.
Oh, oh, yeah.
(To Chorus:)

WILL YOU BE THERE (IN THE MORNING)

Composed by
ROBERT JOHN "MUTT" LANGE

A/C♯
D2
E/G♯
A
E5
be there___ in the morn - ing when I rise._
Ba-by, be there._
Verse:
D2
A
2. Now, who do you
dream a-bout?_____ Are you a-
lone in your sleep?_ To who will you
reach out?___ Oh, let___ it be__ me._ Now, ba-by,
1.
To Next Strain
2.
___ I want._ Don't know what to
do___ a-bout
me lov-in' you,_ but I pray_ to
God______ that you__
___ feel it___ too._ Now, ba-by,
F♯m
you're my ob-ses-sion, my ad-dic
- tion, my drug._ Don't wan-na be with-

A/C♯ D2 E/G♯ A E5 N.C.
out you___ when I wake_ up.__ Will you be there in the
Chorus:
A E A D(2) A F♯m A D(2)
morn - ing? Will you be there when I want_ you?
A E A D(2)
1.
Will you be there when I wake_ up? I need you to be there_ in the morn-
E5 D2 A
- ing. Ba-by, be there!_
D2 A
D.S. 𝄋
2.
E5
3. Now, you're so need you to be there_ in__

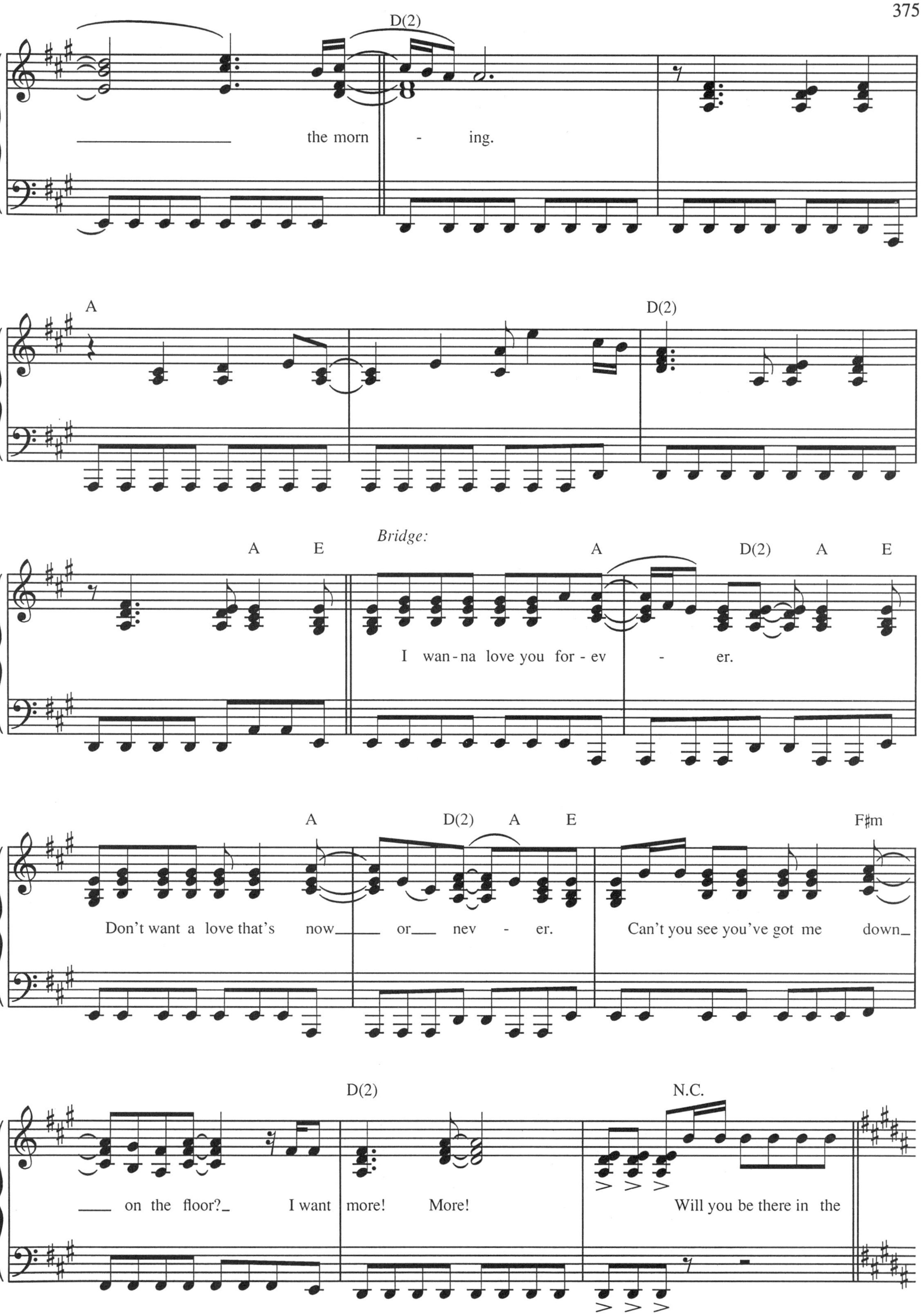

D(2)

the morn - ing.

A D(2)

A E

Bridge:

A D(2) A E

I wan-na love you for-ev - er.

A D(2) A E F♯m

Don't want a love that's now or nev - er. Can't you see you've got me down

Chorus:
B F♯ B E(2)
B G♯m B E(2)
morn - ing?
(with ad lib. vocals 2nd time)
Will you be there when I
want_ you?

B F♯ B E(2)
Will you be there when I
wake_ up?
Will you be there in the

1.
2.3.etc.
Repeat ad lib. and fade
B G♯m B E(2)
N.C.
morn - ing?
Will you be there?
Will you be there in the
Will you be there in the

Verse 3:
Now, you're so close to me, but I feel so alone.
The more I touch you, the more I want.
Don't know what to do about me lovin' you,
But I pray to God that you feel it too.
You're my obsession, my addiction, my drug.
So, let the candle grow into a great fire of love.
(To Chorus:)

THINK TWICE

Words and Music by
ANDY HILL and
PETE SINFIELD

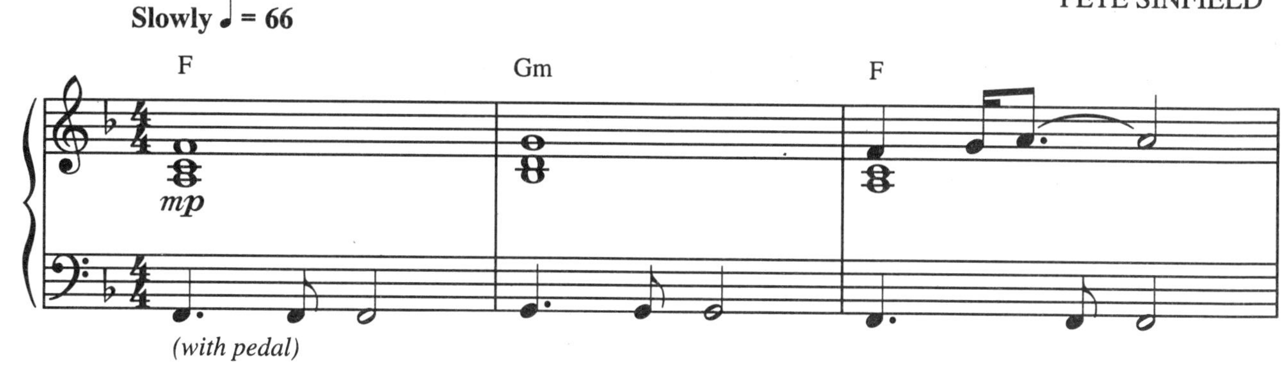
Slowly ♩ = 66
F
Gm
F
mp
(with pedal)

Gm
Verse:
Dm
Gm
1. Don't think I can't feel that there's
some - thing wrong.

C
Am7
3
B♭
Dm
3
You've been the sweet-est part of my
life for so long.
I look in your eyes there's a

Gm
C
Am7
B♭
dis - tant light,
and you and I know there'll be a
storm to - night.

Gm
C
Gm7
This is get-ting ser - i-ous.
Are you think-ing 'bout
cresc.
C
Chorus:
F
B♭
C
you or us? 1.-3.,5. Don't say what you're a-bout to say.
Look back
mf
F
Am
B♭
C
F
B♭
before you leave my life.
Be sure before you close that door,
C
Gm7
1.
B♭
be-fore you roll those dice,
ba-by, think
F
Gm
D.S.
2.
B♭
To next strain
3.4. etc.
B♭
Repeat ad lib. and fade
twice.
2. Ba-by, think
ba-by, think
4. Don't do
5. Don't say

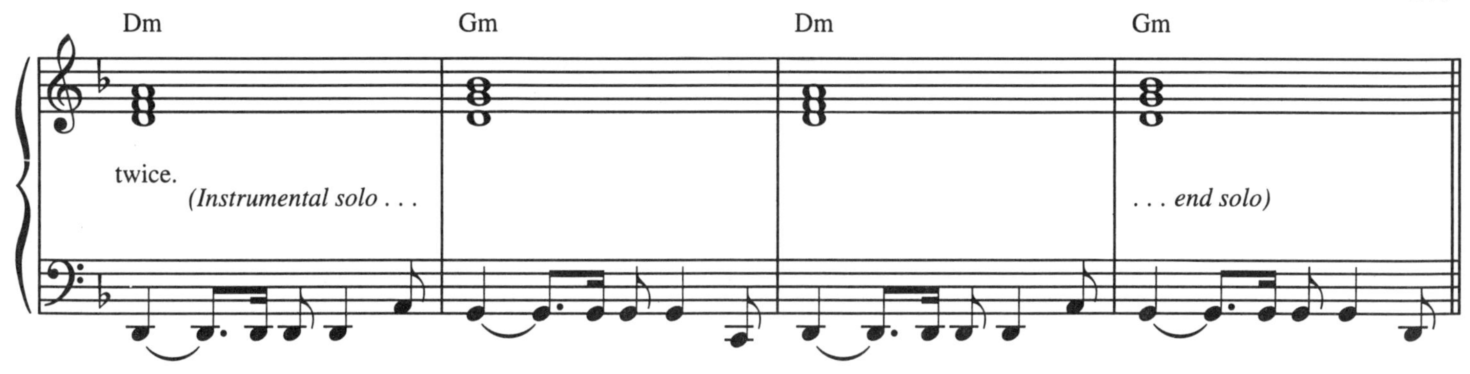

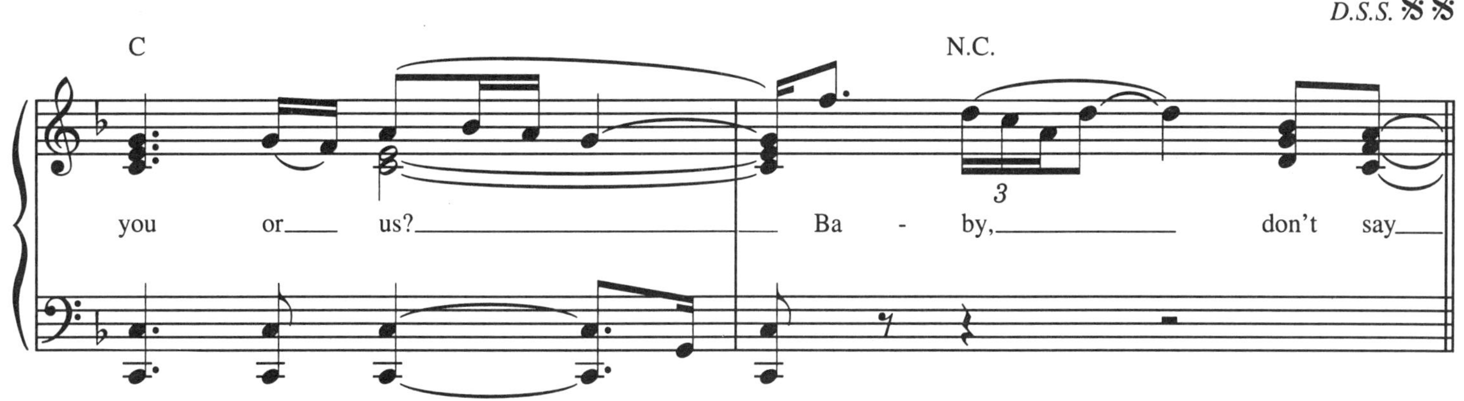

Verse 2:
Baby, think twice for the sake of our love, for the memory,
For the fire and the faith that was you and me.
Baby, I know it ain't easy when your soul cries out for higher ground,
'Cos when you're halfway up, you're always halfway down.
But baby, this is serious.
Are you thinking 'bout you or us?
(To Chorus:)

Chorus 4:
Don't do what you're about to do.
My everything depends on you,
And whatever it takes, I'll sacrifice.
Before you roll those dice,
Baby, think twice.

YOU MAKE ME SMILE

By
DAVE KOZ and
JEFF KOZ

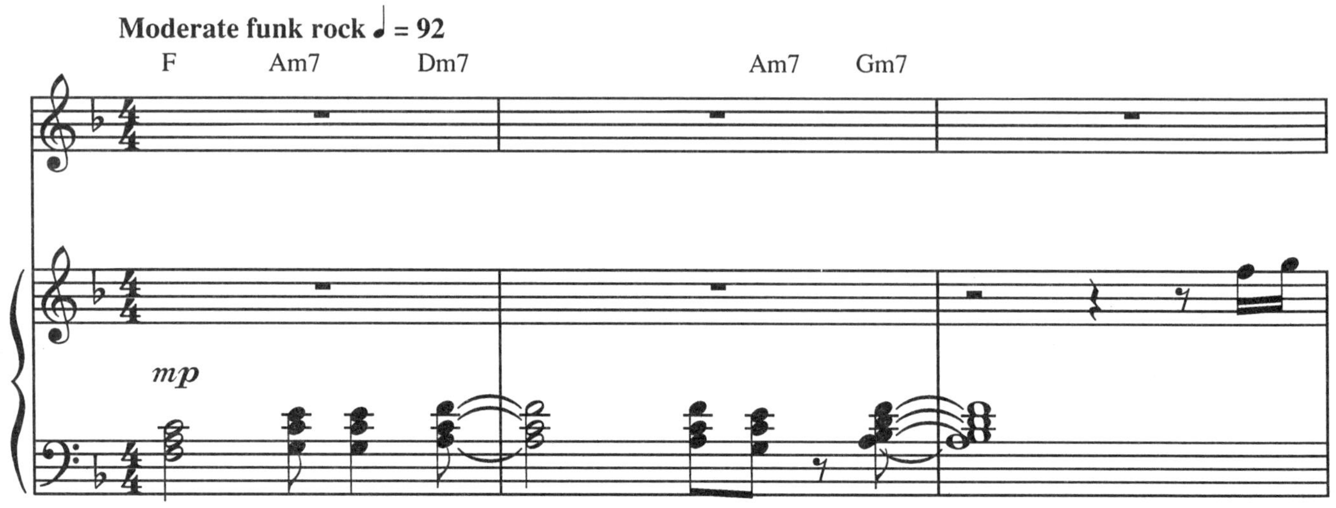

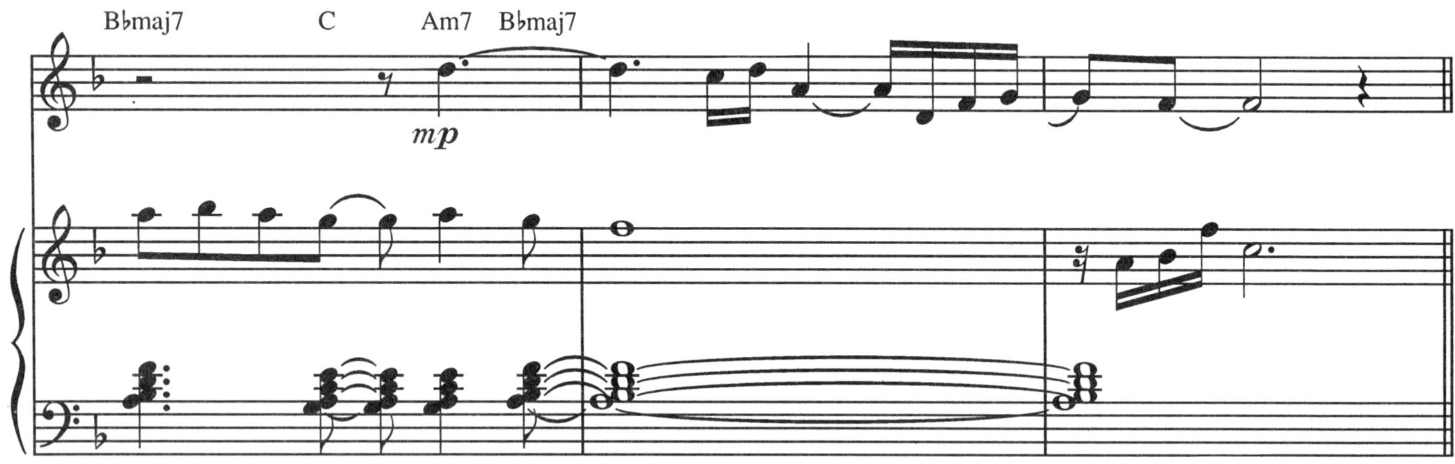

Csus
C7
F
B♭m7
A♭maj7
Csus
C
Fm
E♭/F
Fm7
Cm7
D♭maj7
E♭/D♭
D♭maj7
D♭/E♭
. . . solo ends)
F
Am7
Dm7
Am7
Gm7

To Coda
B♭maj7
B♭/C
F
Am7
Dm7
Am7
Gm7
1.
B♭maj7
C
Am7
B♭maj7
B♭/C
D.S.
2.
B♭maj7
B♭/C
3
F
Am7
Dm7
Am7
B♭maj7
Gm7
3
3

B♭/C
C/D
Bm7(♭5)
B♭maj7
(ad lib. solo)
Dm7
Gm7
D.S. 𝄋 al Coda
Am7
B♭m7
B♭/C

Coda
B♭maj7
B♭/C
C/D
cresc.
cresc.
G
Bm7
Em7
Bm7
Am7
f
f
Cmaj7
C/D
G
Bm7
Em7
Bm7
Cmaj7
Am7
C/D
Repeat ad lib. and fade

YOU MAKE ME SMILE

SOPRANO SAX

By
DAVE KOZ and
JEFF KOZ

Soprano Sax - 2
C/D
D.S. 𝄋
2.
Cmaj7
C/D
3
G
Bm7
Em7
Bm7
Cmaj7
Am7
3
C/D
D/E
C♯m7(♭5)
Cmaj7
Em7
(ad lib. solo)
Am7
Bm7
Cm7
C/D
D.S. 𝄋 al Coda
Coda
Cmaj7
C/D
D/E
cresc.
A
C♯m7
F♯m7
C♯m7
Bm7
f
Dmaj7
D/E
A
C♯m7
F♯m7
C♯m7
Dmaj7
Bm7
D/E
Repeat ad lib. and fade

STREETS OF PHILADELPHIA

Words and Music by
BRUCE SPRINGSTEEN

Moderately, with a beat ♩ = 96
F
Am
1.
2.
mf
1. I was
Verse:
F
Am
3
bruised and bat-tered; I could-n't
tell what I felt. I was
un-rec-og-niz - a-ble to my-
mf
self. Saw my
F
re-flec-tion in a win-dow and did-n't
know my own face. Oh, broth-er are you
Am
gon-na leave me wast-in' a-
way on the streets of Phil-a-
Chorus:
B♭2
del-phi-a.
(bkgrd.) La la la la la
(L.H. cue notes 2nd & 3rd time)

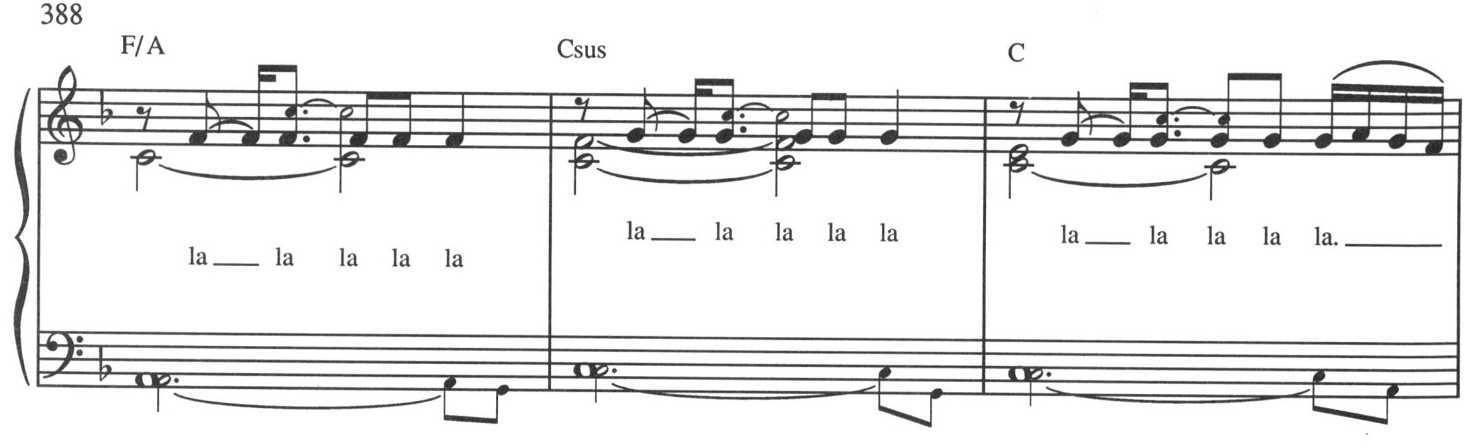
F/A
Csus
C
la __ la la la la
la __ la la la la
la __ la la la la. ______

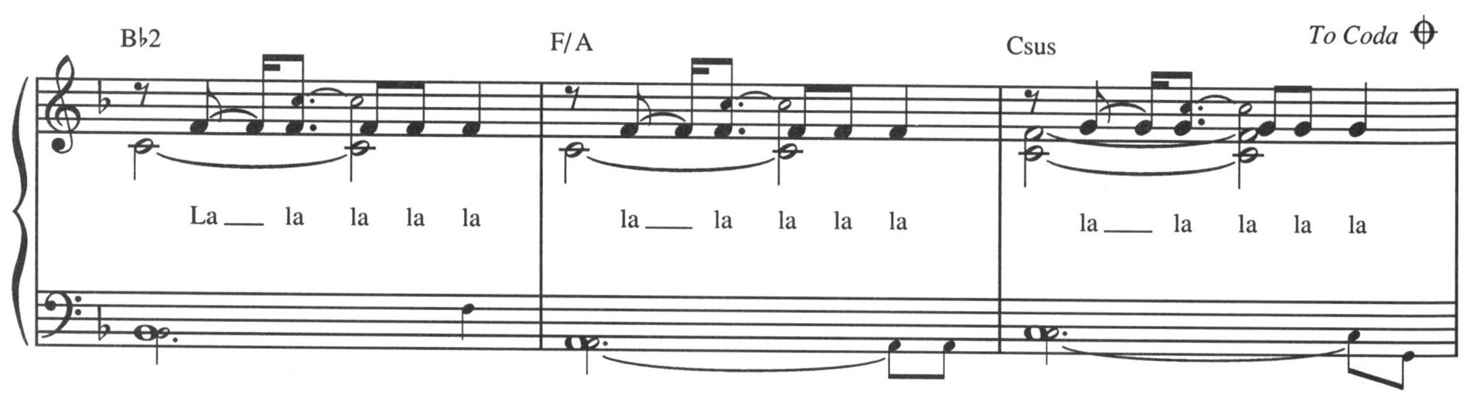
B♭2
F/A
Csus
To Coda
La __ la la la la
la __ la la la la
la __ la la la la

1.
2.
Bridge:
C
C
B♭
la __ la la 2. I walked the
la __ la la la la. ______
Ain't no an - gel gon-na greet
cresc.
f

Dm7
B♭
F
me; ______
it's just you and I, __ my __ friend. ______

Am
B♭
Csus
And my clothes don't fit
me no more; I walked
a thou-sand miles just to

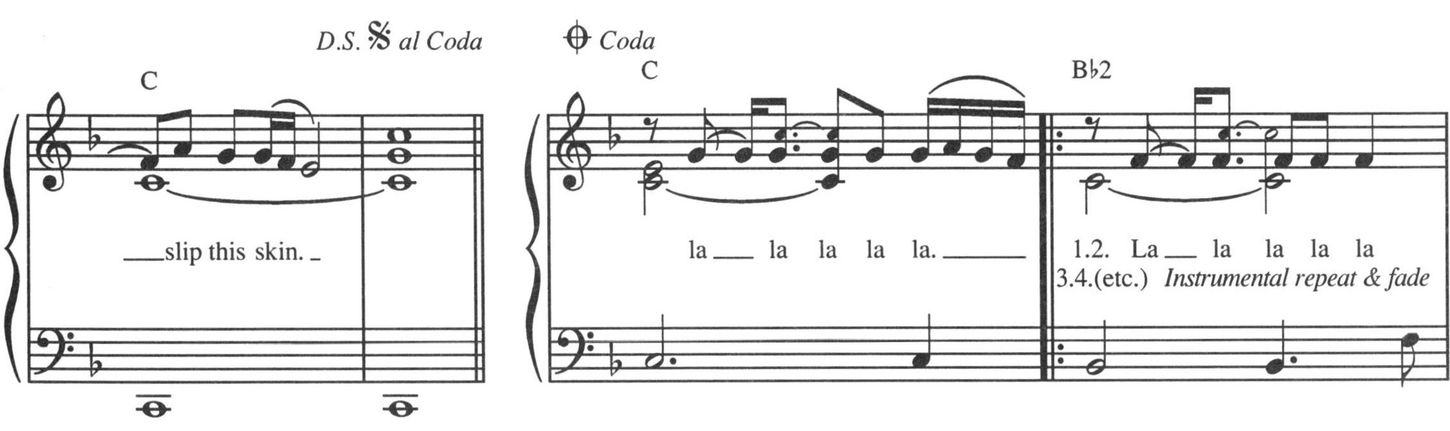
D.S. 𝄋 al Coda
C
slip this skin.
Coda
C
la la la la la.
B♭2
1.2. La la la la la
3.4.(etc.) Instrumental repeat & fade

Repeat ad lib. and fade
F/A
Csus
C
la la la la la
la la la la la
la la la la la.

Verse 2:
I walked the avenue till my legs felt like stone.
I heard the voices of friends vanished and gone.
At night I could hear the blood in my veins
Just as black and whispering as the rain
On the streets of Philadelphia.
(To Chorus:)

Verse 3:
The night has fallen. I'm lyin' awake.
I can feel myself fading away.
So, receive me, brother, with your faithless kiss,
Or will we leave each other alone like this
On the streets of Philadelphia?
(To Chorus:)

MISLED

Words and Music by
PETER ZIZZO and JIMMY BRALOWER

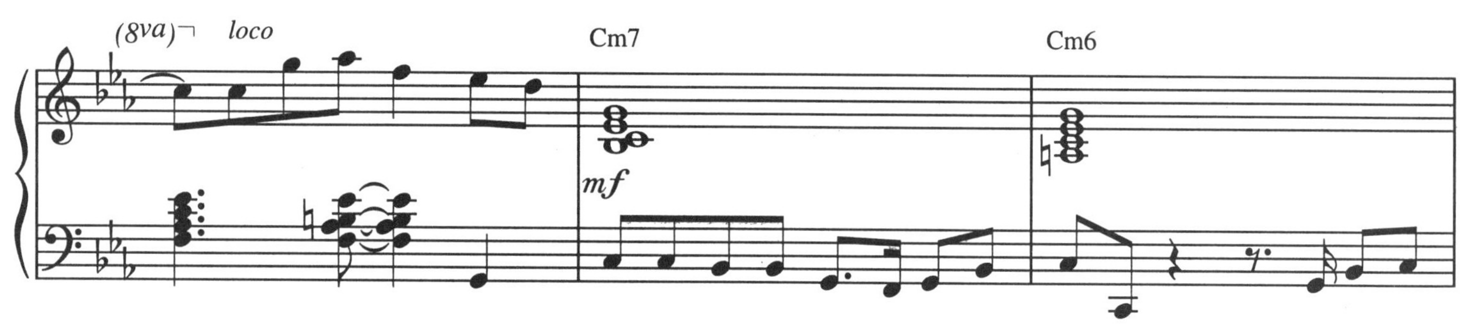

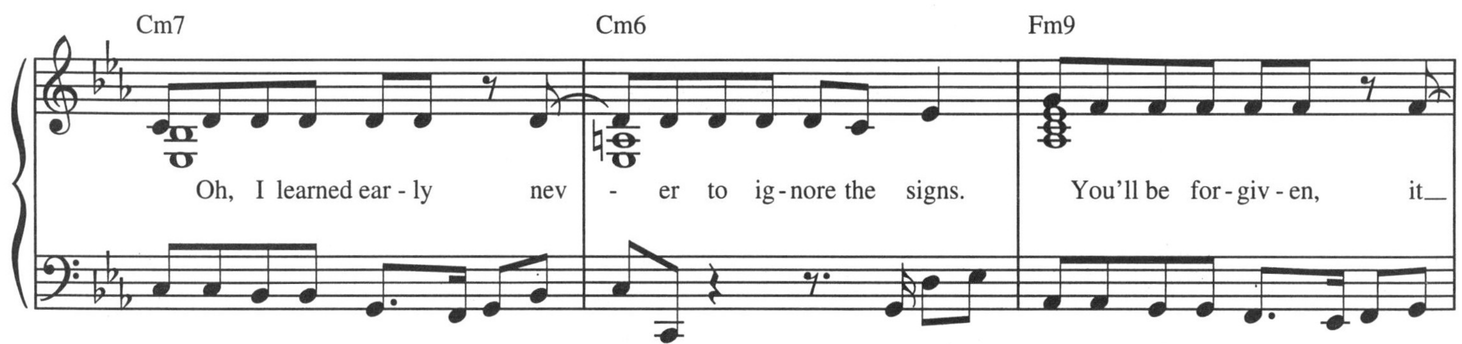
Cm7
Cm6
Fm9
Oh, I learned ear - ly nev - er to ig - nore the signs. You'll be for - giv - en, it

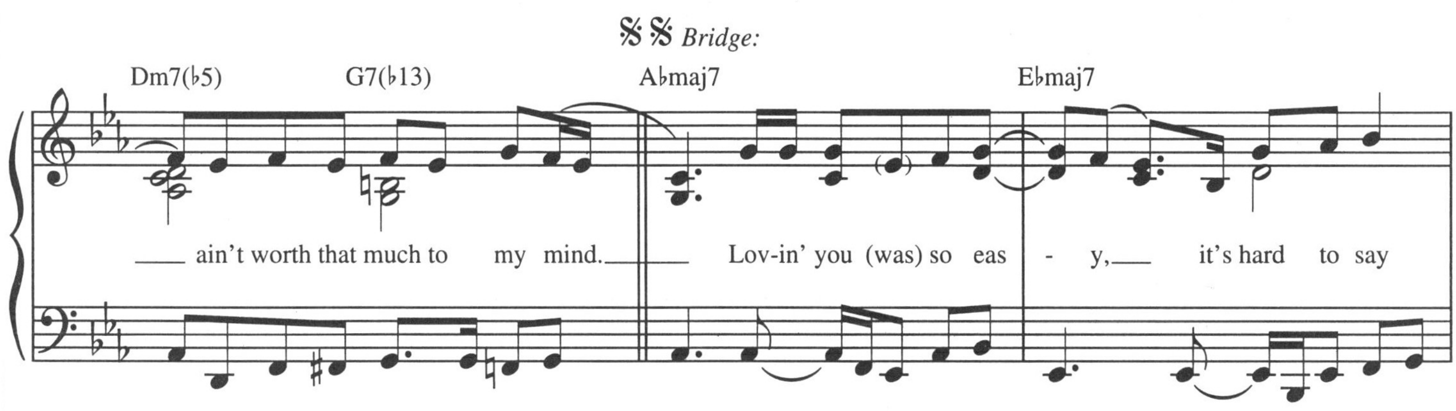
Bridge:
Dm7(♭5)
G7(♭13)
A♭maj7
E♭maj7
ain't worth that much to my mind. Lov - in' you (was) so eas - y, it's hard to say

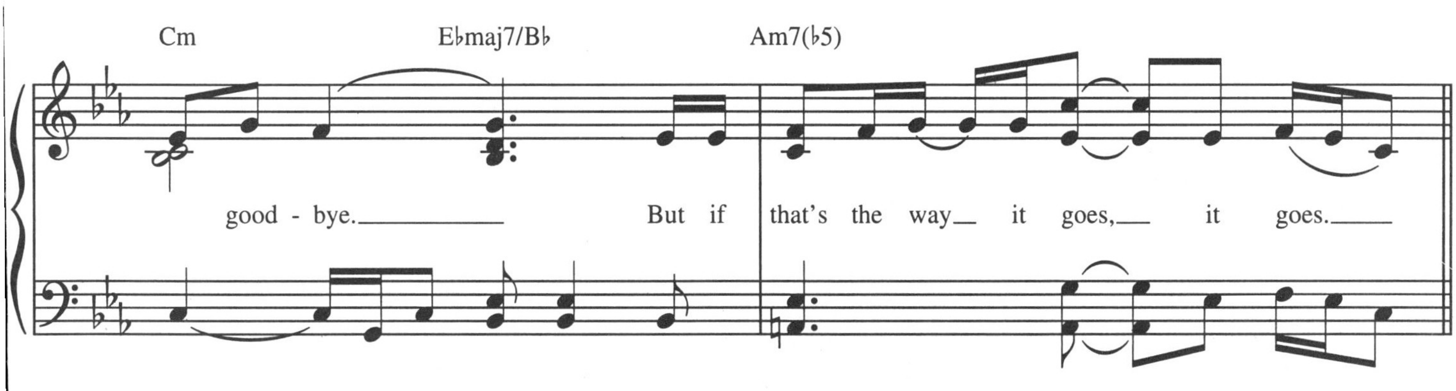
Cm
E♭maj7/B♭
Am7(♭5)
good - bye. But if that's the way it goes, it goes.

Chorus:
Fm7
G7(♭13)
Cm7
Just a page in my his - to - ry. Just

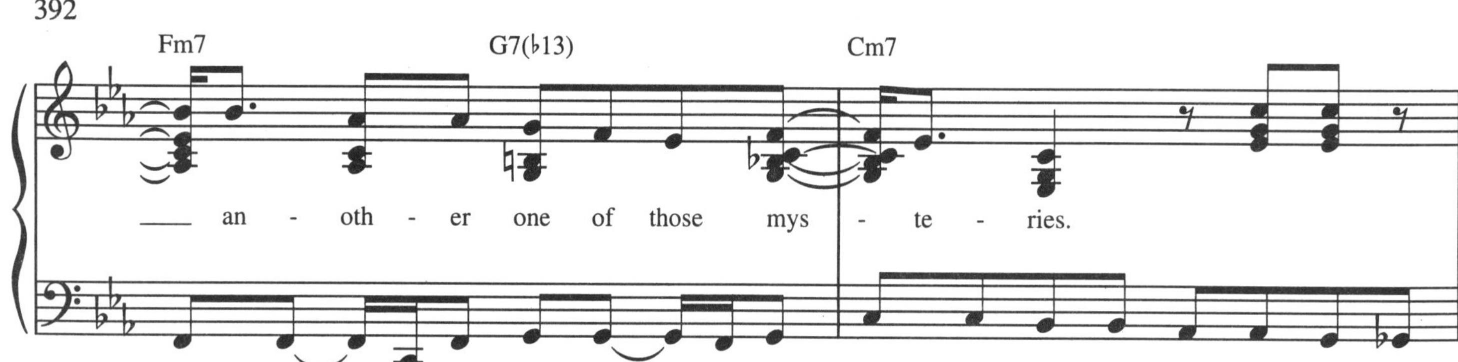
Fm7
G7(♭13)
Cm7
an - oth - er one of those mys - te - ries.

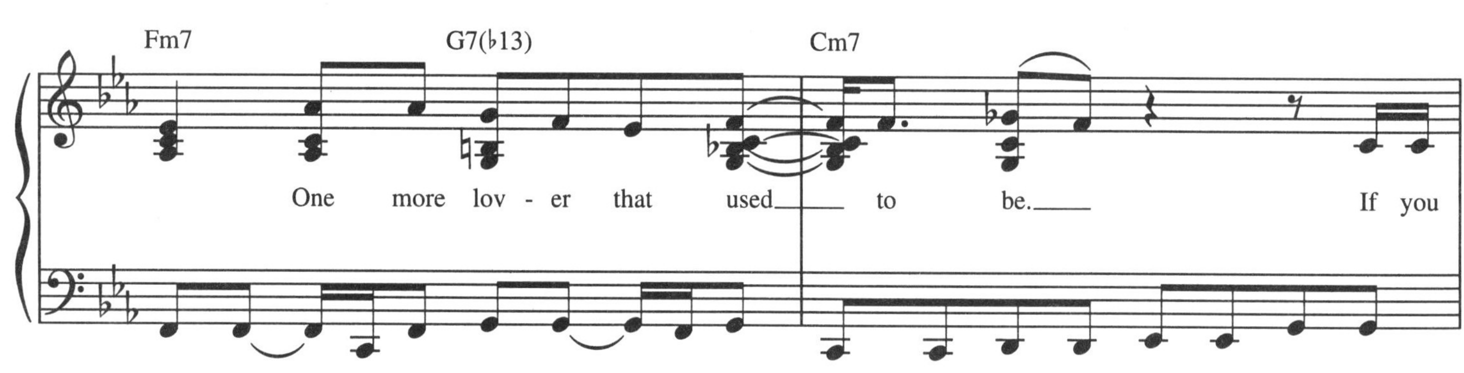
Fm7
G7(♭13)
Cm7
One more lov - er that used to be. If you

Dm7(♭5)
1.2.
To Next Strain
Dm7(♭5)/G
N.C.
think you're in my head, you've been ser - i - ous - ly mis - led.

3.4.
Dm7(♭5)/G
N.C.
5.
Fine
Dm7(♭5)/G
N.C.
ser - i - ous - ly mis - led.
ser - i - ous - ly mis - led.

Verse 2:
Lovin' somebody ain't your average 9 to 5.
It takes conviction, it takes a will to survive.
I'm not somebody who commits the crime and leaves the scene.
But when I've been dissed, I don't spend much time on what might've been.

Bridges 2 & 3:
I'm not about self-pity, your love did me wrong,
So I'm movin', movin' on.
(To Chorus:)

LOVE SNEAKIN' UP ON YOU

Words and Music by
TOM SNOW and
JIMMY SCOTT

D♭/E♭
E♭
Cm7
D♭
think - in' a - bout___ things___ we___ ain't done yet.___
Bridge:
G7
Tell me now,_ I've got to know, do you feel the same?___
B♭7
Do you just light up at the men - tion of my name?_ Yeah.___
Chorus:
D♭/E♭
E♭
D♭/E♭
E♭
Don't wor - ry, ba - by, it ain't noth - in' new.___
Cm7
D♭2
That's just love___ sneak - in' up on you.___ If your

D♭/E♭
E♭
D♭/E♭
E♭
whole world_ is shak - in' and you feel like_ I do,_

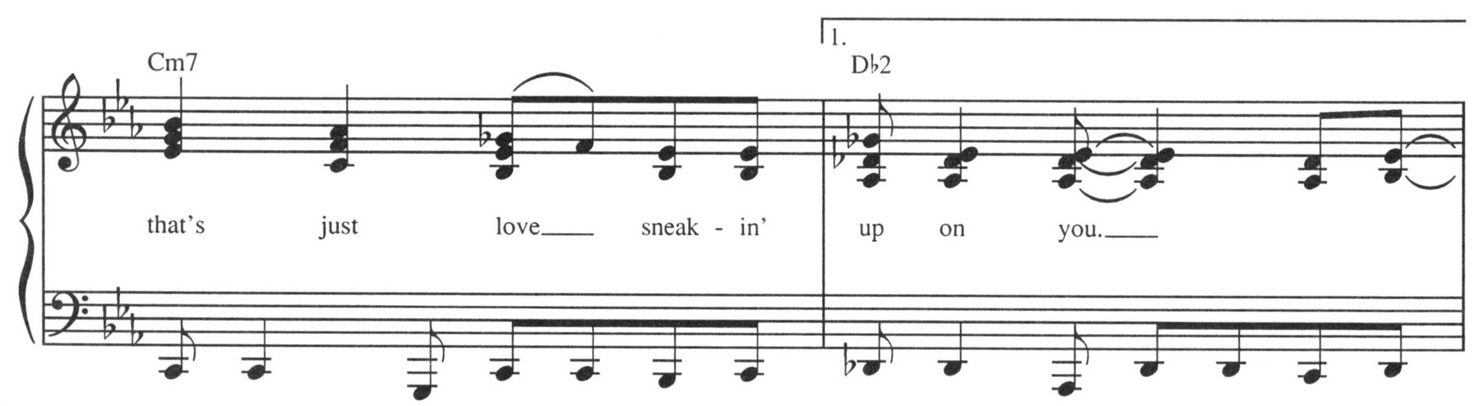
Cm7
1.
D♭2
that's just love_ sneak - in' up on you._

E♭5
D.S. 𝄋
2.
To next strain
D♭2
up on you._

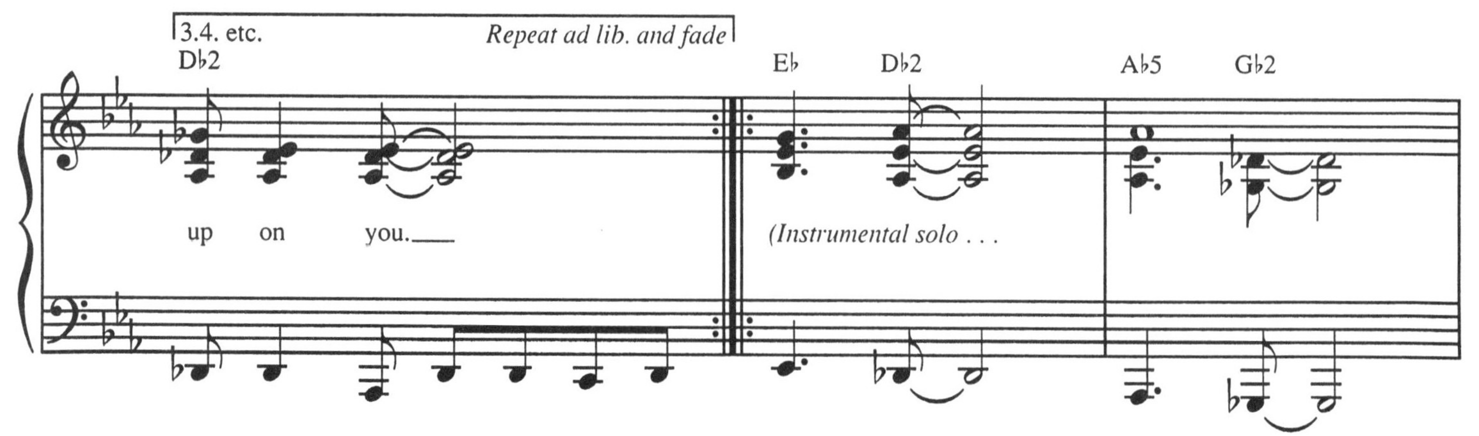
3.4. etc.
Repeat ad lib. and fade
D♭2
E♭
D♭2
A♭5
G♭2
up on you._
(Instrumental solo . . .

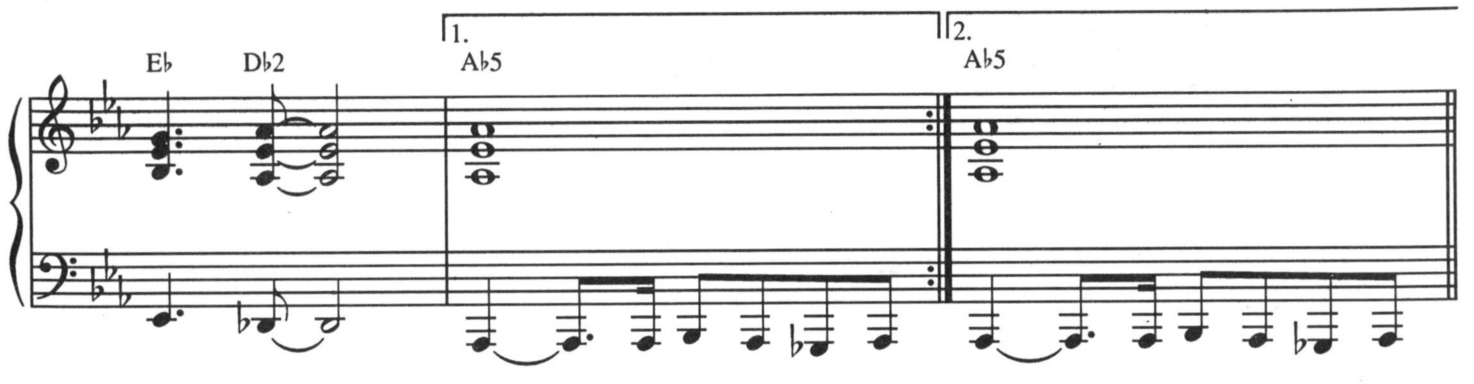

Verse 2:
Nowhere on earth for your heart to hide
Once love comes sneakin' up on your blind side.
And you might as well try to stop the rain
Or stand in the tracks of a runaway train.

Bridge 2:
You just can't fight it when a thing's meant to be.
So, come on, let's finish what you started with me.
(To Chorus:)

DOES LOVE NOT OPEN YOUR EYES

Words and Music by
KURT HOWELL and ERIC KAZ

E♭ B♭/D Cm7 B♭/D E♭maj7 Fsus F
er. What is now, will be for - ev-er. Does
er. What is now, will be for - ev-er.
cresc.
Chorus:
B♭ E♭ F Cm Gm
love not o - pen your eyes, leave you breath-less,
mf
B♭/D E♭ F B♭ E♭ F
warm you in - side? Does love not cra - dle your heart,
Cm Gm B♭/D E♭ F E♭ F/E♭
hold you close, just right from the start? Does love not o - pen your eyes?
1. E♭ F/E♭ D.S. 𝄋 2. E♭ F/E♭ E♭ F/E♭
dim.
Does love not o - n your eyes?

E♭ B♭/E♭ C/E F/A G
Your eyes!
cresc.
f
E7/G♯ Am C/E F G A
3
Does
Chorus:
D G/D D/F♯ G A Em Bm
love not o - pen your eyes, leave you breath-less,
D/F♯ G A D G/D D/F♯ G A
warm you in - side? Does love not cra - dle your heart,
Em Bm D/F♯ G A
Repeat ad lib. and fade
hold you close, just right from the start? Does